CHINA'S RATIONAL ENTREPRENEURS

The ability of China's entrepreneurs to establish firms in the midst of a strangling bureaucratic system is a topic that demands attention, not least because it forms the basis of China's economic development. *China's Rational Entrepreneurs* presents a fresh angle of analysis for understanding the behaviour of Chinese entrepreneurs, and the kind of relations they have with local government in order to secure long-term business success.

Using theoretical approaches informed by neo-institutionalism, institutional economics and cultural studies and a database drawn from extensive fieldwork, the book explores how far these approaches fit the Chinese reality on a micro-level and analyses whether Chinese business behaviour follows the economic rationale, or needs to be explained by its culture and institutions. The overall picture that emerges is of social capital at a local level as the most crucial factor in the emergence of private firms in China. While local governments and private entrepreneurs co-operate in order to establish and manage firms, domestic and international competition limits rent seeking and ensures the expansion of functioning markets. The contributors also suggest that behaviour based on cultural norms and behaviour based on rational decision making are not mutually exclusive in Chinese business relations.

Utilizing a wide variety of perspectives, this book analyses Chinese entrepreneurship by linking theoretical arguments with data collected in open and structured interviews, resulting in an invaluable resource for students of Chinese business and management as well as those studying the Chinese economy.

Barbara Krug is Professor of Economics of Governance at the Erasmus University Rotterdam, the Netherlands. She has published extensively on political economies in China and the Pacific.

ROUTLEDGECURZON STUDIES ON CHINA IN TRANSITION
Series Editor: David S.G. Goodman

CHINA'S RATIONAL ENTREPRENEURS

The development of the new private business sector

Edited by Barbara Krug

Routledge
Taylor & Francis Group

LONDON AND NEW YORK

First published 2004
by RoutledgeCurzon
2 Park Square, Milton Park, Abingdon, Oxfordshire OX14 4RN

Simultaneously published in the USA and Canada
by RoutledgeCurzon
711 Third Avenue, New York, NY 10017

RoutledgeCurzon is an imprint of the Taylor & Francis Group

First issued in paperback 2012

Typeset in Sabon by
Florence Production Ltd, Stoodleigh, Devon

British Library Cataloguing in Publication Data
A catalogue record for this book is available
from the British Library

Library of Congress Cataloging in Publication Data
China's rational entrepreneurs: the development of the new private
business sector / edited by Barbara Krug.
p. cm. – (RoutledgeCurzon studies on China in transition)
1. Small business – China. 2. Entrepreneurship – China.
3. China – Economic conditions – 2000– 4. Business enterprises
– China. 5. Businessmen – China. I. Krug, Barbara, 1950–
II. Series.
HD2346.C6C484 2004
338′.04′0951–dc21   2003013093

ISBN13: 978-0-415-32822-7 (hbk)
ISBN13: 978-0-415-64658-1 (pbk)

CONTENTS

CONTENTS

ILLUSTRATIONS

Figures

Tables

CONTRIBUTORS

Frank Belschak is Assistant Professor in the Department for Social and Organizational Psychology at the University of Cologne, Germany, and holds a research position at the Faculty of Economics at Erasmus University Rotterdam. His main fields of interest are cross-cultural psychology, social capital and emotions within organizations.

Jane Duckett is a Senior Lecturer in the Department of Politics at the University of Glasgow, where she teaches and researches contemporary Chinese politics. Her publications include *The Entrepreneurial State in China (1998)*, and papers in *Pacific Review, World Development* and *Social Policy and Administration.*

David S.G. Goodman is Director of the Institute for International Studies, University of Technology, Sydney. He has recently completed *Provincialism and Democracy* – a study of social and political change in contemporary Shanxi – and is currently engaged in research on the development of Qinghai province.

Hans Hendrischke is Head of the Department of Chinese and Indonesian Studies and Director of the UNSW-UTS Centre for Research on Provincial China of the University of New South Wales and University of Technology, Sydney, Australia.

Gabriele Jacobs is Assistant Professor in the Department for Organization Theory and Personnel of the Rotterdam School of Management, Erasmus University Rotterdam. She specializes in cross-cultural psychology and methodology and is currently engaged in research on the impact of cultural norms on organizational change.

Barbara Krug is Professor for Economics of Governance in the Department for Organization Theory and Personnel of the Rotterdam School of Management, Erasmus University Rotterdam. Her recent publications focus on entrepreneurship, the emergence of norms and the development of private firms and sectors in China. Her publications include papers in the *American Journal of Economics and Sociology,* the *Journal of Institutional and Theoretical Economics,* and *Management International Journal.*

Judith Mehta is Lecturer in Economics, Faculty of Social Sciences at the Open University, Milton Keynes, and Visiting Fellow, School of Economic and Social Studies at the University of East Anglia. Her research interests include industrial organization theory, decision theory and the implications for economic analysis of recent French philosophy.

László Pólos is Szécheny Professor of Applied Logic at the Eötvös University in Budapest, Hungary, a visiting Professor at the Graduate School of Business at Stanford University and Associate Professor of Organization Theory in the Rotterdam School of Management of the Erasmus University Rotterdam. His current publications include 'Foundation of a Theory of Social Forms' in *Industrial and Corporate Change,* 'Reasoning With Partial Knowledge' in *Sociological Methodology* and 'Reducing Uncertainty' in the *American Journal of Sociology.*

Gordon Redding is Senior Affiliate Professor of Asian Business at INSEAD, and prior to that spent 24 years at the University of Hong Kong where he founded and directed the business school. A specialist in Chinese capitalism, he is now working on a general theory of business systems.

1

INTRODUCTION

New opportunities, new sector, new firms

Barbara Krug

Most literature on China at the beginning of the reform era pointed to the necessity for and subsequent development of new industries such as the financial, service or IT sector.[1] Yet economic transformation means much more than the import and integration of new products, technologies, and competence. With the dismantling of the planned economy, new individual and organizational agents such as firms must learn to interact and search for means to facilitate such interaction. The need to establish new firms and new institutions that allow co-ordination of the actions of numerous firms, irrespective of the sector they move in, is crucial if a competitive and innovative private sector should emerge. Only both factors together, the formation of firms (*entrepreneurship*) and the establishment of widely acceptable institutions that co-ordinate individual behaviour in and between different sectors, add up to a *business system.*

What kind of a business system evolves is a crucial question for non-Chinese companies, which consider doing business with or investing in China, or need to reckon with Chinese competitors. Thus, information about how physical assets, financial, human and social capital is allocated in China is as important for Western companies as it is challenging for academics who attempt to distinguish between different business systems.[2]

The (neoclassical) economic literature claims that the *market*, defined as the functioning of the price mechanism, and *hierarchy*, defined as state controlled resources, are sufficient criteria for identifying business systems.[3] In this analysis free prices, private ownership, and voluntary exchange *predate* the emergence of private firms and markets. The management literature and cross-cultural studies on the other hand point to the fact that there are more ways to co-ordinate individual and firms' behaviour than the price mechanism or bureaucratic control. As, for example, Whitley (1990; 1999) has convincingly pointed out factors such as prices, voluntary exchange, or ownership structures are not sufficient to explain the differences between business systems that all have subscribed to a 'market economy'. Factors such as authority and identity form alternative ways to co-ordinate actions and allocate resources (and income) while simultaneously shaping the interaction between the private business sector and the state, as will be argued in the contribution by Redding in Chapter 2. In the business systems literature, but also in evolutionary economics (see Krug and Pólos, Chapter 4) the 'market' is rather the outcome of individual behaviour (of economic agents or firms), voluntary compliance to agreed-upon routines and business practices, as well as the acceptance of state legislation and control. Subscribing to this wider approach the different contributions in this book try to find an answer to the question *what kind of a business system will evolve in China* while sharing the following assumptions:

- The emergence of a new business system in China is an ongoing process; given the transitional nature of the Chinese economy a static view would be of limited value only. Therefore a dynamic analysis going beyond a comparison between the period before reforms and today's state of affairs is needed.
- The development of the business system depends on the behaviour (intentions) of entrepreneurs and the strategies of firms, their interaction, and their relations with government officials in charge of economics affairs at all levels of government. Resources such as technology, competence, financial capital, or raw material and infrastructure, are a (given) constraint in the short run only. In the long run, such as the period between the beginning of the reforms in 1978 and today, searching for new ways as to how these resources can be mobilized and more efficiently employed must be seen as the core of China's economic transformation – and the establishment of a new business system. Therefore the analysis has to look at two forms of entrepreneurship.[4] First, there is the analysis at the individual level dealing with the question *how does an individual Chinese raise the necessary financial, human, or social capital to establish a 'firm'.* Second, an analysis at a more aggregate level needs to ask how individual economic agents and firms look for ways to secure ongoing production and profit. As the success of firms depends crucially on their ability to smoothly (and at low costs) interact with other firms, customers, government officials, and potential investors, another form of entrepreneurship deserves attention. To put it differently, securing long-term business success depends crucially on the ability of economic agents to establish institutions that facilitate private, voluntary exchange and allow the prediction of expected outcomes. In this case *entrepreneurship takes the form of individual contributions to the establishment and functioning of institutions that help to co-ordinate individual activities.* As many Westerners know, irrespective of their

2

own organizational forms or business strategies their business will fail
if they move into an environment hostile to private exchange, or prone
to quick changes in the infrastructure of the business system.

- Established concepts explaining the differences and changes in business
  systems such as the *transformation literature*,[5] *comparative business
  systems*,[6] or *cultural studies*[7] cannot sufficiently enough explain
  Chinese reality. The literature on comparative business systems so far
  has focused on the differences between East Asian economies that
  work within a competitive (market) environment; the literature on
  economic transformation deeply embedded in the German tradition
  of Ordnungspolitik (economic order) offers a normative concept with
  implicit assumptions on European attitudes, tradition, and history,
  while cultural studies focus on long-term trends, too easily underes-
  timating the consequences of 'shocks' and short-term changes on
  economic decisions.[8]

Another stream of literature draws attention to the fact that resources
are *embedded* in social and political ties. Therefore, the necessary re-
allocation of resources and assets remains closely linked to institutional
change at the state level where the winners and the losers of the reforms
will be defined and the 'compensation payments' for the losers are negotiated. However, to claim that social networks established in the recent
socialist past will survive and steer the transformation process is misleading. As the chapters by Duckett and Goodman (Chapters 6 and 7) show,
the assumptions according to which the nascent private sector *reproduces*
the networks between firms that had been established in the socialist past
underestimates the entrepreneurship of state and party cadres.[9] Thus, political science or sociological theories working with pre-defined groups such
as state agencies, state firms or bureaucrats (cadres) cannot catch the
dynamic in the formation of a new business system that developed intended
or unintended outside China's state administration.

All in all, the authors of the book, instead of taking 'models' or theories
to China and searching for data that support (or otherwise) hypotheses formulated by these theories, chose another way: they assumed that what was
needed was empirical and explorative research focusing on questions such
as *How do Chinese entrepreneurs establish firms and business relations?
How do they interact and develop acceptable rules of the game and routines?
How do they redefine their relationship with the still large state sector?*

Legitimization of the theory

Even in an explorative study general theories are needed to illuminate
otherwise obscure observations and to collect data in a systematic way.
When no single theory is at hand, then to select specific concepts from

different theories with the purpose of re-assembling them into a consistent theoretical frame is a good starting point. That is what is done in what follows. The model introduced here works at the interface of *transaction cost theory, cultural studies and organizational ecology*, thus combining approaches based on economics, social psychology, sociology, and political science as applied in the management science literature.

Transaction cost theory supplied the behavioural assumption that Chinese entrepreneurs and firms are intentionally *rational*. At the individual level rationality refers to *calculated risk taking* rather than income maximization; at the level of firms rationality refers to the discovery of courses of action that satisfy a whole set of constraints rather than a strategy for achieving one goal. As Simon (1978; 1979) has pointed out already rationality refers to a *fitness function* and not to utility/income maximization. To start with the assumption that entrepreneurs and other economic agents in China seek to choose that course of action that promises the highest return while facing constraints does not mean that cultural factors determining behaviour get dismissed. It is that part of transaction cost theory commonly referred to as New Institutional Economics that provided useful insights for the following analysis.[10] New Institutional Economics claims that after all, norms, inherited institutions or tradition can establish powerful constraints that function the same way as (market) prices or income (Baurmann 1996; Schlicht 1999; Krug 2002a). On a theoretical level the problem is that we know that rationality and cultural norms interact, yet we do not know how these factors interact in a specific situation or a specific context.

New Institutional Economics argues that transaction cost theory on one side dismisses culture, history, or attitudes and norms, while cross-cultural studies dismiss the notion of rationality *at the individual level*. In the stylized world of models research would be undertaken to prove or dismiss any of these models. In contrast, the contributions in this book follow Redding's analysis, Chapter 2, in which he shows that Weberian rationality is a component of any culture. Subsequently, it is assumed here that both *rationality and cultural features are latent forces that co-exist*. Which one is employed however depends on specific situations and context.

What is needed in a first step is, therefore, to check which cultural features do indeed play a role in Chinese entrepreneurship. Building on the literature in cross-cultural studies[11] the different contributions in this book focus on the following components of culture:

- *Individual behaviour*: whether for example Chinese entrepreneurs reveal a long-term orientation in their business activities.
- *Collectivism*: whether for example entrepreneurs actively search for and contribute to the formation of alliances and networks that promise to facilitate the pooling of resources and securing input.

4

• A specific notion of *authority*: whether for example private entrepreneurs and (local) political entrepreneurs negotiate state–private relations such as agreeing upon the 'state's' entitlements to tax, to regulate, or to control firms.

Thus the empirical problem at stake is to identify cultural factors that will shape behaviour. Relying on the results from cross-cultural studies summarized in the chapter by Jacobs, Belschak and Krug, Chapter 8, six 'cultural' factors were expected to play a role. Data collection and analysis therefore did not attempt to prove that, or the extent to which Chinese entrepreneurs responded to changes in relative (monetary) prices or changing political constraints only, but asked how entrepreneurs and firms acted in certain situations. By doing so, it was expected that common situations would be identified in which entrepreneurs forego the positive returns from individual utility maximization and choose to opt for solutions offering a better fit into the cultural/political environment in the long run.

The contribution of organizational ecology is that it allows conceptually for *diversity* and *selection across time and space*. To start with the former, in China as elsewhere we observe a variety of different organizational forms of firms. Why that should be so cannot be explained by transaction cost considerations alone where it is assumed that there is a dominant organizational form that reflects technology, scarcity, (identical) business practices, and relative prices all of which are exogenously given. Instead it is assumed in what follows that different forms of firms can (and do) co-exist. In the analysis of organizational ecology what kind of organizational forms will evolve and how institutions shape the 'species' of firms depend on the identity and cultural norms or attitudes of all the economic agents involved rather than on competition and market prices.

Whether the future business system in China will offer one or two forms of firms became the topic of debate recently. On one side, there are those who claim that there is still no private sector since state agencies directly or indirectly own most of the fixed assets, and have direct access to profit and cash flow.[12] On the other side, there is the literature based on the Hong Kong, Taiwan, Singapore and overseas Chinese firms, which claims that the new business sector will be dominated by the traditional family business (Yoshira 1988; Wong 1991; Carney 1998, Kiong 1991; Redding 1996a, 1996b, Gibb Dyer Jr 1986, Chan 1982; Chu and MacMurry 1993; Hamilton and Biggart 1988; Hobday 1995, McVey 1992; Wong 1985; Yeung 1994).

New Institutional Economics in this case would argue that both streams of literature underestimate the dynamics of domestic and international competition, assisted by the liberalization of the reform package. On the other hand cultural studies of China argue that there is not one China. Different localities in China developed different cultures to the effect that different forms of firms can be expected in different parts of the country (Hendrischke and Feng 1999; Krug 2002b, Oi 1995, Qian and Weingast 1997; Rozelle and Li 1998; Rozelle *et al.* 2000). Although the data collection aimed at a frame that would capture regional diversity the database underlying the different contributions in this book is too small for employing quantitative methods. Instead two chapters (Duckett and Goodman, Chapters 6 and 7) explicitly deal with one jurisdiction, illustrating with the help of cases the interplay between politics, cultural specificities, and entrepreneurship, while the other chapters treat information from two or three provinces as one dataset.

Organizational ecology further contributes to the conceptual framework by offering the concepts of *selection* and *adaptability*. In order to explain the development of a business system, we need to know something about the dynamics – or learning curve – of economic agents: how entrepreneurs and other agents respond to changes in the environment, whether and why new forms of firms or new/other kinds of institutional arrangements are chosen all need to be explained, as will be attempted in Chapter 3 by Krug and Mehta. Chapter 4 by Krug and Pólos, by focusing on the 'species' of firms (or other organizations) and explicitly addressing the question of diversity, sheds insights into the development and features of Chinese industries and sectors in the future.

Crucial for organizational ecology is the concept of *selection*. Which kind of firm or which kind of institution governing business relations will emerge in the long run depends on a selection process. Organizational ecology overlaps with transaction cost theory as both theories assume that entrepreneurs and firms have an interest to choose that form of firm and that kind of institution that allows the organization of production and all business activities around firms at lowest (transaction) costs. In contrast to (neoclassical) transaction cost theory the assumption of fully informed, neutral, history- and culture-less profit maximizing economic agents is, however, dropped. Instead it is argued that *even if firms were established 'at whim', or without any calculus, the selection process would ensure that only those endeavours survive that come close to intentional rationality at the time they were established.* After all, without generating an added value and without revenues high enough to finance production costs and (re-) investment, firms will lose out in a competitive environment. In other words, selection ensures *ex post* rationality even if the observed *ex ante* rationality is poor. However, in clear contrast to neoclassical economics, organizational ecology insists that the selection process is not the same as, or completely determined by, market competition.

Instead *uncertainty* prevailing at the transitional stage of the Chinese economy will create specific conditions for new firms in China, whereby uncertainty follows the Knight definition in which economic agents find it impossible to even calculate the probability that one outcome will occur. As will be shown in Krug and Mehta, Chapter 3, and Krug and Pólos, Chapter 4, in such a situation firms and entrepreneurs are left with little room to manoeuvre, or anticipate promising business chances. Instead it is assumed that before firms can learn how to adapt, they will meet a 'quick death'. It is the threat of a quick death that forces entrepreneurs to search for other (organizational) forms of firms by which risk can be diversified, or invest in new institutions that promise higher survival chances. In short, the overall performance, if not survival, of a firm depends less on capital or labour productivity, and more on the effectiveness of the organizational form and surrounding institutions to lower transaction costs, and to govern 'business failures'.

While transaction cost theory assumes that the market (competition) is the only selection mechanism, New Institutional Economics and organizational ecology overlap with cross-cultural studies in the sense that they assume that there are other – cultural – factors that influence the selection process. In particular it is the inherited 'political' culture that has a powerful impact on selection. If for example the state can undisputedly claim that some firms or sectors need to be under state control or to be subsidized, then otherwise unproductive firms will be kept alive. Another example is to tolerate 'confiscation' in the form of taxation, extortion or claims on the cash flow of firms as opposed to non-tolerated forms, when state officials refuse to honour private property rights. So long as the inherited institutions from the socialist past or pre-socialist history are assumed to work to the extent that their functional value is not questioned, new 'market' institutions such as for example a 'Western' legal system will remain underemployed. To put it differently, architectured institutions (all those that are new and introduced as an alternative to inherited institutions and business practices) need to offer a high premium in form of monetary returns should they be accepted as a viable alternative to the known and accepted ones. To sum up:

> The economic environment in China asks to embark on two sets of experiments: one is to experiment with new forms for re-allocating 'private' resources and re-organising the division of labour; the other is to create and agree upon new roles for state/party agencies and institutions in different areas and at different levels of society.
> (McDermott 2002a; 2002b)

Finally, organizational ecology can also help to explain why the new business system will not see firms converging on one organizational form or one size. As opposed to functioning markets – or capitalist business systems – where competition causes the co-existence of big and very small firms, in China we find a similar 'resource partitioning', though in this case caused by political institutions. The state will guarantee and subsidize the big state firms, which in a competitive environment would have collapsed years ago, while private entrepreneurs have few incentives to let their successful firms grow into middle-scale companies. As will be seen in Hendrischke, Chapter 5, the confiscation risk, and risk diversification in general, and the incentive to constantly move assets to opportunities that promise high returns create a competitive advantage for networks that establish small companies in different lines of production.

To sum up, the following contributions centre on a model in which it is assumed that both rationality and selection are the driving forces for the development of a new business system. Cultural norms do not offset rationality or (market) selection but need to be seen as indigenous components. Aside from individual norms and attitudes it is in particular inherited political institutions that constitute 'cultural' factors. The search for institutions that facilitate private exchange shapes the development of the Chinese business system and will eventually lead to a specific business system.

The difference between the research agenda on which the following chapters are based and that of other studies on Chinese firms and sectors[13] can be summarized as follows. In the literature on the Chinese economic sector, as in the general organization theory literature, firms are usually identified by structural elements such as ownership, size, sector, scope, age or link to the product market. This set of properties is then employed to assess the comparative advantage and further development, if not the survivability of firms. Seldom are firms identified by their link to other (factor) markets, let alone the blueprint of the architects of firms. But indeed as recent studies have shown, the vision of the founding fathers with respect to organizational forms of firms and their interrelation with the 'environment' do matter (Baron and Hannan 2002).

The approach chosen here concentrates on *the genetic material of firms, namely the intention of the architects of firms and the cultural environment that shapes their intentions and makes them look for the best fit with the environment.* For this reason the interviews do not stop with asking about the 'demographic factors' of firms; instead they explicitly ask entrepreneurs and managers what mechanism, institutional devices, and organizational forms they chose when they set up a firm or searched for a better 'fit' with their economic/political environment.

1   Such a procedure is ambitious in so far as it attempts to use the history of the firm (or local agencies) as a way to looking into the future. The 'mental map' of the architects of new firms is crucial when, for example they need to decide whether to become the sole owner of a firm, even if this would imply remaining small, and limited

by a small resource base so that they would serve a local market only. The alternative, namely incorporating the firm and trading shares for access to scarce resources or mergers, might find its *ex post* explanation in the economic constraints, yet in the last analysis such a decision depends on the personal intention, if not ambition, of the entrepreneurs.

2   To start with the intentions of managers and forms implies seeing the firm as culturally and socially embedded (Granovetter 1992). As the interviews and the experiments in and around Chinese firms clearly show, there is no quasi-technical automatism at work which prompts entrepreneurs and managers to, for example, search purposefully for transaction cost saving devices. How precisely culture influences individual behaviour is still not yet fully explored. As the chapter by Redding, Chapter 2, demonstrates, culture defines 'defaults' for choice. Often enough it remains unscrutinized why certain alternatives are not chosen, courses of action are not taken, the advantage of organizational change is not seen, or institutions are not negotiated. Redding, Chapter 2, provides a thoughtful general frame that focuses on the multi-faceted interplay between culture (i.e. its main components: rationality, identity) and authority, drawing our attention to the many fallacies that accompany any attempt to use either only economic variables or only cultural variables for 'predicting' specific business systems. Jacobs, Belschak and Krug, Chapter 8, take up these issues when instead of (re-)confirming that economic considerations and cultural factors overlap, they offer a first attempt at systematically exploring conditions and situations in which individual actors choose 'traditional', culturally determined action as opposed to ways of action that reflect economic reasoning.

3   The assumption that firms in China gain identity by their cultural and social embeddedness rather than by their structural properties needs to be seen in contrast to transaction costs economics. While for example transaction costs economics would claim that Chinese firms establish networks if these function as transaction cost-saving devices, the embeddedness approach sees the transaction cost advantage as the outcome of organizational learning. In a first step Chinese entrepreneurs with a predisposition to use existing groups for economic purposes used social groups as a 'scaffold' for initiating business relations. After a while they notice the transaction cost advantage when individual activities are co-ordinated by trust and reciprocity. Thus, they have an incentive to broaden the original network as long as this does not mean having to forego the advantage of business relations based on trust and reciprocity. The chapters between Chapter 2, which describes Redding's abstract conceptual frame, and Chapter 8 by Jacobs, Belschak and Krug, try to empirically underpin the choice

between culturally and economically driven choice take up the issue and explore alternative strategies and forms of organization that from the point of entrepreneurs are expected to contribute to the survival of firms.

4   Finally, the assumption that organizational forms or identities will differ depending on the 'mindset' of the architects of the firms but also on the ways chosen to connect the firm to its social environment asks for a geographically and historically restricted data set. The chapters deal with the first generation of private entrepreneurs released under policy changes in the reforms starting in the early 1980s. That firms in, for example, Anhui might differ from firms in Fujian is not hard to see, taking into account the heterogeneity of Chinese culture. The question at stake is however to explore whether and why firms in the same sector, similar in age, scope, or working in the same (provincial) business environment, can attain different identities depending on the blueprints of entrepreneurs and/or their chosen links to political authorities, the scientific community, or other social groups. In short, we expected to find a variety of firms, each with a distinctive identity that can only be explained by the intentional embeddedness in certain networks and enforced practices with respect to allocation of resources and co-ordination of activities. The case studies in the following chapters offer illustrative examples of different forms of firms.

Research methods

Five of the following eight chapters are based on the same research techniques[14] so a general overview seems appropriate. It all started in the middle of the 1990s when two of the contributors went to Shanxi together to interview the new (wealthy) middle class (David S.G. Goodman)[15] and the managers of firms (Barbara Krug). After two years we were confident that more structured interview techniques could be used. A first questionnaire was designed (Judith Mehta and Barbara Krug) and translated, and this subsequently formed the core of the questionnaires used in much of the following empirical research. At all stages of design and translation close co-operation with Chinese colleagues was needed to ensure the unambiguous use of Chinese, and to assist in finding *conceptual equivalence*.

These questionnaires were used three times (1999, 2000, 2001), yet profited decisively from interviews in the years 1996–8. It was during the first years that most of the 'discoveries' that the Western perspective and literature had not prepared us for were revealed.

The questionnaires, written in English and Chinese, consisted of five major parts.

10

Firm and respondent background (questions 1–14A)

Here the bio data of the firms, such as size, line of business, ownership, management etc., were collected. The summary can be found in the Appendix – see Table A1 and Figures A1–A4.

Ownership, capital sourcing, the management of risk (questions 15–69)

The purpose of the questions in this part was to collect information as to how the necessary start-up capital was acquired, what the resource base of the firm was and, ultimately, whether a firm was indeed a private firm. One of the problems was that Chinese respondents have problems with understanding the concept of 'capital', which in their perception refers to financial – if not liquid – capital only. For this reason the questionnaire specifically asked who provided land, machinery, the necessary work force (human capital), and connection to supplier or customer markets (social capital). The questionnaire also distinguished between central government, local government, the community (i.e. the village) and other private groups to avoid answers such as that the 'State' provided the necessary resources. This distinction proved useful at the beginning and helped to show that the retreat of the central state from the economic sector does not mean that state agencies are not involved in the establishment of the new business sector (see Chapters 6 and 7 by Duckett and Goodman). Questions on how profit is calculated and distributed further helped to classify firms: only those which distinguished between pre- and after tax (or compulsory profit transfer to a superior state agency) profit and those which faced a market risk were included in the panel. In other words, being a claimant to residual profit and risk-taking were regarded as constituent factors of private firms. In this respect the definition follows the usage elsewhere in economics. On the other hand, private ownership over fixed capital at the time of the establishment of the firm was regarded as non-decisive for management decisions, and a firm's behaviour. Chapter 3 by Krug and Mehta will discuss the implications of the Chinese business environment at the beginning of the reforms on profit. Chapter 4 by Krug and Pólos will introduce some suggestions as to which modifications of standard assumptions about firms are necessary to catch the specific features of the development of Chinese firms.

A whole set of questions addressed the assumption that the future business system will be dominated by the Chinese form of a family business. Thus, questions were not only asked about the extent to which the family provided the necessary capital and human resources for the start up of a firm; further questions also asked to whom the owner would turn to in case of illiquidity (as opposed to insolvency), or to what extent family connections played a role in business deals or in getting access to networks. Chapter 8 by Jacobs, Belschak and Krug summarizes the findings, while Hendrischke, Chapter 5, offers an explanation for the marginal role of the family in China's emerging business system.

The firm's configuration of business/social relations (questions 70–118)

The aim of the questions in this section was to find out the kind and number of 'stakeholders'. Besides the family business hypothesis, it is also claimed that private firms are still state firms in disguise[16] albeit with a higher share of local state agencies. Therefore the questions explicitly asked about ownership of assets, cross-shareholding, long-term contracts, and the means by which business relations were established. While by definition the data set did not include 'state firms', thus precluding empirical evidence, the contributions by Duckett and Goodman, Chapters 6 and 7, illustrating the interplay between state and private entrepreneurship, show how misleading it is to use Western concepts of private versus public firms, or a private as opposed to a public sector. Their contributions are valuable reminders that the development of the business system is not merely dependent on the intentions and actions of the new private firms.

The section also asked specifically about business relations with other firms or institutions to get a clearer insight about the intensity and scope of competition. During the time of the interviews, it was quickly learned that Chinese firms move beyond their local nexus at an early stage. The interviews confirmed some results of New Institutional Economics, namely that only when firms move beyond their place of origin do questions of monitoring and enforcing behaviour become pressing.[17] A firm's success depends rather on its ability to employ institutions that allow the enforcing of promises or contracts at low costs. For this reason, the interviewees were asked to explain how they 'govern' one specific business relation.

One specific business relation (questions 119–218)

Respondents could choose between a supplier or a customer relation. In the first part of this section they were asked about kind, value and location of the business relation. In the second part respondents had to indicate 'how important' preceding social contacts had been for the selection of the business partner, to which extent credible commitments, such as the partner's willingness to invest in the relationship, determined the establishment of a business and which mechanisms of enforcement were used.

In a third part, the content of written and unwritten contracts was examined. This set of questions led to many answers when the use of standard national contracts became national law and when provincial governments decided to implement the use of the contract law. It is worthwhile mentioning that the national standard contracts do follow contract practices in the West.

In a final section the respondents were asked why they had embarked on a business relation with their partner(s):

- to broaden the firm's resource base
- vertical integration or product diversification
- cost advantages
- competitive advantages.

Agreements and disputes (questions 219–56)

The final part of the questionnaires concentrated on agreements and disputes, asking how promises and contracts were enforced. Respondents were asked whether they would use

- *economic sanctions*, such as exist in the form of ending the existing contract or switching to other partners;
- *legal sanctions*, i.e. taking the dispute to court;
- *trust*, assuming that the problem does not indicate ill-intent therefore leading to renegotiation of the contract;
- *networks*, i.e. private arbitration by somebody both partners would trust.

Crucial for the overall analysis of entrepreneurship in China was, however, the one 'open' question in the questionnaire in which the respondents were asked to recall the history of the firm up to the day of the interview. The answers to this question brought forward one of the most important results of the research, namely that *the development and growth of Chinese firms is accompanied by frequent changes in the organizational form (ownership, line of production, diversification)*. This is in striking contrast to the notion of firms in the literature where it is assumed that the form of a firm, for example a family firm, or a state controlled firm, reveals a considerable level of organizational inertia. Another result is that Chinese firms show a *weak organizational identity*. Often they can hardly be identified by product, core business, or ownership. In order to illustrate the remarkable flexibility by which Chinese entrepreneurs give up firms, re-allocate resources to start another one, change ownership structure and 'fish' for additional business opportunities, case studies are used and included in the book.

The life history of firms is presented by *cases*, each of which attempts to illustrate a specific feature. For example the cases in Chapter 5 by

Hendrischke show that corporatization of the firm was (and is) regarded as an effective means to attenuate private property rights, while the cases in Goodman, Chapter 7, illustrate the impact of state sponsored localism on the establishment and operation of firms.

Data collection

All empirical research in China relies on finding and collaborating with a Chinese partner institution, which, aside from assisting in the conceptualization of the study, is needed to help select and find interview partners. In the case of those studies that based their analysis on the standard questionnaire the Chinese research staff consisted of two or three academics plus one interpreter. Before the interviews started the Chinese partners made themselves familiar with the questionnaire and the fundamentals of interviewing techniques. The selection followed the principles described in Chapter 3 by Krug and Mehta and discussed with the Chinese partners beforehand. The sample centred on the emerging private sector with respect to output and industry. The insistence on interviewing some business failures met problems and pointed to one specific feature of Chinese entrepreneurship: unsuccessful entrepreneurs often have a 'second chance'. Underperforming firms, instead of going bankrupt, see their assets transferred to another organizational form (see Hendrischke, Chapter 5).

It was quickly learned that in order to secure completely filled out questionnaires all 256 questions had to be read aloud. As time consuming as such a procedure may be the advantage is that it allows respondents to ask when something is not clear or not quite understood. The risk that interpreters pre-formulate the answer by their way of explaining the question can be countered by having one person on the English-speaking side of the team who is proficient enough to double-check the answers. This can be best described as a *translation–re-translation* procedure aiming at reducing linguistic and conceptual ambiguity.

Collaboration at the Western side, and for this book, reflected two considerations: first, sufficient competence and interest for the conceptual setting as described above; second, knowledge about the location in which the field study was executed. The importance of the last factor can hardly be underestimated. One of the major problems in attempting to systematically explain Chinese business behaviour is to distinguish between observed differences caused by differences in local culture as opposed to differences caused by the different speed by which local authorities implement economic reforms. A third connected problem was that during the years in which the field studies were executed overall policy changed. To give an example, objections to the use of contracts in business deals were more frequent in the early years, such as 1999. That this objection declined later should not be interpreted as a change in behaviour but rather reflects the stricter implementation of a policy that made written contracts compulsory in business deals.

In order to get a 'feeling' for the possible influence of different policies, the two (Chinese and Western) research teams usually met before the interviews started but also during the evenings in order to discuss influences that were not captured in the questions.

The procedure of the interviews was as follows. The research team would drive to the company site where after a short introduction the interviews started. The size of the questionnaire implied that the interviews lasted for two or two and a half hours depending on the length of time needed for recalling the history of the firm. While most of the data were processed in China and double-checked with Chinese colleagues, both the selection and writing of cases, as well as the statistical analysis, was left for later.

Characteristics of the database

The overall database of 74 firms, on which 5 of the 9 chapters in this book depend, can be shortly summarized as follows (statistics can be found in the Appendix):

- The respondents, managers of firms or owner/managers, were aged between 27 and 61 years old, and many were young: 25 per cent of the respondents were younger than 35 years and half of the respondents were younger than 40 years (see Figure A2 in the Appendix).
- Figure A3 in the Appendix shows that private firms were young. Almost 50 per cent (48.6 per cent) were no older than 6 years, two thirds (68.9 per cent) no older than 11 years at the time of the interview.
- The firms were not small by Western standards. As Figure A4 shows 36 per cent employed more than 200 people; almost half of the firms were 'medium-sized', meaning that they had between 25 and 200 employees.
- Data on turnover was hard to collect. The respondents either refused to answer, or, amazingly, did not 'know for sure'. As far as they are available (one third of the firms interviewed) the numbers indicate that two thirds of the firms had a turnover of between 10 and 100 million RMB (in the year preceding the interview or the year before); one quarter claimed a turnover between 100 and 500 million RMB.
- The interviewed firms operate in different sectors, which the economic reforms had singled out as *complementary market sectors* as Table A1 shows.

The different contributors to this book offering empirical research made different use of the data set, or subsets, where they did not rely on their own or additional data. Table 1.1 gives the overall position.

Table 1.1 Authors' use of subsets of the database

	Pre-sample period, open interviews in Shanxi 1996–8	Shanxi 1999	Zhejiang 2000	Jiangsu 2001	Other data, interviews, places
Krug, Chs 1 and 9	Yes	Yes	Yes	Yes	Plus informal talks, 1996–2001
Redding, Ch. 2	–	–	–	–	
Krug/Mehta, Ch. 3	Yes	Yes	–	–	–
Krug/Pólos, Ch. 4	Yes	Yes	Yes	Yes	–
Hendrischke, Ch. 5	–	–	Yes	Yes	Plus informal talks 2000–1
Duckett, Ch. 6	–	–	–	–	Tianjin, 1992–3 and 1996–7 Open interviews
Goodman, Ch. 7	Yes	–	–	–	Plus other interviews 1999–2001
Jacobs/Belschak/ Krug, Ch. 8	Yes	Yes	Yes	Yes	–

A final remark: on one side it might be argued that the following contributions add up to an analysis that is still far from a comprehensive quantitative study of China's business system. Moreover, it cannot be doubted that a larger data set would offer much additional value so long as the conceptual problems described in all the chapters are not solved. On the other hand, analysing the same database from different perspectives and relying on different concepts allows a more systematic inquiry into the specific features of the emerging Chinese private sector and business system.

Acknowledgements

I gratefully acknowledge the financial support of the Royal Dutch Academy of Science, the Vereniging Trustfonds of the Erasmus University Rotterdam, and the ERIM Research School. More colleagues and friends have commented on preliminary drafts than I can possibly mention. I particularly want to thank Bart Nooteboom, Bruno S. Frey, Peter Bernholz, Michael Hannan and Uskali Maeki. Each of them offered helpful comments to one or more of the chapters. I also want to thank the participants and audiences at various workshops at the Erasmus University where drafts of some of the chapters were first presented. Special thanks to Li Tsin

May and Diederik Dorst who provided effective assistance in compiling and editing the book.

Notes

1 The best overview is to be found in the different contributions to Joint Committee, Congress of the United States (1993) *China's Economic Dilemmas in the 1990s*, Armongk, NY: M.E. Sharpe; Nolan 2001; Krugman 1994; Lardy 1995.
2 The literature centres on Whitley 1995; Whitley 1990; Whitley 1999; Redding 1990; Redding 1996a; Hamilton 1996; Hofstede 1991; Hofstede 1993.
3 In the Anglo-Saxon world this stream of literature became known as the neo-liberal view of transformation. In continental Europe this stream of literature blended with the 'ordo-liberal' tradition of the old Austrian Historian School, which concentrates on a normative theory of economic policy. For a general discussion of the neo-liberal concept see McDermott 2002b. The ordo-liberal debate can be found in the journals quoted in footnote 20 in the chapter by Krug and Pólos. See also Williamson 1985; Qian and Roland 1998; Cheung 1996; Lipton and Sachs 1990; Shleifer 1998; Lin *et al.* 1996.
4 A useful introduction into the concepts of entrepreneurship can be found in Bhidé 2000; Swedberg 2000.
5 The best overview can be found in the different volumes of the *Journal of Institutional and Theoretical Economics*, in particular vols. 149 (1994), and 156 (2000). See also Powell 1990.
6 Mentioned above, see Note 2.
7 See literature cited in Chapter 8 by Jacobs, Belschak and Krug.
8 See literature in Chapter 4 by Krug and Pólos, footnote 14.
9 This assumption was formulated first by David Stark. See Stark 1996; Stark 1998; Grabher and Stark 1997. For China see Nee 2000. This assumption is also behind the notion of a 'corporatist' model in China. See Unger and Chan 1995.
10 The best introduction can be found in Furubotn and Richter 1997.
11 The literature relevant for China can be found in the contribution by Jacobs, Belschak and Krug, Chapter 8.
12 See chapter 7 by Goodman and the literature cited therein.
13 For example Nolan (2001). On the other hand, Guthrie (1999) and Yep (2001) seem to aim at a similar research agenda without making the approach explicit.
14 Krug and Mehta, Chapter 3; Krug and Pólos, Chapter 4; Hendrischke, Chapter 5; Jacobs, Belschak and Krug, Chapter 8; Krug, Chapter 9.
15 The analysis is published in Goodman 1996.
16 See literature in the chapters by Duckett and Goodman, Chapters 6 and 7.
17 The best analysis can be found in Greif 1993.

References

Baron, J.N. and Hannan, M.T. (2002) 'The Economic Sociology of Organizational Entrepreneurship: Lessons from the Stanford Project on Emerging Companies', in V. Nee and R. Swedberg (eds) *The Economic Sociology of Capitalism*, New York: Russell Sage.

Baurmann, M. (1996) *Der Markt der Tugend. Recht und Moral in der liberalen Gesellschaft*, Tübingen: J.C.B. Mohr.

Bhidé, A.V. (2000) *The Origin and Evolution of New Business*, Oxford: Oxford University Press.

Carney, M. (1998) 'A management capacity constraint? Obstacles to the development of the overseas Chinese family business', *Asia Pacific Journal of Management*, 15:137–62.

Chan, Wellington, K. K. (1982) 'The organisational structure of the traditional Chinese firm and its modern reform', *Business History Review*, 56:218–35.

Cheung, S.N.S. (1996) 'A simplistic general equilibrium theory of corruption', *Contemporary Economic Policy*, 14.

Chu, T.C. and MacMurray, T. (1993) 'The road ahead for Asia's leading conglomerates', *McKinsey Quarterly*, 3:117–26.

Furubotn, E.G. and Richter, R. (1997) *Institutions and Economic Theory: The Contribution of the New Institutional Economics*, Ann Arbor: University of Michigan Press.

Gibb Dyer, Jr, W. (1986) *Cultural Change in Family Firms, Anticipating and Managing Business and Family Transitions*, San Fransisco: Jossey-Bass Publishers.

Goodman, D.S.G. (1996) 'The People's Republic of China: The Party-State, Capitalist Revolution and New Entrepreneurs', in D.S.G. Goodman and R. Robinson (eds) *The New Rich in Asia: Mobile Phones, McDonald's and Middle Class Revolution*, London: Routledge:225–45.

Grabher, G. and Stark, D. (eds) (1997) *Restructuring Networks in Post-Socialism: Legacies, Linkages, and Localities*, Oxford: Oxford University Press.

Granovetter, M. (1992) 'Economic action and social structure: the problem of embeddedness', in M. Granovetter and R. Swedberg (eds) *The Sociology of Economic Life*, Boulder: Westview Press:53–81.

Greif, A. (1993) 'Contract enforceability and economic institutions in early trade: the Maghribi traders coalition', *American Economic Review*, 83(3):525–48.

Guthrie, D. (1999) *Dragon in a Three-Piece Suit: The Emergence of Capitalism in China*, Princeton: Princeton University Press.

Hamilton, G.G. (1996) *Asian Business Networks*, New York: Walter de Gruyter.

Hamilton, G.G. and Biggart, N.W. (1988) 'Market culture and authority: a comparative analysis of management in the Far East', *American Journal of Sociology*, (94):52–94.

Hendrischke, H. and Feng, C. (eds) (1999) *The Political Economy of China's Provinces: Comparative and Competitive Advantages,* London: Routledge.

Hobday, M. (1995) 'East Asian latecomer firms: learning the technology of electronics', *World Development*, 23(7):1171–93.

Hofstede, G. (1991) *Cultures and Organizations: Software of the Mind*, London: McGraw-Hill.

—— (1993) 'Cultural constraints in management theories', *Academy of Management Executive*, 7(1):81–94.

Journal of Institutional and Theoretical Economics, 149 (1994), and 156 (2000).

Kiong, T.C. (1991) 'Centripetal Authority, Differentiated Networks: The Social Organization of Chinese Firms in Singapore', in G. Hamilton (ed.) *Business Networks and Economic Development in East and Southeast Asia,* Hong Kong: Centre of Asian Studies, Occasional Papers and Monographs, 99:176–200.

Krug, B. (2002a) 'Norms, numbers and hierarchy', *The American Journal of Economics and Sociology*, 61(2):555–62.

—— (2002b) 'Why Provinces?', in J. Fitzgerald (ed.) *Rethinking China's Provinces*, London: Routledge:247–76.

Krugman, P. (1994) 'The myth of Asia's miracle', *Foreign Affairs*, November–December:62–78.

Lardy, N.R. (1995) 'The role of foreign trade and investment in China's economic transformation', *The China Quarterly*, 144:1065–1082.

Lin, J., F. Cai, and Li, Zh. (1996) *The China Miracle: Development Strategy and Economic Reform*, Hong Kong: The Chinese University.

Lipton D. and Sachs, J. (1990) 'Creating a market economy in Eastern Europe: the case of Poland', *Brookings Papers on Economic Activity*:75–147.

McDermott, G.A. (2002a) 'Institutional change and firm creation in East-Central Europe: an embedded politics approach', paper presented at the 18th EGOS Colloquium, July 2002.

—— (2002b) *Embedded Politics: Industrial Networks and Institutional Change in Post Communism*, Ann Arbor: University of Michigan Press.

McVey, R. (1992), 'The Materialization of the Southeast Asian Entrepreneur', in R. McVey (ed.) *Southeast Asian Capitalism*, New York: Cornell University Southeast Asia program:7–34.

Nee, V. (2000) 'The role of the state in making a market economy', *Journal of Institutional and Theoretical Economics*, 156(1):66–88.

Nolan, P. (2001) *China and the Global Economy*, Basingstoke: Palgrave.

Oi, J.C. (1995) 'The role of the local state in China's transitional economy', *The China Quarterly*, 144:1132–49.

Powell, W.W. (1990) 'Neither market nor hierarchy: network forms of organizations', *Research in Organizational Behaviour*, 12:295–313.

Qian Y. and Roland, G. (1998) 'Federalism and the soft budget constraint', *American Economic Review*, 88(4):1143–62.

Qian Y. and Weingast, B.R. (1997) 'Federalism as a commitment to preserving market incentives', *Journal of Economic Perspectives*, 11(4):83–92.

Redding, S.G. (1990) *The Spirit of Chinese Capitalism*, New York: Walter de Gruyter.

—— (1996a) 'The distinct nature of Chinese capitalism', *The Pacific Review*, 9(3):426–40.

—— (1996b) *Weak Organisations and Strong Linkages: Managerial Ideology and Chinese Family Business Networks*, New York: Walter de Gruyter.

Rozelle, S. and Li, G. (1998) 'Village leaders and land-right formation in China', *American Economic Review*, 82(2):433–8.

Rozelle, S., Park, A., Huang, J. and Xin, H.H. (2000) 'Bureaucrat to entrepreneur: the changing role of the state in China's grain economy', *Economic Development and Cultural Change*, 48(2):227–52.

Schlicht, E. (1999) *On Custom in the Economy*, Oxford: Clarendon.

Shleifer, A. (1998) 'State versus private ownership', *Journal of Economic Perspectives*, 12(4):133–50.

Simon, H. A. (1978) 'Rationality as process and as product of thought', *American Economic Review*, 68(2):1–16.

—— (1979) 'Rational decision making in business organizations', *American Economic Review*, 69:493–513.

Stark, D. (1996) 'Recombinant property in East European capitalism', *American Journal of Sociology*, 101:993–1027.

—— (1998) *Postsocialist Pathways: Transforming Political and Property in Eastern Europe*, New York: Cambridge University Press.

Swedberg, R. (2000) *Entrepreneurship: The Social Science View*, Oxford: Oxford University Press.

Unger, J. and Chan, A. (1995) 'China, corporatism, and the East Asian model', *Australian Journal of Chinese Affairs*, 33:29–53.

Whitley, R. D. (1990) 'Eastern Asian enterprise structures and the comparative analysis of forms of business organization', *Organization Studies*, 11(1):47–74.

—— (1995) 'Eastern Asian Enterprise Structure and Comparative Analysis of Forms of Business Organisation', in P.N. Gahuri and S.B. Prasad (eds) *International Management*, London: Dryden Press:191–212.

—— (1999) *Divergent Capitalism: The Social Construction and Change of Business Systems*, Oxford: Oxford University Press.

Williamson, O.E. (1985) *The Economic Institutions of Capitalism*, London: Macmillan.

Wong, S.L. (1985) 'The Chinese family firm: a model', *British Journal of Sociology*, 36:58–72.

Wong, G. (1991) *Business Groups in a Dynamic Environment: Hong Kong 1976–1986*, Hong Kong: Centre of Asian Studies, University of Hong Kong.

Yep, R. (2001) 'Manager empowerment: political implications of rural industrialization in reform China', Ph.D. thesis, London: Routledge.

Yeung W.C.H. (1994) 'Hong Kong firms in the ASEAN region: transnational corporations and foreign direct investment', *Environment and Planning*, 26:1931–56.

Yoshira, K. (1988) *The Rise of Ersatz Capitalism in South-east Asia*, Oxford: Oxford University Press.

2

RATIONALITY AS A VARIABLE IN COMPARATIVE MANAGEMENT THEORY AND THE POSSIBILITY OF A CHINESE VERSION

Gordon Redding

Introduction

The challenge of analysing management in China is affected by large influences which make its circumstances unique. In the first place change has been very fast. The period from 1980 – when private business was conducted furtively on pavements watching out for policemen, or in whispers between conspirators – to the point now – where it accounts for half the economy and where party membership is possible for business owners – has been a period of immense growth at blinding speed. This makes the economy a moving target as far as analysis is concerned. The second distinct feature is the persistent role of the state in the economy, reflection perhaps of a historical sense of state duty to maintain order. This means that market logics have so far played a muted role in much that has occurred. The third feature which singles out China from other nations is the legacy of a major social catastrophe – the Cultural Revolution – and its unvoiced influences on people's minds and attitudes, at least now among those who lived through it when they consider the thirty million who did not.

The main idea in this paper is that societies, in making sense of their surroundings, come to different agreements in the process of interpreting reality, and that these different mental landscapes shape the behaviour of people in them in ways which produce different economic structures and behaviour. The case is developed of how a Western form of rationality was central to the evolution of Western capitalism. By examining how this took place, the ground is laid for proposing the possibility of a Chinese alternative.

21

There have been three research stimuli for this re-examination of the role of rationality in the explanation of managerial and organizational behaviours and structures comparatively. The first has been the demonstration by Whitley (1992a; 1992b; 1999a; 1999b) of the validity of the business systems approach as a means of explaining the variation in systems of capitalism globally. This approach, which places strong emphasis on the historical emergence of distinct institutional fabrics in societies, has been instrumental in grounding ideas such as those of Granovetter (1985) on the embeddedness of economic action, and the creation of a sociology of firm behaviour. The second influence has been that of Child, partly in the light of his work with Boisot (1988; 1996; 1999) and Boisot's (1995) own work in analysing the role of the codification and diffusion of information as a cultural determinant of societal infrastructures, but also in his reviews of the comparative management field (Child 1981; 2000), where he calls for an integration of ideas, and the incorporation into a single framework of the material logics of economics and technology, and the ideational logics of culture. In the more recent of these reviews he advocates a return to some of the pioneering and sophisticated insights of Weber on this complexity, many of which remain widely acknowledged but relatively unused.

This latter issue may well be affected by the somewhat inaccessible nature of many of Weber's ideas, due to their complexity, their continual evolution throughout his writing, and the widespread publications in which they appeared. Even so, their persistent appeal, despite their age, is a tribute to a quality of insight and understanding which has rarely been exceeded, and which continues to seem relevant to theorists in this field. The third decidedly less ethereal stimulus has been from the teaching of comparative management, in which I find it increasingly valuable to include the notion of 'the purposes for the existence of the firm' in explaining global variety. More generally, progress in the field of socio-economics has also brought such issues to the forefront of attention, for instance Smelser and Swedberg 1994).

The explanatory challenge exists against a background of conflicting paradigms, and the constantly running convergence debate. At one end of the spectrum lies the field of economics generally, in which its normal science assumption is that economic rationality, seen metaphorically as *homo oeconomicus*, is the central driver of economic action universally. This assumption also penetrates many related fields whose core theories are forms of applied economics, or at least are outcomes of the positivist epistemology, which tends to be its natural and inseparable companion. This would include now much of management theory, especially in strategy (Rumelt *et al.* 1991; Porter 1991), but also organization theory (Penrose 1995; Williamson 1985; Barney and Ouchi 1986), the management of trust and networking (for instance Casson 1997; Burt 1997) and, obviously, the variations on managerial economics in much of the work on operations, technology, productivity, and distribution.

At the other end of the spectrum are the more purely cultural approaches, using ethnographic insights, and based on interpretive methodologies. These tend, as is inevitable, to be rich in insight but weak in generalizability. Exceptions here are contributions such as those of Hofstede (1980; 1991) and Trompenaars (1993), which provide overarching theories of the role of culture as a determinant of economic behaviour, at least at a first-stage level of analysis. The middle ground, in which one might see integration, is difficult terrain for two reasons. First, there is the problematic issue of the unit of analysis, and the consequent social science challenge of achieving understanding. Generalizations across the global terrain will run into local variations, which undermine them. They also tend to extract issues for study and to have to take them out of context, and this deracination makes for a handicapped form of explanation. Local studies, by contrast, will have findings which may not travel. The solution offered by Ragin (1987) to this dilemma, for the study of 'wholes' comparatively, has been a creative resolution of the issue, but has also proven difficult in practice, partly on account of the second reason. This is the simple practical fact that the discipline-bound reputation systems of much academic research inhibit the occupation of the no-man's land, which has to be inhabited if multi-disciplinary work is to proceed.

At the level of business practice, the impetus towards globalization has tended to carry with it certain, often inarticulated, assumptions about the universal applicability of a particular system of organizing and managing economic behaviour. So, in recent years, the rise of the US form of capitalism to its present position of great strength in the command of wealth has carried with it ideas about its universality. The World Bank and the IMF (International Monetary Fund) have played a part in the transmission of this message. This tendency has been exacerbated by two other forces: the Asian crisis had a seriously negative effect on the reputation of alternatives (at least for those who saw it as not greatly contributed to by erratic flows of loose Western cash); and the revolution in information technology has tended, so far at least, to create the same impression. The language of the Net is predominantly English, and the communication norms and culture of the Net, if one can posit such an idea, appear to owe much to its West Coast origins.

It is, then, perhaps appropriate to consider again the possibility of a unifying theory which could deal with the questions posed by these trends, and those questions might be identified as follows:

1   What are the most appropriate units of analysis with which to explore the questions of convergence versus divergence?
2   Inside one of those units of analysis what key sets of phenomena ought to be studied to achieve improved understanding?

3   How can comparison of economic systems be achieved at a minimum
    level of complexity?

Business systems theory

There was a long gap between Weber's specification of the ideal type as
a conceptual tool in societal analysis (Weber 1988), and the beginning of
its use for the analysis of alternative systems of capitalism. Different ways
of managing have been the subject of a very large comparative management literature analysing specifics, either globally or locally, but unifying
frameworks have been few. The first well grounded studies based on the
comparison of such wholes date from recent years (Whitley 1992a; 1992b;
Albert 1993; Orru *et al.* 1991; Dore 2000) and the contribution of collections of empirical work relating to the issue has grown (McCraw 1997;
Berger and Dore 1996; Crouch and Streeck 1997; Whitley and Kristensen
1996; Hollingsworth and Boyer 1997; amongst others).

A notable attempt to revisit Weber was Stinchcombe's (1974) analysis
of the social sources of administrative rationality in a study based in Latin
America, which acknowledged the idea of the degree of rationality of
economic life as a variable capable of determining the economic progress
of a society. There has also been a large literature in economic history
and in the study of development and modernization which has included
many attempts to describe the components needed in a successful case
(for instance Landes 1998; Innes 1994; World Bank 1993), but these tend
to have stopped short of general explanatory models for comparative
purposes containing patterns of determinacy, and the explication of the
variations in the tracks pursued by different societies.

At the same time, the consciousness of variety in economic systems has
grown. Granovetter's (1985) paper on embeddedness has been influential
in legitimizing the study of social fabrics as the contexts of economic
action. The notion of path dependency and of evolutionary theory in
economics has inevitably brought variety into the account, but as Nelson
concludes from a review of that field: 'We are far from a powerful theory
of the evolution of economic institutions. Undoubtedly in part this reflects
the still primitive state of our ability to work with cultural evolutionary
theories' (Nelson 1994).

Whitley's (1992a) initial study of different systems of capitalism in East
Asia was based on an evolutionary view of business systems, and their
emergence as distinct systems was presented as a result of their interaction with particular societal fabrics. Thus Japanese, Korean and regional
ethnic Chinese ways of co-ordinating economic behaviour were seen as
products of societal histories of development and institution building which
differed markedly from each other. The business system is seen in this
theory as a combination of three interacting features: the way in which

24

structures of ownership, typical of that society, bring together the elements needed to construct a functioning enterprise, or an equivalent unit of co-ordinated behaviour; the way such enterprises typically co-ordinate economic action among themselves across an economy; and the way that styles of managing an enterprise result in different forms for the co-ordination of their employees into co-operative relations with the unit's purposes. Using these characteristics it is possible to delineate the main ideal typical differences between, say, the *keiretsu*, the *chaebol*, and the Chinese family business. As Whitley points out:

> Each business system can therefore be seen as systematic, inter-related responses to the three fundamental issues of any market-based system. These are: first, what sorts of economic activities are to be authoritatively integrated and coordinated towards what competitive priorities? Second, how are market relations of compe-tition and cooperation to be organized and firm's activities connected? Third, how are economic activities to be managed in authority hierarchies?
>
> (Whitley 1992a)

These business systems are seen as explicable in terms of their interde-pendence with dominant social institutions, including established beliefs and values, and such key institutions cannot be understood without reference both to political contexts and to the pre-industrial formation of both primary and secondary institutions. Among such aspects are authority and subordination relations, structures of trust, and the degree of insti-tutional differentiation present in a society. Political systems, forms of elite legitimacy, and especially the presence or absence of pluralism and decentralization, are particularly relevant for such accounts (Whitley 1992a).

In his later treatment of the institutional features which structure business systems Whitley (1999a) identifies them within four categories: the state; the financial system; the skill development and control system; and trust and authority relations. Their contents are seen as follows:

- *The state*
  Dominance of the state and its willingness to share risks with private owners
  State antagonism to collective intermediaries
  Extent of formal regulation of markets.
- *Financial system*
  Capital market or credit based.
- *Skill development and control system*
  Strength of public training system and of state–employer–union collab-oration

Strength of independent trade unions
Strength of labour organization based on certified expertise
Centralization of bargaining.
* *Trust and authority relations*
Reliability of formal institutions governing trust relations
Predominance of paternalist authority relations
Importance of communal norms governing authority relations.

In this formulation we have three sets of features which Whitley sees as 'proximate', in other words more directly connected with practice, and these are the first three. The last category he would see as 'background' institutions in that their influence is less direct (Whitley 1992b). The explanatory model which connects these institutional elements with the business system features takes full account of issues of reciprocal determinacy, and of the complex interconnections between factors. It is also used to analyse dynamic processes in the entire structure and so to deal with change. In this regard it is especially valuable in being able to illustrate the nature of path dependency at the societal level, and to assist with clarifying questions of convergence (or as the argument is put, the continuing of divergence).

It should be noted here that, in the case of China, the role of the state has been so strong up to now that the evolutionary path followed by the economy cannot be said to have been 'free' or 'normal'. The laws of the market have had only a recent influence, and are still constrained, and for that reason the path of evolution needs to be seen as heavily conditioned. This is of special relevance when making comparisons with other systems, and when making predictions as to what happens next.

The role of culture

Semantic problems abound in classifying any approach in this field. It is inappropriate to consider Whitley's work as representing an 'institutionalist' perspective when so much of his explanation rests on factors such as authority and trust. This is because his interpretation of culture is as a set of institutions, a position with a strong pedigree (for instance Berger and Luckmann 1966). Nevertheless it might be worth examining the range of factors within this and other socio-economic models in order to pose these questions: Have all the key cultural (or institutional) variables been accounted for? Is there a significant piece missing from the jigsaw? Especially, as a point of focus, I would wish to follow up the challenge posed by Whitley to illuminate the question of *what competitive priorities* are typically pursued by firms in these varying ideal type national systems. In simple terms what is the firm for? What are the purposes for its existence as it is conceived, and acted upon, by those who set and manage its behaviour?

26

The purely culturalist explanations, such as those of Hofstede (1980; 1991), and Trompenaars (1993), although they do not lead to such complete explanatory results as will furnish an understanding of distinct capitalist systems, nevertheless attempt to be reasonably exhaustive on the question of cultural determinants of economic structures. For Hofstede this force is expressed as five dimensions of the collective programming, or software, of the mind, as follows: power distance; individualism/collectivism; masculinity/femininity; uncertainty avoidance; and long versus short-term orientation (or Confucian dynamism). These mental frameworks are said to predispose individuals in a society to organize and relate in certain ways. A large body of supporting empirical literature is available to illustrate the workings of these patterns of determinacy, and some theorizing is available to connect with organization theory more generally (Hofstede 1991), but the absence of an ability to address the more direct determinants in the 'proximate' institutional fabric leaves the contribution of this work to be substantial but essentially supportive.

The work of Trompenaars uses a different conceptual framework from that of Hofstede, who worked inductively from a large empirical base. Trompenaars operationalized the components of culture as conceived in the classic sociology literature, relying largely on the Parsonian pattern variables. The main dimensions used were: universalism/particularism; individualism/collectivism; neutral/emotional; specific/diffuse engagements; achievement/ascription; perception of time; and activism/fatalism. He also sees culture as being manifest as choices of emphasis between alternatives, each of which might remain present, rather than as positions on a set of linear continua. The implications of this set of cultural features have been analysed as determinants of seven cultures of capitalism (Hampden-Turner and Trompenaars 1993), but again without addressing fully the mechanics of determinacy or the range of ancillary causal features.

Specific aspects of managing in different societies have been the subject of decades of work and reviews of it have consistently advocated more theoretical development (Roberts 1970; Barrett and Bass 1976; Child 1981; Beaty and Mendenhall 1991; Boyacigiller and Adler 1991; Triandis 1992; Redding 1994; Child 2000). Progress in the study of societal effects on management in a fuller sense was pioneered by the work of Abegglen (1958) in Japan, and Maurice *et al.* (1982) in Europe, and has now given rise to a flowering of interest, much of it centred on the European Group for Organization Studies (EGOS) (for instance Foss 1999) and in the field of New Institutionalism (Hodgson 1994). In most of this work, however, there is little open discussion of questions of managerial purposes. They may well be implicit in many accounts, but issues surrounding the reasons why key economic actors do things are rarely dealt with directly. DiMaggio's (1994) review of work in the field of culture and the economy saw culture as playing many roles in economic life and specifically

27

'constituting economic actors and economic institutions, defining the ends and means of action, and regulating the relationship between means and ends'. In particular he saw it as crucial to the understanding of matters central to economics: the formation and stability of preferences; and change and innovation in economic institutions.

If 'the formation of preferences' is cultural and important, and if the choice of competitive priorities by actors is key to understanding business systems, then it is perhaps appropriate to go back to the issue of rationality, not as it is conceived by economists, but as it was seen by Weber.

Disaggregating rationality

Rationality has an air of unassailable virtue. It is taken by most to be one of the principal foundations of economic and societal progress, at least in the Western world, and the key to much of current Western civilization. Thus Stinchcombe (1990) observes: 'The achievement of civilization could be formulated as the successful detachment of the faculties that make people rational from the limiting context of personal goals, so that they can be applied to the improvement of social life.'

So too Gellner, in discussing 'rationality as a way of life' and in discussing the philosophers of the Age of Reason, has noted that:

> The thinkers who theorized about the nature of this alleged inner cognitive and moral guide, the repository of our identity, were also, in effect, knowingly or otherwise, codifying the rules of comportment of a newly emerging civilization, one based on symmetry, order, equal treatment of claims and of evidence. They were helping to bring about such a civilization.
>
> (Gellner 1992)

Rationality is usually seen in conjunction with bureaucracy, the latter providing the discipline needed to generate the co-operation and the labour of large numbers of people. In this, rationality becomes a property of the system, in that it isolates economic decision making from personal influences, and causes it to be driven by calculation and the logical pursuit of pre-defined purpose. Weber saw that people would behave more rationally in some circumstances than in others, and that those circumstances were determined in large measure by societal conditions. He saw that the development of Western societies had been accompanied by an increase in the quantum of rationality, and that it was thus a variable in one straightforward sense. But he additionally saw that it was a variable in another sense. He saw that the purposes towards which a rational system could direct effort could also vary. He referred, for instance, to the 'specific and peculiar rationalism of Western culture' and explained, by way of illustration, that there could be a rationalization of mystical contemplation which, viewed from other departments of life, could seem specifically irrational. Each field, with its own rationality, could be so 'in terms of very different ultimate values and ends, and what is rational from one point of view may well be irrational from another' (Weber 1930). This feature of his theory, and especially its implications for the comparative analysis of societally defined economic systems, seems not to have been given the degree of acknowledgement it would appear to deserve.

The literature on rationality is not always clear in its terms. There is rationality, reason, and rationalism, and the qualifying of the basic notion as formal, substantive, instrumental, calculative, and value-based. I shall use the term *rationality* to mean the application of reasoning (and in some forms the addition of calculation) to the achievement of specified ends. *Reason* will be taken as that more abstract quality of thinking which is being applied. *Rationalism* will be seen as the social tendency to apply reason by processes (including mental) of rationality. The other qualified sub-categories will be defined as the argument proceeds.

Human action can be said to be rational when purposes are achieved in the most efficient way possible, in other words with the least expenditure of costs, or effort, or dissatisfaction. In the context of the economy, stress has normally been given to the use of money as the basis of the calculations, which will serve to drive behaviour to desired ends. In referring to the achievement of purposes, however, it is necessary to acknowledge that they do not come attached to the pursuit of them. The determining of purposes is a separate act from the calculated decisions about how best to achieve them, and it is an act which may be communal, and which arguably is more significant than the calculated pursuit of them. At the same time, even though purpose and logical pursuit are distinguishable, they are closely intertwined as ends and means.

For this reason a distinction is commonly made between *formal* and *substantive rationality*. The first of these is the objective, scientific, value-neutral calculation of the best means to achieve something. It is an abstract notion independent of the application of it in particular circumstances. Thus the mathematics and the reasoning behind the concept of a price–earnings ratio exist separately from the use of the concept by analysts, and an entire reservoir of such calculi lies available for use by those wishing to apply them. The derivation and refinement of them is regularly pursued by abstract analysis based on some collective agreement about the nature of the efficiency seen as the aim of the system. Formal rationality has, in addition to content, a certain style. The main components of this are a methodical approach, the scrupulous use of objectivity and logic, and the formality of debate.

Substantive rationality has a different nature. It deals with the purposes of the economic system, and more specifically with how the system's benefits are to be allocated, i.e. who gets what. This lies at the heart of a culture's system of power. In Weber's (1922) terms it is: '. . . the degree to which the provisioning of given groups of persons with goods is shaped by economically oriented social action under some criterion (past, present, or potential) of ultimate values, regardless of the nature of these ends'.

Weber further acknowledged that the idea introduced ambiguities. Instead of assessment being monopolized by formal calculation, it would be subject to criteria of ultimate ends. These might be ethical, political, utilitarian, hedonistic, feudal, egalitarian etc. The results of economic action would be measurable against these scales of *value rationality* or *substantive goal rationality*, there being an 'infinite number of possible value scales for this type of rationality'.

The way in which Weber saw this second main aspect of rationality (i.e. the substantive as opposed to the formal working) was via two processes. In the first of these, standards of judgement would be derived from the system of societal values, examples of which might be social justice, equality, status distinction, perceptions of national power. These would then be used as bases from which to judge the outcomes of economic action. Current examples come to mind in the assessment of companies' records on environmentalism, or directors' fees, or products perceived as harmful.

In the Chinese context it is arguable that defence against insecurity is a deep-seated major driver of behaviour, and that this is occasioned by specific historical experience, and legitimated broadly within society by Deng Xioaping's comments encouraging the pursuit of wealth.

In the second form, judgements might come to be made, from an ethical, ascetic, or aesthetic point of view, of what Weber termed the 'mentality', as well as the instruments of economic activity. One can imagine examples of the mentality being greed, discrimination, cronyism, and examples of the instruments monopoly, corruption, and non-disclosure. In transferring societal values into the assessment of economic behaviour, the formal rationality of calculation might become quite secondary, or even inimical to these alternative ends. But, in that process of transfer, a society would be shaping its economic and associated institutions to reflect its collective ideals. In this sense the process is rational. It interprets the society's purposes and delivers what is desired. During such a process, the parallel mechanisms of formal calculative rationality are simply instrumental and secondary, and the way they are used depends upon the substantive conditions, in other words the criteria of ultimate ends.

Rationality in context

As this argument proceeds it will be necessary to break down further the workings of substantive rationality, and to identify its constituents, but before doing so it will perhaps be useful to locate the entire concept of rationality within a schema for the explanation of comparative economic behaviour. The detail may then benefit from being seen in context. For this purpose it is proposed that Whitley's framework should be used as the template, but that it should be amended in three ways. First, there should be a distinction, in the interests of conceptual convenience, between the institutional level of his model and a level seen as cultural. This does not challenge the idea of cultural features being conceived as institutions, as the elasticity of both categories is likely to remain unresolved by theorists. What it does, more modestly, is to return certain categories of analysis, particularly those of authority and trust, to the domain in which they are more commonly seen. This is also more in line with Weber's separation of ideas from institutions as I shall explain later. It does not in any sense change the arguments about determinacy which have been developed, except to strengthen the implication that the features seen here as cultural are in some sense 'prior' to the emergence of the more concrete institutional fabric of a society.

Second, I would propose that rationality, in the sense to be developed further in this paper, should be treated as a component of this cultural layer. This then leaves the treatment of culture as being represented in three main components:

- *rationality*, which covers the question of the purposes for economic action as they are adopted by a society, and the preferences for certain ways of achieving those purposes;
- *identity*, which covers the way in which a society derives and maintains its form of horizontal order, including the structuration of trust;
- *authority*, which covers the way in which a society structures and legitimates its form of vertical order.

Reasons for the implied assumption that these three categories are exhaustive for the cultural contribution to the larger explanation, are presented elsewhere (Redding 2001), but they are based on the notions that societal structures derive essentially from the choices made over what Polanyi (1994), after Malinowski, saw as the two core elements of reciprocity and redistribution, in other words the use of relationships and the use of power. In a similar way, Platteau (1994) has argued for the core salience to a society of the same factors, in his case termed 'mutuality of agreement', and the 'structure of basic property rights'. Weber, similarly, has been represented by Schluchter (1981) as conceiving the integration of societies in terms of two challenges: social integration, which is largely about identity and horizontal connections; and system integration, which is concerned with the distribution of power within and among partial groupings.

31

Third, I would propose to re-label the main institutional components in Whitley's model to reflect their nature as facilitating, or transformative agents, in line with Eisenstadt's (1968) suggested amendment of Weber's interpretation of the workings of Protestantism. Thus they are referred to here as capital, human capital, and social capital. This removes government from the list of core institutions and requires justification. I see the role of government as being formative, alongside parallel roles of individuals such as entrepreneurs, and civil society generally, in interpreting societal values into institutional structures. This does not detract from government's role in a number of cases as principal determinant of the resulting business system, as, for instance, would be necessary in explaining the managed markets of East Asia, or the economy of France. The case of China is clearly one where government remains the prime mover.

A final minor addition is the inclusion of specific reference to external influences beyond those strictly bounded within one society. These are fully acknowledged by Whitley in various accounts, and it is simply a matter of order to specify them here. They are seen as the 'material' logics of economics, especially price, and of technology, on the one hand, and on the other, the 'ideational logics' of other cultures and philosophies, which may well be influential. This derives from a review by Child (2000) of the challenges of analysing both national organizations, and also organizations which are themselves built across nations.

The model containing this context is given as Figure 2.1. In this, the emergence of alternative systems of capitalism is depicted in three layers. For a specific society there is a base layer of culture, seen here as a composite of rationality, identity, and authority.

Rationality serves to formulate ends and to shape the adoption of means. Identity is concerned with the shaping of horizontal order. Authority is concerned with the shaping of vertical order. This basic cultural conditioning influences the creation of institutions in a process of complex historical interaction, which includes individuals, governments, and the bodies of civil society. The institutions of particular relevance to the shape taken by the business system are those which serve to amplify or suppress access to the core requirements of that system. They are the facilitating structures, which control access to capital, human capital, and social capital.

The emergence of a distinct business system is a matter of the historical interaction between these 'proximate' and 'background' determinants and the structures for co-ordinating economic behaviour, seen here in Whitley's terms, but named more cryptically, as the forms of ownership, networking, and management. The external influences are also seen as permanent features of the reciprocal flows of influence.

Rationality has been expanded in this diagram to make clearer the distinction between its 'absolute' and 'relative' components. The absolutes are the objective, mathematical logics, which underpin the practices of

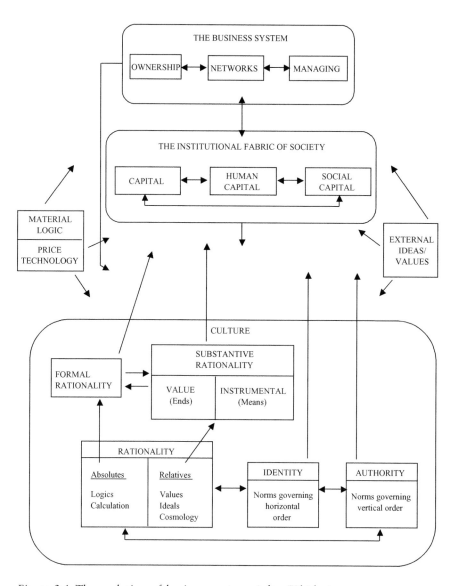

Figure 2.1 The evolution of business systems (after Whitley)

calculation, and they include notions of efficiency, which are, as it were, scientific. These absolutes, examples of which might be algebra, or mathematics itself, are available to all cultures and might be thought to exist independently of culture, unless one takes account of the historical differences in their formulation in different locations. The relative components in rationality are seen as varying between societies, and to act as the determinants of the different ends and means selected by societies in their evolution. In the cases of most interest to management analysts this evolution is in the direction of 'progress' in some form, but the defining of the shape of such progress begins here with core values, ideals, and the society's adopted cosmology.

Swedberg (1998) has observed that 'Weber is far ahead of contemporary economic sociology in his analysis of *rationality*' and that his 'concept of rationality is unique, not only among sociologists but also among economists'. Seeing it as historically emergent, and as variable, not just between societies but among the parts within a society, he posed challenges which have not yet been taken fully into account in the use of the concept. It is, in the light of such comment, worth probing further into how Weber conceived the workings of this force.

The mechanisms whereby these two aspects of rationality assist in shaping the institutional fabric of society are analysable in two categories. The absolutes are manifest in formal rationality. Specifically, in the Western case (see Figure 2.2), this has been a matter of money-based calculation, of applying the principle of accountability, and of logically co-ordinating the pursuit of efficiency. These are seen as independent of the specification of particular ends and particular means. Formal rationality is applicable in principle to whatever ends may be specified, and whatever means chosen.

The choosing of ends and means is a matter of the substantive rationality referred to by Weber (see Figure 2.1). The German adjective is *materielle* and this conveys much of the meaning in this elusive but important concept. It suggests rationality being put to use in practice, and manifest in its application. It is, as the English translation implies, rationality given substance, as opposed to rationality lying available for use in an abstract mathematical formula. In analysing this, Weber made a crucial distinction between two components within it: *value rationality* is concerned with ends ; and *instrumental rationality* is concerned with means (i.e. two subsets within substantive rationality). The crucial defining aspect of instrumental rationality is that it proceeds by deliberate planning. It is in other words about making things happen. As interpreted by Schroeder (1992) 'it is instrumental in that practical and worldly goals are pursued by direct means'. Weber saw, however, that action which is instrumentally rational (*zweckrational*) does not account exhaustively for the sum of resulting economic behaviour. There is also much traditionalism in economic action, and this is not instrumentally rational – it is in other words not consciously planned. Instead it is *value rational (wert-rational)*. Noting that Weber introduced no specific term for the kind of economic action which flows from value rationality, Swedberg (1999) considered that Weber's intention was to treat the distinction between value and

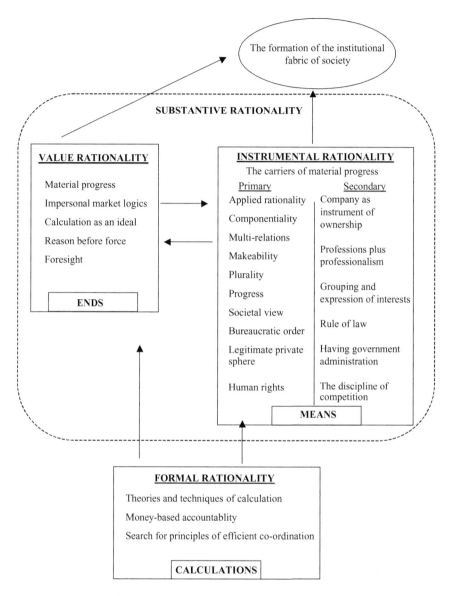

Figure 2.2 The workings of Western-style rationality (an interpretation of Weber)

instrumental rationality in a similar way to the distinction at a more general level between formal and substantive rationality; in other words to see them as not necessarily coinciding in all respects. They work in parallel but in different ways, and they are intertwined.

For this reason, at this first-stage level of consideration, they are seen as the two components of the general category substantive rationality. The value component is related to setting societal goals, and to the expression of the values and ideals, which derive largely from the cosmology. The instrumental component is that which is concerned with planning and implementation, effective co-ordination of action, and the shaping of the institutional fabric.

Alongside rationality as components of a culture, are the collections of values and norms which serve to shape a society's horizontal and vertical order. It is an analytical convenience to make such separations, and the interpenetrations between them are acknowledged, but the specific understanding of, in simple terms, (a) the societal setting of purposes, (b) horizontal order, and (c) vertical order is perhaps helpful in the work of conceptualizing phenomena of such complexity. Acknowledgement is also given that patterns of determinacy are inevitably reciprocal, and that the cultural features are as likely to be shaped and remoulded by the institutions designed to facilitate economic action, and by economic behaviour and its results, as they are to do the shaping. The material and ideational logics penetrating from outside are also inseparable from any full understanding.

The workings of rationality

It is now necessary to proceed to a last stage of unpacking of the concept of rationality, in order to provide a clearer understanding and to illustrate meaning. Figure 2.2 shows more specifics and also introduces a final subdivision within instrumental rationality. As guiding labels for the main subdivisions, formal rationality is associated with *calculation*, value rationality is associated with *ends*, and instrumental rationality is associated with *means*. These are of course convenient simplifications and acknowledged as such, but they do convey key general distinctions. For purposes of explanation the details in Figure 2.2 are about the case of Western development seen broadly, and are not intended to be taken as relevant to all societies. The fact that they have worked successfully in many Western cases does not necessarily demonstrate their universality in any normative sense.

Formal rationality has been described already and requires no further elaboration. It has its own abstract existence as an available tool and a set of logical principles and forms of calculation. Its use may well vary in both extent and intensity.

Value rationality is essentially about the derivation and application of a society's notions of what is important to it. It is the ethical sphere, and this includes cosmology and religion and their effects on priority setting. In locating it in the larger context, Weber (1922) added a significant

36

clarification to an earlier work, as follows: 'Interests (material and ideal) not ideas directly determine man's action. But the world views, which were created by ideas, have very often acted as the switches that channelled the dynamics of the interests.'

The distinction made here between the material and the ideal is essentially that between (a) human concerns for their well being, health, and longevity, and (b) their search for meaning or salvation. The search is for both material and spiritual goods. This search ends with the institutional realm which, in Schluchter's (1981) term, 'mediates between ideas and interests', being embedded in constellations of both, and 'only through institutionalization do material and spiritual wants receive a socially relevant solution'. It is worthy of note here that Weber claimed relative autonomy *(Eigenrecht)* and its own dynamics, for the institutional sphere.

Value rationality: the rationale for ends

There is no systematic account in Weber of the institutional realms and value spheres, but Schluchter (1981) proposes a summary in terms of four partial orders, which he believes do not distort Weber's reasoning. These are:

1   The 'natural' order, which is tied to natural reproduction, especially family and kinship, and which is at the core of a much larger order, the educational order.
2   The economic order, which meets the recurrent, normal wants of everyday life.
3   The cultural order, of which religion is the most important element.
4   The political order, which protects social life on a territorial basis internally and externally.

Within these, it would be possible to fit, reasonably exhaustively, the processes of evolution of institutions and to study the way in which societal ideas and values over time come to shape the institutions of capital, human capital and social capital. The quality of these institutions as facilitators determines the material success of the business system. The quality of these institutions as reflectors of the core values of the society determines their legitimacy as cultural artefacts and will have a bearing on their adaptiveness under both local and external pressures to change. To take an illustration, the Japanese system of financing industry, i.e. the institutional category of capital in the Japanese case, grew out of ideals for the formation of society which left the state in a key co-ordinating but not commanding role in capital allocation. It also included notions of corporate identity, which assumed networking and widespread collaboration. It also assumed long-term perspectives on risk, and strong ethical obligations to key employees. It assumed the transfer of private savings, based on family thrift, into the industrial capital system. It saw the essential purpose of the firm as the long-term stable employment of a core set of people, and the respect accorded executives was based largely on their capacity to live up to that ideal. Related values affecting the psychology of competition, both locally and internationally, would shape the details of the workings of the capital system. The closeness of fit between the Japanese value sphere and the consequent institutional realm is suggested in the very distinct nature of the Japanese capital system (Calder 1993). The difficulty it now has in adjusting is a natural consequence of this embedding.

The Chinese case presents a stark contrast to that of the Japanese. The Chinese state took command. It planned welfare into the economic structure and chose to ignore market effects. Its current transition is to an undefined alternative.

Turning now to the Western case in the illustration, it is proposed that five components of value rationality might serve to illustrate the workings of the evolutionary process. These are 'habits of the mind' of special significance in shaping Western capitalism. They express important ideals around which the economy is shaped. They define 'what it is about'. They are therefore selected from a wider and more general set.

The idea of material progress

To pursue material progress with the intensity witnessed in the Western case a society must have a fundamental belief in the possibility of such an advance, a mindset in contrast with that described by Foster (1965) for the great majority of the world's peasant populations. This mindset is seen by him as 'the image of limited good' and it is founded in the experience of subsistence living in relatively closed communities, and the consequent coming to terms with a surrounding universe in which the total quantity of good available to the society is perceived as fixed, and social ideals form around living with that. In the Western societies which have developed up to now, there has grown an understanding that progress, growth, invention, betterment are not just possible but central to the economic system. The total amount of good is permanently expandable.

In a sense this becomes its core rationale. Firms must grow, people must attempt to accumulate greater wealth, quality of life should keep on improving. For China, the full (as opposed to temporary) means implications of such a 'Western' mentality might include, over time, the dismantling of the social structures of reciprocity which are traceable to that earlier mindset. The systemic nature of such social systems is such that you cannot choose to change one component and ignore the side effects.

The impersonality of the market

The market is impersonal in that someone entering as a buyer or seller does not carry into the transaction a set of signals about his or her social position which affect that transaction. More or less anyone can buy from anyone. The people transacting are seen in the abstract. They are also free and independent. Their rights and duties are strictly equal and their personal circumstances mainly irrelevant. In the pre-industrial condition, social status determined largely what an individual did, not the other way around, and it was the contribution of the capitalist market system to reverse this. The source of such reformulated identities was money, which allowed entire populations to detach themselves from their backgrounds and re-invent themselves. This was a radical redesign of the basic ordering framework of society (Platteau 1994) and it released huge volumes of new energy which served to legitimate it. But it rested on a collective understanding of its value, in other words the contribution it made to achieving what was believed to be a better society. Adam Smith's *Wealth of Nations* would become its bible, and its impact on value formation in many countries would be high. At the centre of this set of beliefs is the core ideal of personal freedom.

In the case of China, the depersonalizing of market transactions would be as radical a redesign for the society as it was for the West. But the difference in their starting points, in terms of values, and the absence in China of incipient forms of institutional trust support in civil society suggest that both (a) the trajectory of movement and (b) the end result in economic structures are likely to be different.

The use of calculation

It has been noted earlier that formal rationality, in a set of calculative techniques, exists independently of the use of it. At the heart of rationality in the world of business is commercial book-keeping as the basis of capital accounting, and this mechanism is served by three ancillary ideals: (a) the continual adaptation of means to ends; (b) the intelligent calculation of probabilities; and (c) the reliability and standardization of information. In each of these activities questions and answers are most commonly formulated in money terms. To say that accounting is the language of business is to say that it defines the terms, and their meanings, with which business issues are debated and decided. In the process it establishes the key value of scientific calculation as the basis for deciding matters.

Reason and argument replace force

This is a wider extension of the principle of calculation. Gellner (1992) makes the point that reason is not just a mental route to a supposed truth or set of legitimate principles, but it is also a lifestyle. It rests on method and precision, tidiness and order, above all in thought. Separable issues are dealt with one at a time, so as to avoid conflating criteria. The latter have to be impartial and stable, not arbitrary. Achievement is steadily progressive. Procedures are de-sacralized. Innovation is adopted when needed. Labour is divided and specialized. A rational accounting for success and failure is sought. Dealings between people are guided by the free choice of ends by both parties, and by their individual assessment of the advantages. The organization of society is not given, but is the sum of the free and rational contracts. Such an ideal, with all its manifestations, is not permanently on display in all cases in a Western economy, but it is unquestionably established as one of the most influential sets of guiding principles for personal, social, and organizational conduct. The historically recent capacity of China to deviate from this is visible in the Cultural Revolution and the Tienanmen Square massacre.

Foresight

Foresight stands in contrast to mental worlds of seemingly more focused vision, in which the future does not need to be brought forward into the present. The kind of consciousness of time which is capable of spanning past, present, and future, and is measurable on a wristwatch 'is drastically alien to the overwhelming majority of traditional societies in the Third World, and quite possibly to all of them' (Berger *et al.* 1973). There are arguably two main drivers of the habit of using foresight. First, the use of technology has tended to raise the level of investment needed in most economic processes, and has increased the significance of forecasting risk into the future. Second, administration, as manifest in bureaucracy, is largely a means of reducing uncertainty, and of bringing under control, in predictable patterns, the behaviour of potentially very diverse components. The diversity includes people and their behaviour, but also less animate features such as currencies, commodity values, and technical changes. Such attempting of control will inevitably lead to taking a view forward into the new period being prepared for. The value being expressed here is, at base, that of mastery.

The examples just given of components of value rationality in the Western case could be supplemented with others whose sources might be psychological, or political, or legal, or ethical. They are offered not as a comprehensive statement of the workings of this aspect of culture, but more as a means of illustrating the shaping of a core set of purposes by the fusion of separate contributions. The 'end' to which they all point, in the Western case, is the central, driving purpose of material progress based on principles of open competition, and the incorporation of individual contribution and motivation via systems which express the principles of reason and of personal freedom. Mastery of the natural world, seen in the use of science and technology, is a component of the same set of ideas. Ethical principles, such as fairness and equality, and political ideals, such as democracy, might appear as qualifiers at different times and places. Although there is a widespread assumption that such ends are universal to all societies, there is counter-evidence that the world is not so simple. Of course societies will normally wish collectively to improve their conditions, but the meaning of 'improvement' may be subject to wide interpretation. No discussion of Korean 'ends' would be complete without reference to the centrality of state identity and performance comparative to other states. No explanation of German managerial ideology could exclude the communitarian nature of much thinking. For Japan, the ethics of the Tokugawa period, and especially the consciousness of specific bounded social responsibilities, would need to be included as a component of the overall aim being sought. As Lodge and Vogel (1987) have shown, national ideologies are both complex and constantly shifting, and they also have very complex interconnections with what we are referring to here as the institutional fabric of society. They conclude, from a study of nine industrialized countries, that:

> Because ideological systems have such great staying power, they greatly affect how leaders, managers, and ordinary citizens analyse and respond to their environment. The ideological framework may be implicit and people may not even be aware of the assumptions they are making, but the impact of ideology is nonetheless profound.
>
> (Lodge and Vogel 1987)

To consider the largely non-industrialized world of Islam, or the complex value domains of India and China, is of course to add greater variety again, and such contrasts are now having to be folded in to the world of business practice, as globalization proceeds to carry into those arenas the Western assumptions of so many corporations.

Instrumental rationality: the rationale for means

The second of the divisions of substantive rationality is what Weber termed instrumental. The phrase is suggestive of devices for the accomplishment of purposes, the shaping of the instruments to achieve the ends envisaged. This is about 'means' and why they are chosen. These are the ideas which become intimately associated with the formation of institutions, and which, in some versions of explanation, are themselves institutions. For instance, is bureaucracy an idea, or an idea operating as an institution? Without entering a complex debate, it is proposed to simply assume here that even though culture and institutions are intertwined, it is convenient to consider ideas as cultural and ideas manifest as regular patterns of behaviour as institutions. The justification for examining the contents of instrumental rationality is simply that attention needs to be paid to the *rationale within institutions* if their evolution is to be comprehensible and predictable. Such rationale deserves understanding, and so is identified here as a field of analysis and influence. The ideas are taken to be distinguishable from the social structures they produce.

The primary carriers of modernization have been proposed as two: technological production; and the bureaucratically organized state (Berger *et al.* 1973). These have been supplemented by a series of secondary carriers such as: urbanization; a 'mobilized' stratification system; the 'private sphere' as a key context of individual life; scientific and technological innovation; mass education; and mass media. The primary carriers are seen not just as the main agents of modernization but also as the 'primary carriers of modern consciousness'. They are in some sense 'stronger' than the secondary carriers because there are more intrinsic linkages between them and clusters of consciousness. As Berger *et al.* (1973) observe, they are 'more firmly "tied together" and therefore more difficult to take apart'. Any attempt to restructure consciousness will succeed in inverse proportion to its closeness to the primary carriers. The 'themes of the symbolic universe of modernity' which derive from these two primary carriers are seen as follows:

- *From technological production*
  1. The application of rationality
  2. Componentiality: reality in separable components
  3. Multi-relationality: an enormous variety of relations with people, objects and abstract entities
  4. Makeability: life as a problem-solving enterprise
  5. Plurality: multiple spheres of meaning
  6. Progressivity: onward and upward, and acceptance of change.
- *From the bureaucratically organized state*
  1. Society itself seen as both problematic and manageable
  2. Bureaucratic order as a means of absorbing plurality
  3. Private sphere legitimized alongside the public sphere
  4. Human rights related to bureaucratically identifiable rights.

It is important here to consider the way in which this set of primary carriers, and their clusters of subsidiary rationales, are different from the earlier category entitled value rationality. There is, at first glance, some overlap between the sets, as for instance between 'material progress' within value rationality and 'progressivity' within instrumental. The answer lies in the difference, proposed here for analytical convenience, between ends

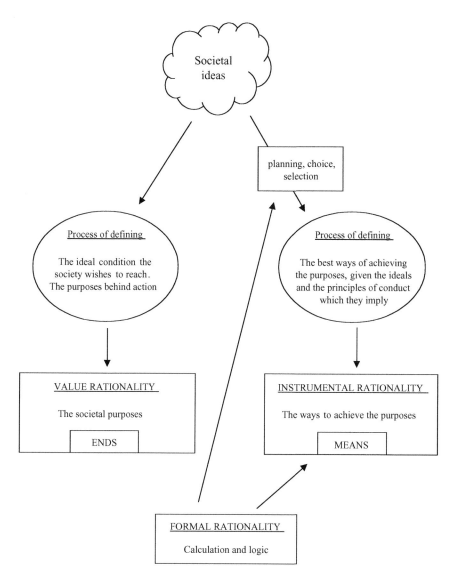

Figure 2.3 The separation of ends and means and the fields of rationality

and means. In practice much running together occurs, and the separation is not always clear, but the two frameworks of thinking do have different ramifications for social reality. The description, given earlier, of the general intention of Western societies as they develop, was an amalgam of the ideals given under value rationality. It said nothing about the mechanisms whereby the achievement was to be pursued. The same general ideals can now be interpreted at a different level of analysis as inputs to the specification of means of delivery. This distinction is illustrated in Figure 2.3. This shows value rationality as the repository of those aspects of societal ideals which contribute to the design of the purposes of the economic system. It shows instrumental rationality as the arena in which choices are made about the instruments of delivery. The making of choices as a conscious act justifies a reminder here of Weber's means of distinguishing the two rationalities, noted earlier. *Wert-rational* (the value form) may well introduce unplanned elements of factors such as traditionalism into the equation. It is, in other words, unconstrained. The design of the economic features is of necessity a connected part in a much larger framework of ideas which penetrate it. On the other hand *zweck rational* (the instrumental form) is based upon planning, and thus on selection and choice of method. It is consequently shaped by some incorporation of formal rationality into its processes, a feature largely absent from the value form.

The useful distinction between primary and secondary carriers (see Figure 2.2) allows for greater clarity in understanding the inner workings of instrumental rationality. It is not intended here to examine in any detail the interplay between the primary and the secondary, as the complexity of that requires separate treatment, but a set of examples of the secondary is proposed, from which the process of influence may be deduced. Note that these remain in the realm of ideas, or guiding principles, and that they coincide with (and may be constrained by) some of their primary precursors, but they are seen as being more focused, in a sense more pragmatic, and more closely bound up with the institutions which they sponsor. These secondary carriers of the West's ideals, which directly facilitate the creation of institutions in the context of the economy, and which serve its core purpose of material progress, are seen as follows:

1   the idea of the company as an instrument for ownership
2   the profession seen as a standards-setting and maintenance device
3   the grouping and expression of interests
4   the rule of law
5   having government administration
6   the discipline of markets.

Discussion

Progress in comparative management may be claimed in a number of respects in the past two decades. Increasing clarity has been achieved in the understanding of the key dimensions of culture, and in their measurement in different societies. As initiator of much of that work, Hofstede has regularly maintained that much more understanding is needed of how such differences come to be formed, but also of their implications for societal structuring. Those vacuums in understanding remain to be filled, but occupy widespread attention in a number of related disciplines working empirically.

Elster points to 'one of the most persisting cleavages in the social sciences' as that between the lines of thought initiated by Adam Smith, in which behaviour is guided by instrumental rationality, and those initiated by Durkheim, in which behaviour is dictated by social norms (Elster 1989). He sees three solutions to resolving the opposition between these camps: first, to take one of the eclectic views that either (a) some behaviours are explained by one and some by the other, or (b) that both rationality and social norms are operating to influence most actions; second, to include norm oriented action as a form of rational, or, more generally, optimizing behaviour; third, to reduce rationality to one social norm among others. For Elster, the distinction between rationality and norms lies in the way that rationality is outcome oriented and norms are not, a division which accords with that in this paper between value and instrumental rationality, in that although the former is labelled as concerned with ends, it is not until it comes to be operationalized through its instrumental counterpart that it could be characterized as outcome oriented.

On those grounds, it may be possible to see two advantages in the adoption of the framework suggested here. One is that it could possibly help to persuade together the two approaches (rationality or norm based) by requiring their acknowledgement of the other's contribution to a fuller analysis. This is not to say that it pre-defines integrated methodologies, or that it gives full theoretical treatment to mechanisms of determinacy explaining linkages, outcomes, and feedbacks, but it at least divides up the causal process into units which encompass the two main paradigms.

Secondly, it may go some way towards a more complex use of the concept of rationality within the economics based approach, and in particular the partial dismantling of the implied universalism of the *homo oeconomicus* model. Elster (1989) offers the comment that the modern Western emphasis on instrumental rationality may not be present in all cultures: 'We adopt it because we are socialized into thinking in this manner, even when it is actually counterproductive in its own instrumental terms.' But he also makes the point that this view has not been clearly articulated by anyone so far. It was a view clearly at the centre of Weber's work, and the extreme difficulty of researching it remains visible in the complexity, and sometimes the obscurity, of his thinking about it. But that framework of basic thinking may be worthy of recall if the socio-economics agenda is to face the challenge of placing in context the 'specific and peculiar rationalism of Western culture' and its massive implications for economic behaviour worldwide. Whitley's analysis of the origins of alternative business systems remains rare in its willingness to take on that question. This addition to it is intended to sponsor focus on the role of culture specifically, but in doing so to supplement the logics of that schema, not amend them.

The case of China is fascinating for its capacity to illustrate the possible evolution of an alternative economic system to that of the West. Much of that fascination stems from the experimental nature of the process, 'wading across the river, feeling with your feet stone by stone' (Deng Xiaoping). In considering this experimentation, the role of a distinct form of Chinese rationality has been largely ignored by researchers. The mental maps of the architects of China's new enterprises were not acquired elsewhere. They may prove in the end to be the ultimate determinants of very distinct forms of economic co-ordination and control.

Acknowledgements

The support of the Institute for the Study of Economic Culture, Boston University, and of its Director, Peter Berger, is most gratefully acknowledged. Also much appreciated has been the support of the Euro-Asia Centre, Insead, and the INSEAD Research Committee.

References

Abegglen, J. (1958) *The Japanese Factory*, Glencoe: Free Press.
Albert, M. (1993) *Capitalism vs. Capitalism*, New York: Four Walls Eight Windows Press.
Barney, J. and Ouchi, W.G. (1986) *Organizational Economics*, New York: Jossey Bass.
Barrett, G.V. and Bass, B.M. (1976) 'Cross-cultural Issues in Industrial and Organizational Psychology', in M.D. Dunnette (ed.) *Handbook of Industrial and Organizational Psychology*, Chicago: Rand-McNally.
Beaty D.T. and Mendenhall, M. (1991) 'Theory building in international management: an archived review and recommendations for future research', in paper delivered at the Academy of Management Annual Meeting, San Francisco.
Berger, P., Berger, B. and Kellner, H. (1973) *The Homeless Mind: Modernization and Consciousness*, London: Penguin.
Berger, P. and Luckmann, T. (1966) *The Social Construction of Reality*, London: Penguin.
Berger, S. and Dore, R. (eds) (1996) *National Diversity and Global Capitalism*, Ithaca, New York: Cornell University Press.
Boisot, M. (1995) *Information Space*, London: Routledge.
Boisot, M. and Child, J. (1988) 'The iron law of fiefs: bureaucratic failure and the problem of governance in the Chinese economic reforms', *Administrative Science Quarterly*, 33:507–27.
—— (1996) 'From fiefs to clans: explaining China's emerging economic order', *Administration Science Quarterly*, 41:600–28.
—— (1999) 'Organizations as adaptive systems in complex environments: the case of China', *Organization Science*, 10(3):237–52.

Boyacigiller, N. and Adler, N.J. (1991) 'The parochial dinosaur: organization science in a global context', *Academy of Management Review*, 16(2):262–90.

Burt, R. (1997) 'The contingent value of social capital', *The Administrative Science Quarterly*, 42(2):339–65.

Calder, K. (1993) *Strategic Capitalism*, Princeton: Princeton University Press.

Casson, M. (1997) *Information and Organization*, Oxford: Clarendon.

Child, J. (1981) 'Culture, Contingency and Capitalism in the Cross-national Study of Organizations', in B. Staw and L.L. Cummings (eds) *Research in Organizational Behaviour*, Vol. 3, Greenwich CT: JAI Press.

—— (2000) 'Theorizing about Organization Cross-nationally', in J.L.C. Cheng and R.B. Peterson (eds) *Advances in International Comparative Management*, Vol. 13, Stanford CT: JAI Press.

Crouch, C. and Streeck, W. (eds) (1997) *Political Economy of Modern Capitalism: Mapping Convergence and Diversity*, London: Sage.

DiMaggio, P. (ed.) (1994) *Meaning and Measurement in the Sociology of Culture*, Amsterdam: North-Holland/Elsevier Science.

Dore, R. (2000) *Stock Market Capitalism: Welfare Capitalism*, Oxford: Oxford University Press.

Eisenstadt, S. (1968) 'The Protestant Ethic Thesis in an Analytical and Comparative Framework', in S.N. Eisenstadt (ed.) *The Protestant Ethic and Modernization: a Comparative View*, New York: Basic Books.

Elster, J. (1989) *The Cement of Society: A Study of Social Order*, Cambridge: Cambridge University Press.

Foss, N. (ed.) (1999) 'Preface: Perspectives on business systems' and 'The challenge of business and the challenge to business systems', *International Studies of Management and Organization*, 29(2): 3–8 and 9–17.

Foster, G. (1965) 'Peasant society and the image of limited good', *American Anthropologist*, 67:293–315.

Gellner, E. (1992) *Reason and Culture*, Oxford: Blackwell.

Granovetter, M. (1985) 'Economic action and social structure: the problem of embeddedness', *American Journal of Sociology*, 91:481–510.

Hampden-Turner, C. and Trompenaars, A. (1993) *The Seven Cultures of Capitalism*, New York: Currency Doubleday.

Hodgson, G. (1994) 'The Return of Institutional Economics', in N. Smelser and R. Swedberg (eds) *The Handbook of Economic Sociology*, Princeton: Princeton University Press.

Hofstede, G. (1980) *Culture's Consequences*, London: Sage.

—— (1991) *Cultures and Organizations*, London: McGraw-Hill.

Hollingsworth, J.R. and Boyer, R. (eds) (1997) *Contemporary Capitalism: The Embeddedness of Institutions*, Cambridge: Cambridge University Press.

Innes, S. (1994) 'Puritanism and Capitalism in Early Massachusetts', in J.A. James and M. Thomas (eds) *Capitalism in Context*, Chicago: Chicago University Press.

Landes, D. (1998). *The Wealth and Poverty of Nations*, New York: Norton.

Lodge, G. and Vogel. E.F. (eds) (1987) *Ideology and National Competitiveness*, Boston MA: Harvard Business School Press.

Maurice, M., Sellier, F. and Silvestre, J-J. (1982) *The Social Foundations of Industrial Power: a Comparison of France and Germany*, Cambridge, MA: MIT Press.

McCraw, T.K. (ed.) (1997) *Creating Modern Capitalism*, Cambridge, MA: Harvard University Press.

Nelson, R. (1994) 'Evolutionary Theorizing about Economic Change', in N. Smelser and R. Swedberg (eds) *The Handbook of Economic Sociology*, Princeton: Princeton University Press.

Orru, M., Biggart, N.W. and Hamilton, G.G. (eds) (1991) *The Economic Organization of East Asian Capitalism*, London: Sage.

Penrose, E. (1995). *The Theory of the Growth of the Firm*, Oxford: Oxford University Press.

Platteau, J. (1994) 'Behind the market stage where real societies exist. Part I: the role of public and private institutions. Part II: the role of moral norms', *Journal of Development Studies*, 30(3):533–77 and 753–817.

Polanyi, K. (1994) *The Great Transformation*, Boston: Beacon Press.

Porter, M. (1991) 'Towards a dynamic theory of strategy', *Strategic Management Journal*, 12:95–118.

Ragin, Ch. (1987) *The Comparative Method*, Berkeley: University of California Press.

Redding, S.G. (1994) 'Comparative management theory: jungle, zoo or fossil bed?', *Organization Studies*, 15(3):323–60.

—— (2001) 'The cultural component of business systems', *Euro-Asia Centre INSEAD Research Series*.

Roberts, K. (1970) 'On looking at an elephant: an evaluation of cross-cultural research related to organizations', *Psychological Bulletin*, 74(5):327–50.

Rumelt, R., Schendel, D. and Teece, D. (1991) 'Strategic management and economics', *Strategic Management Journal*, 12:5–30.

Schluchter, W. (1981) *The Rise of Western Rationalism: Max Weber's Developmental History*, Berkeley: University of California Press.

Schroeder, R. (1992) *Max Weber and the Sociology of Culture*, London: Sage.

Smelser, N. and Swedberg, R. (eds) (1994) *The Handbook of Economic Sociology*, Princeton: Princeton University Press.

Stinchcombe, A. (1974) *Creating Efficient Industrial Administrations*, New York: Academic Press.

—— (1990) 'Reason and Rationality', in K.S. Cook and M. Levi (eds) *The Limits of Rationality*, Chicago: Chicago University Press.

Swedberg, R. (1998) *Max Weber and the Idea of Economic Sociology*, Princeton: Princeton University Press.

—— (ed.) (1999) *Max Weber: Essays in Economic Sociology*, Princeton: Princeton University Press.

Triandis, H. (1992) 'Cross-cultural Industrial and Organizational Psychology', in M.D. Dunnette (ed.) *Handbook of Industrial and Organizational Psychology*, Vol. 4, Palo Alto: Consulting Psychologist Press.

Trompenaars, A. (1993) *Riding the Waves of Culture*, London: Nicholas Brealey.

Weber, M. (1922) *Economy and Society*, Tübingen: J.C.B. Mohr.

—— (1930) *The Protestant Ethic and the Spirit of Capitalism*, London: Urwin.

—— (1988) *Gesammelte Aufsätze zur Soziologie und Sozialpolitik*, Tübingen: J.C.B. Mohr.

Whitley, R. (1992a) *Business Systems in East Asia*, London: Sage.

—— (ed.) (1992b) *European Business Systems: Firms and Markets in their National Contexts,* London: Sage.

—— (1999a) *Divergent Capitalisms: The Social Structuring and Change of Business Systems,* Oxford: Oxford University Press.

—— (1999b) 'Competing logics and units of analysis in the comparative study of economic organizations', *International Studies of Management and Organization,* 29(2):113–26.

Whitley, R. and Kristensen, P.H. (eds) (1996) *The Changing European Firm: Limits to Convergence,* London: Routledge.

Williamson, O. (1985) *The Economic Institutions of Capitalism,* New York: Free Press.

World Bank (1993) *The East Asian Miracle,* New York: Oxford University Press.

3

ENTREPRENEURSHIP BY ALLIANCE

Barbara Krug and Judith Mehta

Introduction

Recent years have seen the introduction of markets and a system of private property rights in China with a view to changing the composition of production and demand and enhancing welfare. Central to the success of these reforms is the rise of entrepreneurship with its potential to set the economy on a higher growth path by supplying the products which consumers need and want, creating new employment opportunities, and introducing new and more efficient technologies of production. But to what extent can we expect to see entrepreneurs in China behaving like their counterparts in the advanced industrial economies of Western Europe, Japan, and the United States? This is the question we address in this chapter. In our view, the reform programme has, indeed, opened up new opportunities for private enterprise activity; but idiosyncrasies of the business environment are at the same time generating novel institutional arrangements in support of entrepreneurs' investments. We agree, therefore, with Herrick and Kindleberger when they assert: 'Development ought not to be viewed as a monotonic, stylised path, ever onward and upward, historically established and invariably repeated' (Herrick and Kindleberger 1983).

In this chapter, we analyse modes of entrepreneurship in one particular province, Shanxi, which lies to the north-east of Beijing. We claim that six idiosyncratic features of the business environment generate a particularly high level of economic and institutional uncertainty for would-be entrepreneurs in this province; these are:

- a dual economy
- missing and poorly functioning markets
- poorly developed institutional arrangements
- incomplete private property rights
- a weak regulatory regime
- the 'newness' of private enterprise.

50

We suggest that the high transaction costs associated with uncertainty, together with resource constraints, are responsible for pushing entrepreneurs into alliances with others. This is because alliances raise the probability of success and the expected level of profits in the new private sector. Under these conditions, the establishment of a firm and its expansion path turn on the ability of the entrepreneur to identify, and form alliances with, the 'right' kind of others.

Our account is supported by twenty-seven case studies of entrepreneurs acquired through fieldwork in Shanxi province in 1999. The age and principal productive activities of respondents are described in Table 3.1. Shanxi province was selected for fieldwork because it has an extremely fast-growing private sector but has not been a major recipient of foreign direct investment or preferential treatment by the State. Growth has therefore been endogenous. Interviews were semi-structured and lasted for at least two hours (and sometimes much longer) with the aim of capturing qualitative data.[1] It cannot be claimed that the sample of respondents is representative by the usual social-scientific standards of Western research practice since we were dependent for access to entrepreneurs on three mediating agencies: the principal commercial bank of the region, a university in the provincial capital, and local Party officials; each of these agencies is likely to have applied their own filters to the sample. The alternative would have been to wait for the time it takes for Western sampling methods to be acceptable and practicable. Nonetheless, we suggest the resulting data set is rich in information and offers a unique glimpse of key features of entrepreneurship in Shanxi province at this stage of the reform programme.

The chapter is organized as follows. The first section describes the particular features of uncertainty which characterize the business environment and which generate high transaction costs for would-be entrepreneurs. The next section describes the impact of uncertainty on profit, investment, and product mix. The claim that high transaction costs, together with resource constraints, push entrepreneurs into alliances with others is developed in the subsequent section, and the concluding section discusses some of the ramifications of our findings. To add substance to our claims, short case studies of four representative entrepreneurs are presented at the end of the chapter.

The business environment

The economic, social and political environment facing a potential entrepreneur in the newly reformed China has distinct transaction cost-generating features. These features need to be regarded as interrelated but, for expositional purposes, they can be described under the following six headings.

The dual economy

China is characterized by the co-existence of a socialist sector where economic activity continues in large part to be co-ordinated by centrally planned quotas and low state-controlled prices, and a competitive, free-enterprise sector where activity is co-ordinated by the price mechanism with (relatively) free entry to private entrepreneurs. Producers would face far less uncertainty if just one sector predominated, and if that sector manifested some stability. As it is, both the socialist sector and the free-enterprise sector are in a state of flux. Negotiating the divide between sectors is a primary source of transaction costs since time and money must be spent cultivating access to, and good relations with, those bureaucrats and Party officials in the state sector who have control over key resources. But success has high rewards: an individual who succeeds in buying inputs at low state prices while selling their own goods in competitive markets can appropriate the profits accruing to arbitrage (Nee and Matthews 1996; Nee and Su 1990; Nee 2000).

Missing and poorly functioning markets

The emerging market situation in China is characterized at best by poorly functioning markets, and at worst by missing markets, for capital funds, other factor inputs, risk management, and information of all kinds (Stigler 1989; Boisot 1995). This situation necessarily adds to the costs of undertaking transactions.

Commercial banks, for example, simply do not have sufficient capital available to meet the needs of all budding and actual entrepreneurs, nor are they practised in assessing the risks and managing the insurance associated with all the novel ventures presented to them. Banks are not the only source of capital; but locating other sources is difficult for would-be entrepreneurs. Information relating to the availability, price and location of other inputs to production (for example, appropriately skilled labour and intermediate goods) is similarly either lacking altogether or disaggregated. All of the twenty-seven entrepreneurs whom we interviewed spoke of the inadequacy of the services provided by commercial banks, and/or described access to capital, appropriately skilled labour, and information as key problem areas.[2]

However, on the positive side, the newly unleashed desire for consumption in China means that an individual can earn high profits *if* they can acquire access to factor inputs and can identify ways of establishing business relations across markets and provinces. A budding entrepreneur, then, faces high deterrents to market entry but also robust incentives to succeed.

Poorly developed institutional arrangements

China is short of the kind of public and private sector agencies which are found in plentiful supply in a mature industrial economy and which support the co-ordination of market activity; these include employment agencies, law and accountancy firms, commercial banks, insurance agencies, and chambers of commerce. Islam and Chowdhury (1997), for example, report that there are only 75,000 lawyers and 6,000 law firms across China. In economies with a long experience of private sector production, these agencies act as repositories of information and expertise, and as intermediaries in the negotiations between potential business partners. But where they exist in China, the experience of personnel, and the information and other resources available to them, are severely limited.

The demand for intermediaries is high; as one of our respondents pointed out, China has an inadequate capital base and intermediaries are needed to locate sources of capital and to broker agreements. New agencies are, indeed, evolving and they resemble their counterparts in the West in terms of their structure and organization, and the services they seek to supply. And, certainly, through their activities a range of quasi-institutional business arrangements has been engendered, such as laws and legal precedents, accountancy procedures, capital markets, and guidelines for business practice. As such, the new agencies would appear to contribute to a reduction of the transaction costs associated with the management of risk, the acquisition of capital funds, the enforcement of contracts, and the dissemination of information. However, they are inadequate to the task of lubricating the wheels of private enterprise. Since the arrangements engendered by the new agencies do not emanate from the State at its centre, their status is undetermined and at best equivocal, particularly where transactors seek to cross provincial boundaries. And since the experience of personnel is limited, and the coverage of exchange relations is incomplete, the capacity of the new agencies to broker and subsequently to enforce the wide range of novel transactions is commonly recognized by entrepreneurs to lack substance.

Incomplete private property rights

In the period 1980–4, legislation was introduced to establish private property rights as a way of supporting private enterprise activity. For the first time in recent history, individuals and enterprises of various kinds now find they can have lawful private ownership of both physical and financial assets. Under the legislation, the State guarantees that asset holders can exclude others from use of the same asset. In the Western legal sense, this guarantee does not constitute a complete private property right, but a *possessory* right (Furubotn and Pejovich 1974; Posner 1980; Fukuyama 1995), which is legally binding only when resources are used within the politically defined market sector and where effective law enforcement agencies exist.[3] Despite these limitations, the legislation has had the desired effect on investment by raising the expectations of individuals that they can appropriate the returns to their ventures.

The impetus to invest is evident both in urban areas where the state manufacturing sector is concentrated and in the countryside. In the case of the former, a variety of state agencies are taking advantage of their new-found entitlement to become the lawful owners of physical and financial assets. In the case of the latter, the village has been established as the *natural owner* of all assets within village boundaries, with the further assignment of private property rights to individuals taking place contingent on negotiations within the village or its next superior administrative unit (Rozelle and Li 1998). Three procedures have come to dominate the transfer of assets into private hands.

First, control over resources and possession is commonly recognized as the first step towards the acquisition of private property rights. This procedure can be thought of as one of *cold privatization*; it is the means by which state cadres previously in control of resources are able to transform themselves into the managers, if not the owners, of those resources. The second procedure is to acknowledge past investment into a resource. Thus, land which hitherto was farmed by a group of households under the People's Commune System is apportioned and assigned to private households within that original group. However, at its best, this second procedure secures sharecropping and similar lease contracts while full, legally enforceable private property rights are still missing. From the early 1990s, a third procedure has emerged. Those entrepreneurs seeking to acquire land without some original association with it have been permitted to purchase a lease, if local politicians and Party cadres are pliant and sanction the use to which the land will be put. However, security of tenure beyond the period specified in the lease, the right to change of use, and the right to transfer ownership remain uncertain.

It is true to say, then, that opportunities for private enterprise activity have, indeed, expanded with the introduction of private property rights. But procedures for the assignment of rights to individuals mean that bureaucrats, Party cadres, and other local politicians continue as a force to be reckoned with in determining who can do what with land which is in private hands (Oi 1996; Unger 1995).

A weak regulatory regime

The reform process in China has been characterized by on-going shifts in the regulatory regime across a number of dimensions.

While regulations are negotiated and agreed in the first instance at the centre in Beijing, China is *de facto* a decentralized (that is, federalist) state in that each locality enjoys the leeway to modify, manipulate – and even create – its own regulatory regime. As a consequence, entrepreneurs do not face a unified system of taxes, laws and regulations but a variety of systems which differ from province to province and, sometimes, even from county to county within a single province. The heterogeneity of systems, and their lack of stability, add to the uncertainties associated with production and exchange, particularly where entrepreneurs seek to transact across provinces. At the same time, within a locality, the regulatory regime is experienced as a *soft* and eminently malleable constraint on economic activity, with the tax base, the tax rate, and the application of regulations open to negotiation – at least, to those with influence. As Oi observes:

> Local officials routinely manipulate regulations to allow local enterprises to receive the maximum tax advantages and exemptions. This keeps more revenue within the locality and adds to the competitive advantage of the enterprises, which also means that of the locality. . . . [the county tax bureau] may also use its connections to influence other agencies, such as banks, to bend the rules in favour of a particular enterprise.
>
> (Oi 1996)

Despite encouragement of private enterprise from the State at its centre, and despite advances in the assignment of private property rights, economic activity continues to take place under considerable risk of confiscation as a result of opportunism and/or where private enterprise is frowned upon by the local political leadership. In the early days of the reform programme, confiscation involved the seizure of physical assets or bank accounts from private firms or households; more recently, it can take the form of *ad hoc* taxation once net profits are known, and can involve the sudden appearance of Party cadres on the doorstep asking for a share of the returns (Krug 1997; Gambetta 1993; Boisot and Child 1988). During fieldwork, respondents provided enough anecdotal evidence to suggest that *ad hoc* systems of taxation, or 'invitations' to contribute to local community facilities, are a real threat.

The risk of confiscation of assets, together with the malleability of the regulatory regime, has implications not only for the conduct and performance of private enterprise once it is up and running but at the planning stage when the decision is taken about whether or not to proceed with a business venture. Arguably one of the most dramatic differences between the business environments to be found in China and in the mature economies of the West is that the expected returns to an investment cannot be calculated solely by reference to economic parameters: the political climate, and the control of local politicians over the regulatory regime, both have to be taken into account. As one of our respondents remarked, 'Everything depends on the government'.

The newness of private enterprise

Private enterprise activity is still relatively novel in China and so the very newness of the private firm as an organizational form generates a high level of uncertainty for would-be entrepreneurs (Krug and Pólos 2000). There are several dimensions to this kind of uncertainty.

First, budding entrepreneurs are endowed with a low level of expertise with regard to the organization of production and the management of the private firm. However enthusiastic the current generation is to embrace private enterprise, the formal education they received did not equip them with the expertise and acumen which might be thought necessary for sound business practice in a market environment. There is little awareness of the mechanics of demand and supply, and price and income elasticities, even at an intuitive level, and there is no systematic knowledge base which could help entrepreneurs to identify, and subsequently to quantify, the risks associated with their ventures. Second, the newness of the private sector means business practices are heterogeneous. Thus, there is no obvious model of best practice to imitate and there are no standardized routines of business practice which entrepreneurs can rely on for the smooth passage of transactions. And, finally, in the absence of a history of experience of business strategy, there is no collective memory about what can go wrong and how to resolve problems when they arise.

Institutional uncertainty

Chinese entrepreneurs have robust incentives to succeed in their private sector business activities. There is growing domestic demand for final and intermediate goods, a low level of competition from indigenous suppliers in most markets, and (as yet) relatively poor penetration of markets by foreign firms. Yet the six features of the economy we have described in this section all point to a high level of *institutional uncertainty*. We use this term in order to emphasize two facets of the business environment which potentially constrain entrepreneurial activity. First, weak institutions are unable to reduce uncertainty in the business environment to the level experienced by entrepreneurs in a more mature market economy. And, second, the very co-existence of a multiplicity of different institutional forms and practices, many of which are in flux, is a source of uncertainty itself.

Under these conditions, the transaction costs accompanying production and exchange relations are high, and mistakes are expensive. In particular, customer and supplier firms, employees, and other business partners cannot be expected to act according to well-established and, hence, predictable patterns of behaviour, as they might in a more mature and stable environment. The rational entrepreneur can therefore expect instead to elicit a large variance in the responses of economic agents to his or her actions, and a large variance in the responses of business partners to external shocks (Stinchcombe 1965). Moreover, while the potential exists for costly principal–agent problems (that is, the problems of adverse selection and moral hazard), it is not within an entrepreneur's power to enforce a specific kind of behaviour since social and legal mechanisms of enforcement are unstable, can change rapidly over time, and are likely to vary from one locality to another. What do these factors imply for the practice of entrepreneurship?

The impact of uncertainty on profit, product mix and investment

Fieldwork reveals that entrepreneurs are keen to ensure their investments will generate a steady stream of profits over time. This objective translates into the pursuit of long-term business relations in factor and product markets in order to minimize the risks of opportunism and to transcend the mere 'wheeling and dealing' of spot markets.[4] In these respects, the aspirations of entrepreneurs in China are similar to those of their counterparts elsewhere (Sako 1992; Lyons and Mehta 1997). But as we have already observed, it is particularly difficult in China to assess the level of risk associated with a business venture: is this the right product of the right quality? Will the market prove to be profitable? How should costs and revenues be calculated? Can business partners be relied upon to abstain from opportunism? Will local government approve of the enterprise, or frustrate it? How secure are profits and assets? These economic and institutional uncertainties have ramifications for the behaviour of actual and potential entrepreneurs.

The relationship between uncertainty and profit

High uncertainty in the business environment means it would be rational for potential entrepreneurs to expect a large variance in the profits from their business ventures. Consequently, all but those who are the most adventurous, imaginative and risk-loving will be eliminated from the subset of those who actually proceed to production. It follows that any action on the part of the potential entrepreneur which results in less uncertainty will increase the expected net returns to a venture and reduce the variance in residual profit, thereby lowering the boundary on entrepreneurship. This being the case, we may predict that the set of actual entrepreneurs will only include those who are best placed to reduce the level of economic and institutional uncertainty.

But success in production also confers a positive externality on the wider population of potential entrepreneurs in an evolutionary fashion

(Nelson 1996; 1997). *Ceteris paribus*, the larger the number of private firms which become established in an emergent market, the better that market functions for all its actual and potential participants, both on the supply side and the demand side. Once again, the boundary on entrepreneurship is lowered. Not only do prices and profits begin to act as reliable signals, but successful entrepreneurship adds to the knowledge base of the economy and offers new models of behaviour to be imitated. Success also exposes new opportunities to supply which, if exploited, generate efficiency gains and raise profit margins. Thus, the market may reach a point where for certain inputs it becomes efficient to switch from the internal hierarchy of the firm to new sources of supply. In other words, as factor and final goods markets become established through successful entrepreneurship, it may be expected that the gains to specialization associated with an increasing division of labour can be realized. Given the early stage of the reform process, it will be some time before markets are so competitive that profit margins start to be squeezed.[5] Thus, success in entrepreneurship simply adds to the opportunity set faced by the population of would-be entrepreneurs (Nelson 1996).

The relationship between uncertainty and product mix

In a situation of emergent markets and where there are political as well as economic uncertainties, two special risks attach to the concentration of activity on a single product, and these call for special kinds of insurance. First, through a combination of poor information, miscalculation, and insufficient expertise, entrepreneurs may find themselves operating at the margin where they are at risk of being driven out of the market, for example, where start-up costs have been under-estimated, revenues are less than expected, or the wrong product has been produced. Second, unanticipated changes in the political climate or to the regulatory regime can quickly change business conditions for the worse in a particular market or locality; for example, an entrepreneur may suddenly find their personal and corporate assets at risk of confiscation or actually confiscated. Under these conditions, it becomes rational to consider not only current but future options on business activity by creating and maintaining a portfolio of *real options*, that is, a wide-ranging set of production possibilities such that resources can be diverted to additional or alternative activities at minimum cost and at the optimal moment (Chang 1996; Trigeorgis 1993).

The attention given by entrepreneurs to current and future production possibilities is exemplified by the perplexity of respondents when asked to specify their core business activity. The notion of *core competence* turned out to be irrelevant to respondents in deciding which activities to engage in. For the most part, a firm is known, not by *what* it produces, but by *who* stands behind it, and that individual will seize on *any* profitable opportunity which presents itself, with scant regard for any core competence the firm may, or may not, have. Case number 16, for example, began his career in the private sector selling colour television sets and subsequently moved into car and motorcycle sales, real estate, brick production, and the recreational services sector; and Case number 17 began in the coal and iron industry and expanded into biological engineering and the supply of biological products.

The relationship between uncertainty and investment

Institutional uncertainty also has implications for the forms taken by investment. Fieldwork reveals that a rational entrepreneur will invest in forms of capital which enhance the ability to move rapidly from one sector to another, or from one locality to another, without the loss of large sunk costs. It might be argued that a necessary requirement for the building up of a core business is *tradable* input; but as long as a wide range of inputs cannot be safely traded due to the weakness of private property rights and an unstable political climate, a firm needs to exploit *any* valuable asset it happens to possess. Thus, unlike the modern Western-style firm which tends to concentrate investment on firm-specific or product-specific know-how, entrepreneurs in Shanxi concentrate their investment on *transferable assets*. And the single most transferable asset which entrepreneurs have is themselves and their social capital in the form of the ability to mobilize allegiances.

The assets which are embedded in the person of the entrepreneur are secure from confiscation which means they can easily be transferred into alternative income-generating activities and from one locality to another. This facet of successful entrepreneurship can explain why most of the individuals encountered in fieldwork were endowed with wide-ranging personal attributes or endowments, such as charm, charisma, and persuasiveness, as well as intelligence, adaptability and imagination; these attributes are immensely valuable in securing co-operation with others. As we shall see below, it is the ability of the entrepreneur to form alliances, and the subsequent rents from co-operation, which are crucial to the establishment and on-going profitability of firms. Thus, success in entrepreneurship calls for more than a bright idea, a good product, and the willingness to accept risk. Without heavy investment in the kind of alliances which minimize transaction costs, the future of the firm will always be in serious jeopardy.

Alliances

It was not until 1994 that banks would give loans to private entrepreneurs and, as we have seen, even now capital markets are poorly developed and supported by an inadequate capital base. Yet obtaining access to financial capital, while clearly important, is not the crucial element in successful entrepreneurship. The potential entrepreneur begins their career in the private sector with a small personal endowment, the single most valuable component of which is his or her *social* capital.[6] This is because the key to success in entrepreneurship is access to resources. At this stage of the reform process in which information is disaggregated, contractual security is weak, and the assignment of private property rights is incomplete, the ability to gain access to resources translates into the ability of the entrepreneur to locate, and then to affiliate themselves with those with whom there exists the potential to reap mutual benefits. The Western concept of *entrepreneurship* is focused on the ability of the individual to identify profitable opportunities (Kirzner 1973; 1985). But, in China, the key factor in successful entrepreneurship is *the ability to form an alliance* with those economic agents who possess or control the financial assets, physical assets, or specific human capital needed for brokering market entry, that is, for starting production, securing supply, and gaining access to distribution channels (Cheng and Rosett 1991; Nee 1989; Boisot 1995). These alliances render value to the budding entrepreneur, not only by making production possible in the first instance, but by reducing the level of risk and increasing the expected net returns to a venture.

First, the difficulties associated with *the dual economy* can be overcome by the entrepreneur if entry to the erstwhile socialist sector can be secured. This translates into the need to form an alliance with those politicians or bureaucrats who control entry to the socialist sector. Entry can then be secured through a series of bribes or a share of the profits to a venture, or some other mutually beneficial exchange.

Second, the difficulties associated with *weak institutional arrangements* can be overcome by forming an alliance with those able to promote and sustain a stable business environment. This can be understood as a form of private collective action. An effective alliance has four transaction cost-saving properties in this respect:

1   It provides access to insider information which allows the entrepreneur to anticipate changes in the regulatory framework, and to acquire information relating to factor and final goods markets.
2   By generating its own influential codes of behaviour, the effective alliance is able to supplement the inadequate legal system with social and political sanctioning thereby providing a higher level of contractual security than would otherwise be the case.
3   The effective alliance provides room for experimentation in two ways: it ensures that an entrepreneur can fail once yet return for a second attempt, and it forms a buffer against failure in the first instance.
4   The effective alliance imparts a positive externality: it acts as a form of collective memory, ensuring that a single failure need not be

constituted simply as one individual's loss of investment but as an experience which others can learn from.

Numbers count in the performance of these transaction cost-saving tasks: the greater the number of economic agents who participate in the alliance, the more effective it will be in the dissemination of information, the management of risk, and the monitoring and sanctioning of business practice. With these significant benefits at stake, the fortunes of the entrepreneur are heavily dependent on their ability to form alliances with bureaucrats, political leaders and other significant parties in the business environment.

Third and finally, the ability to form the *right* kind of alliances can mitigate the transaction costs associated with the newness of private enterprise. The problems associated with newness include not only missing institutions, such as the banking services or tort laws which normally support private sector exchanges, but also missing business practices, such as the norms, conventions and routines which determine how things are done. These practices constitute a form of tacit knowledge which is present in the mature economy but missing in the newly reformed China. The effective alliance performs a crucial role in the development of tacit knowledge by creating and promoting a stable set of expectations of good business behaviour. Once again, numbers matter: the greater the number of economic agents who have internalized the same practices of behaviour, the more smoothly and efficiently can business be transacted and the lower the monitoring costs. Conversely, the more heterogeneous the business environment is (that is, the more different practices that co-exist), the higher the transaction costs because each new exchange relation must be negotiated afresh to avoid misunderstandings and ambiguities. Entrepreneurs in China are aware of heterogeneities in their business environment; as several of our respondents indicated, they expect people from other regions to behave differently, and even to speak in dialects they cannot understand. And they are sensitive to the need to create mechanisms to deal with difference, chief of which is the alliance of like-minded individuals who see the value of establishing common practices.

Discussion and conclusion

We have suggested that entrepreneurial success in Shanxi turns crucially on a system of alliances. This system can be understood as a means of creating and mobilizing the economic, social and political capital required to lubricate the wheels of private enterprise in an environment characterized by a high level of economic and institutional uncertainty. Within this system, the identities and personal attributes of individuals are key elements, which would explain why we observe a large number of firms with weak organizational identities combined with the high exposure and strong personal charisma of the owner. The right kinds of alliances help to overcome resource constraints and to minimize transaction costs through the pooling of both tangible and intangible assets, the spreading of risk, the monitoring and enforcement of business deals, and the creation of a stable business environment. Alliances are also valuable because they offer patronage and trust-generating mechanisms, and because they reduce search costs. Thus, alliances function as a repository of knowledge about business opportunities and the location of human resources.

This account of entrepreneurship is distinctive in that it raises the profile of the *processes* which take place prior to the establishment of the firm and downplays the significance of the production function in its subsequent behaviour. In contrast, the Western-style neoclassical account, which only begins with a production function, and which presupposes that it is economic factors alone which determine the activities of the firm, is inadequate to the task of modelling behaviour. The neoclassical model has been criticized in the West by institutional economists, and by managerial and behavioural theorists, for its treatment of the firm as a 'black box' (Bradach and Eccles 1989; Furubotn and Pejovich 1974; Granovetter 1985; Pratten 1997; Williamson 1993). The criticism is particularly apt in China where personal identities and the broader architecture of the business environment are crucial factors in the determination of productive activities and the level of profits.

Our account is supported by fieldwork which reveals that entrepreneurs are discriminating in their choice of who to form an alliance with and seek out those who offer the highest expected returns. It follows that the expansion path of firms is driven by differential access to alliances; for example, if an entrepreneur has access to alliances which can broker influence in the state sector, he or she is likely to move into productive activities where bureaucratic controls are greatest. In other words, the forms taken by social capital are a driving force in the development of the private sector.

Fieldwork also reveals, in contrast to claims in the literature (Redding 1996; Fukuyama 1995), that the family does not play a major and ongoing role in the firm. In those cases where a member of the family had given a loan, it was repaid as rapidly as possible, and we came across no instances of a loan being accompanied by legal entitlement to a share in either the risks or the profits associated with the venture. Moreover, a loan did not grant authority in decision making. These features indicate that neither party regards the loan as an *investment* and, hence, that the family cannot be regarded as a capital-pooling institution.

Given the role of alliances, why is it that entrepreneurship in China has not become prone to the business practices to be found in the countries of the old Soviet Union and, in particular, of Russia, where a single alliance – the Mafia – predominates? Our fieldwork to date has been restricted to one province only and so we can only speculate as to the answer.

One local explanation may be that Shanxi province was traditionally dominated by state-run heavy industry, notably coal; this history has bequeathed powerful alliances centred on the Party. Our fieldwork certainly provides evidence of the influential role of Party cadres and other local officials in private enterprise activity, a practice described by Oi as *local state corporatism* (Oi 1996). We would also suggest that under the conditions we have described in the section on the business environment, the mutual gains to co-operation are highest in the presence of a multiplicity of alliances and where there is an element of competition between alliances. This being the case, individuals and alliances have no incentive to see a single alliance (such as the Mafia) rise to dominance or to limit their allegiance to a single alliance. Certainly, our fieldwork in Shanxi province suggests that no single alliance has the monopoly on all business transactions and that competition between alliances is characterized by a form of *product differentiation*. Ex-army colleagues, for example, specialize in their ability to locate certain kinds of qualified labour and thus provide a pool for engineering and mining skills and expertise with chemicals. We also came across evidence of the part played by alumni clubs in providing access to distribution channels; for example, networks of old classmates were used as reliable contacts by two respondents wanting to market products in distant provinces. Entrepreneurs, for their part, face strong incentives to gain entry to more than one alliance but, because of the positive costs of entry, they aim to be discriminating; they would appear to seek out the combination of alliances which promises the highest returns on membership, rejecting those they have no use for. Of course, it remains to be seen if this system will survive further stages in the transition process.

In venturing these claims, we do not suggest that cultural difference is the single most important factor in explaining the forms taken by entrepreneurship in different environments.[7] We would argue instead that it is the nature, level and source of *uncertainty* which determines the particular way in which private markets and their associated institutional practices emerge. Clearly, further comparative work elsewhere in China is needed in order to develop this thesis. But, certainly, our fieldwork so far points to flaws in the neoclassical framework which takes the already-existing firm as the unit of analysis and begins its story there. In our view, a deeper understanding of entrepreneurship may be acquired by treating the firm and its expansion path as an evolutionary *process* in which the conditions for success and failure are laid down well before an actual firm comes into being.

Acknowledgement

The authors gratefully acknowledge the support of the Royal Dutch Academy of Sciences and the Vereniging Trustfonds of Erasmus University Rotterdam.

Four illustrative case studies

Note: respondents' names have been changed to protect their anonymity.

Case 3.1 Mr Chen

Mr Chen is 37. He is Chairman of the Board of a large group of companies with 1,500 employees. He began his career in the private sector in 1986 with the import and sale of textiles using personal savings of 5,000 RMB (about €400 at the time of interview). He formed an unregistered (that is, unofficial) private company in 1989 when he established a small electronic equipment shop, followed by a car repair shop in 1991. Since then, his company has expanded rapidly to embrace: the distribution and sale of car parts and accessories; a car customization service; the manufacture of car parts; car importation; car rental; hotel and restaurant services; and advertising services. The major source of capital to fund expansion has been a group of one hundred partners, but Mr Chen is 'the big boss' (as one of his aides describes him); he has a charismatic personality, takes all major decisions himself, and commands complete loyalty. With his success, the capital offered by banks to Mr Chen has increased ('I could get 20 million RMB easily') such that about 30 per cent of current assets are in the form of bank debt; but Mr Chen uses a network of different banks 'so they have to compete for me'.

Mr Chen has use rights of the land on which his buildings are located; these can be purchased for 50 years at a time. Mr Chen states that the kind of use to which the land is put is vulnerable to political intervention at any time, but he says he is confident that, with his connections and influence, intervention is unlikely.

Mr Chen's business deals are accompanied by written agreements; but he says that trust and co-operation, supported by his personal reputation, conventions of business practice (which Mr Chen has played a part in establishing), and the size and robust market position of the company are primary factors in enforcing the good behaviour of business partners.

Mr Chen is a key figure in the development of the private sector, both in Shanxi province and beyond. He says he travels frequently to Beijing and the US to maintain his contacts. He is vice-president of his local Association of Industry and Commerce; he is a member of a Youth Enterprise Association (with links to local schools and

---

training organizations), the Council of Private Enterprise, the Auto-mobile Engineering Institute, and a Gentlemen's Club (which meets in his hotel). Mr Chen describes his relationships with state-controlled firms, a variety of other firms, and the village community as important to his success; but he describes his relationships with key individuals as essential. Mr Chen is well connected to the Party: 'If there's a policy problem, we'll ask the government for help and urge them to modify their policy'. A key tool of leverage is his willingness to pay taxes and the large amount paid.

Case 3.2 Mr Wang

Mr Wang is a graduate of the prestigious Shanghai University. In 1992, he opened a small restaurant with personal savings of 10,000 RMB (about €1,250) enabling him to save a further 100,000 RMB with which he opened a larger restaurant. Mr Wang observes that the mid-1990s saw an increase in the level of uncertainty in the sector and so he diverted his resources into the production of industrial coal and pig-iron when he saw an opportunity for entry into this erstwhile state-monopolized sector. His brother helped with a loan. Mr Wang says that his brother had already formed a private firm offering taxa-tion services, and he transferred his business networks and debts to Mr Wang's firm. All loans and debts incurred via the brother were rapidly repaid from profits. Mr Wang says that his major problem with expansion has been gaining access to capital funds at the right time. Mr Wang now has 250 employees, the majority of whom he says he picks up as excess labour from the state-controlled sector. Employees receive generous wages as a reward for good performance, but also in bad times 'to encourage them'. Mr Wang says that he particularly values their willingness to alert him to investment opportunities.

Mr Wang faces serious problems in obtaining enough land to meet his expansion plans, and insecurity in its use as a result of poorly defined land rights.

Mr Wang's business deals are supported by verbal agreements. He observes that monitoring is easy because most products are stan-dardized, but that mutual trust, co-operation, and flexibility, together with his personal reputation and honesty, are vital to the success of his ventures.

Mr Wang says that his relationships with firms and individuals in the state sector are vital to his success since he is dependent on them for access to key resources and for market entry; for their part, the state-owned enterprises must barter for Mr Wang's products due to lack of cash. He says he is also dependent on good relations with township governments, village heads, and villagers in the areas where his factories are located since otherwise 'they will cause trouble' over land use and transport issues. Mr Wang says his relationship with his brother was essential when he first began as an entrepreneur because he was deemed to be an outsider as a result of his period in Shanghai; he says that this connection is less important 'now that I have established my own networks'. He says that township and village enterprises are important customers; these are linked into a network and, since it is the network with which he conducts business, his personal reputation and connectedness within this network are vital to the success of his transactions.

Case 3.3 Mr Xiang

Mr Xiang is 67. His firm was originally the state-owned enterprise which employed him for most of his life and which was founded in 1957 with six employees. Mr Xiang recounts how ten months ago, the firm was bought out by its forty-five managers, each of whom had a small amount of personal savings; but Mr Xiang is the largest shareholder (with 60 per cent of shares) and the principal decision-maker. The firm now has more than 1,000 employees, most of whom had been discarded by state-owned factories in the locality. The firm produces iron moulds, cast-iron clamps, and zinc-plated fittings and machinery, which are supplied to customers throughout China and in Europe. It has a robust market position which Mr Xiang claims is due to his willingness to introduce Western technology and his loyalty to the Party.

Agreements to trade are supported by written contracts, and regular inspections of Mr Xiang's premises. But he says that since many of his customers are 'old friends', mutual trust, co-operation and flexibility play a major role in the success of the firm.

Mr Xiang clearly builds on his long-established connections with the State and within state-owned enterprises to maintain the valuable customer and supplier base he inherited and has since expanded. He is a member of the Committee for Power Line Materials of the Ministry of Power, and has been appointed the sole manufacturer of power armour clamps for the Ministry. Mr Xiang says he drew on personal connections in order to secure the private water and power supplies which are vital to his rurally located operation. Good relations with the village authorities recently enabled him to build a road connecting to the main highway. Mr Xiang observes that human resources are most important to the success of his business and that he has good relations with the Workers Union, as well as the Consumers Association and his Trade Association. Political influence at the local level is also important to Mr Xiang's enterprise; he is a loyal Party member and proud of the large pictures of Marx, Lenin, Engels, and Mao displayed in his office.

Case 3.4 Mr Zhu

Mr Zhu is 36. He began his career in the private sector 15 years ago when he set up a boiler repair shop with seven employees. He says that old-style boilers were noisy and his innovation was to make them work quietly. Mr Zhu says he has never turned to the bank for loans but uses the cash paid in deposits on boilers as capital for expansion. He states that his firm is immune from political events 'because I have influence' and that his dominant position in the market is protected because 'I am too big'. Mr Zhu describes himself as 'the Boiler King'. He portrays his expansion to an enterprise with nine branches in different provinces, 1,672 employees, and a turnover of 300 million RMB, as seamless. In fact, Mr Zhu had forgotten that he had been interviewed by one of the authors two years previously, shortly after he had been declared bankrupt following entry into the supermarket sector and investment in a shopping mall. This event was widely known since it was reported in the press. Senior Party cadres had introduced us to Mr Zhu as a 'model entrepreneur'. Mr Zhu and the Party cadres only reluctantly confirmed this earlier business failure, pointing both to its insignificance and to 'the difficult trading conditions' prevailing at the time. Soon after this admission, the authors politely brought the interview to an end. Responses to questions were becoming incoherent, perhaps due to the quantity of alcohol being imbibed by Mr Zhu and the Party cadres. Drinking was accompanied by toasts to the Party, and to China as represented by the boiler industry. The authors concluded that the relationship between Mr Zhu and the Party has been of major significance in Mr Zhu's economic activities, although the precise nature of the relationship remains unclear.

Appendix

Table 3.1 Age and principal private sector activities of respondents, Shanxi province, 1999

Case no.	Age	Principal private sector activities
01	36	wholesale supply of electrical appliances for bakeries; retail sale of electrical appliances and furniture
02	33	wholesale and retail supply of cars and low-quality pick-up trucks
03	35	retail supply of high-quality cars
04	38	wholesale and retail sale of truck tyres; in-house production of metal rims for tyres
05	30	production of chemicals
06	42	production of heating boilers and air conditioning systems; wholesale supply of digital televisions
07	47	breeding and cultivation of seed; wholesale and retail seed merchant
08	46	wholesale supply of food additives
09	33	design and supply of 'intelligent buildings'; supply of hardware and software engineering services; wholesale and retail supply of office and communications equipment
10	45	chain of supermarkets; wholesale supplier of specialist noodles
11	49	photographer
12	34	restaurants; production of industrial coal and pig iron; trade in coal, iron and minerals
13	48	manufacture of gold and silver jewellery, and tourist souvenirs
14	37	import and sale of textiles; retail sale of electronic equipment; car repair shop; hotel and restaurant services; advertising services
15	43	real estate; construction
16	35	retail supply of cars and motor cycles; real estate; brick production; supply of recreational facilities
17	35	trade in coal and iron; production of biological engineering products
18	40	educational services (private school for children aged 5+)
19	45	production of aluminium and electrolysis processors; aluminium processing and plating
20	36	boiler repair shop; design and production of boilers
21	38	production of preserved fruit and fruit products, and soft drinks
22	67	production of iron moulds, cast-iron clamps, and zinc-plated fittings and machinery
23	50	manufacture of pigments
24	50	manufacture of cast-iron fittings
25	49	manufacture of cast-iron fittings
26	37	coal-mining; iron and coal traders
27	37	retail sale of sportswear and sports equipment

Notes

1 A copy of the interview schedule is available from the authors on request.
2 The seriousness of these problems was openly acknowledged by the senior representative of one of the largest banks in the province who introduced us to many of our respondents.
3 According to standard economic theory, complete private property rights require a bundle of rights over a good to be defined. Thus, a good is private property if there is: the exclusive right of use, implying the right to exclude others; the exclusive right to receive any income generated by the good; the right to change the form and substance of the good; and the right to transfer ownership. In addition, the transaction costs associated with the enforcement of rights through the courts must be zero or sufficiently low to ensure the pursuit of enforcement is worthwhile. Any divergence from these conditions means that economic agents are unable to realize the full value of their property and, hence, there is a diminishing of the incentive to invest in production.
4 While the wheeling and dealing which takes place in spot markets constitutes a form of private enterprise, it may be regarded as conceptually distinct from the more enduring forms of business activity which characterize entrepreneurship and which involve the establishment of a firm and capital accumulation.
5 The profit margins of several respondents were protected by a strong position resulting from a first-mover advantage and/or a total monopoly of the market. When asked whether new entry would place the firm in jeopardy, sixteen respondents (59 per cent) answered positively, but only two respondents were actually facing new competition, and one further respondent said he would actually welcome new competition because of the benefits in terms of new technology and ideas. However, we suggest a more significant finding is that new entry is universally seen as a less important factor in success than government policy and local Party attitudes with respect to private enterprise. One entrepreneur, for example, pointed out that his firm's control of the market was directly attributable to local government protection. Another respondent said that a barrier to the entry of foreign-owned enterprise into his market (biological engineering products) was created by a central government policy of import substitution; since this policy was actively supported by the Academy of Sciences, the crucial factor in this firm's success was perceived to be the maintenance of good relations with the Academy.
6 One respondent made an explicit distinction between *financial* and *social* capital.
7 The claim that Chinese culture is the driving force behind the emergence of *network capitalism* is discussed in Boisot and Child (1988 and 1999).

References

Boisot, M. (1995) *Information Space: A Framework for Learning in Organizations, Institutions and Culture*, London and New York: Routledge.

Boisot, M. and Child, J. (1988) 'The iron law of fiefs: bureaucratic failure and the problem of governance in Chinese economic reforms', *Administrative Science Quarterly*, 33(4):507–28.

—— (1999) 'Organisation as adaptive systems in complex environments: the case of China', *Organisation Science*, 10(3): 237–52.

Bradach, J.L. and Eccles, R. (1989) 'Price, authority and trust: from ideal types to plural forms', *Annual Review of Sociology*, 15:97–118.

Chang, S.J. (1996) 'An evolutionary perspective on diversification and corporate restructuring: entry, exit, and economic performance during 1981–89', *Strategic Management Journal*, 17:587–611.

Cheng, L. and Rosett, A. (1991) 'Contract with a Chinese face: socially embedded factors in the transformation from hierarchy to markets, 1978–1989', *Journal of Chinese Law*, 5(2):143–244.

Fukuyama, F. (1995) *Trust: The Social Virtues and the Creation of Prosperity*, New York and London: The Free Press.

Furubotn, E. and Pejovich, S. (eds) (1974) *The Economics of Property Rights*, Cambridge, MA: Balinger.

Gambetta, D. (1993) *The Sicilian Mafia: The Business of Protection*, Cambridge, MA: Harvard University Press.

Granovetter, M. (1985) 'Economic action and social structure: the problem of embeddedness', *American Journal of Sociology*, 91(3):481–510.

Herrick, B. and Kindleberger, C. (1983) *Economic Development*, London: McGraw-Hill.

Islam, I. and Chowdhury, A. (1997) *Asia-Pacific Economies*, New York: Routledge.

Kirzner, I.M. (1973), *Competition and Entrepreneurship*, Chicago: University of Chicago Press.

—— (1985) *Discovery and the Capitalist Process*, Chicago: University of Chicago Press.

Krug, B. (1997) 'Moving the Mountains: Transformation as Institution Building from Below', in J. Backhaus, and G. Krause (eds) *The Political Economy of Transformation: Country Studies*, Marburg: Metropolis.

Krug, B. and Pólos, L. (2000) 'Entrepreneurs, enterprises, and evolution: the case of China', paper presented at the Annual Meeting of the International Society for New Institutional Economics, Tübingen, September 2000.

Lyons, B. and Mehta, J. (1997) 'Private Sector Business Contracts: The Text Between the Lines', in S. Deakin, and J. Michie (eds) *Contracts, Cooperation, and Competition*, Oxford: Oxford University Press.

Nee, V. (1989) 'Peasant Entrepreneurship and the Politics of Regulation in China', in V. Nee, and D. Stark (eds) *Remaking the Economic Institutions of Capitalism*, Stanford: Stanford University Press.

—— (2000) 'The Role of the State in Making a Market Economy', *Journal of Institutional and Theoretical Economics*, 156(1):66–88.

Nee, V. and Matthews, R. (1996) 'Market transition and societal transformation in reforming state socialism', *Annual Review of Sociology*, 22:401–35.

Nee, V. and Su, S. (1990) 'Institutional change and economic growth in China', *Journal of Asian Studies*, 49:3–25.

Nelson, R.R. (1996) *The Sources of Economic Growth*, Cambridge, MA: Harvard University Press.

—— (1997) 'How new is new economic growth?', *Challenge*, 40(5):29–59.

Oi, J.C. (1996) 'The Role of the Local State in China's Transitional Economy', in A.G. Walder (ed.) *China's Transitional Economy*, Oxford: Oxford University Press.

Posner, R. (1980) 'A theory of primitive society, with special reference to law', *Journal of Law and Economics*, 23(1):1–53.

Pratten, S. (1997) 'The nature of transaction costs economics', *Journal of Economic Issues*, 31(3):781–803.

Redding, S.G. (1996) 'The distinct nature of Chinese capitalism', *The Pacific Review*, 9(3):426–40.

Rozelle, S. and Li, G. (1998) 'Village leaders and land-rights formation in China', *American Economic Review*, 82(2):433–8.

Sako, M. (1992) *Prices, Quality and Trust*, Cambridge: Cambridge University Press.

Stigler, J.E. (1989) 'Markets, market failures, and development', *American Economic Review*, 79:197–203.

Stinchcombe, A.L. (1965) 'Social Structure of Organizations', in J.G. March (ed.) *Handbook of Organizations*, Chicago: Rand McNally.

Trigeorgis, L. (1993) 'Real options and interactions with financial flexibility', *Financial Management*, autumn:202–24.

Unger, J. (1995) 'The decollectivisation of the Chinese Countryside: A Survey of Twenty-Eight Villages', in J. Ravenhill (ed.) *The Political Economy of East Asia: China, Korea and Taiwan, Volume II*, Aldershot: Edward Elgar.

Williamson, O. (1993) 'Calculativeness, trust and economic organization', *Journal of Law and Economics*, 36:453–86.

4

EMERGING MARKETS, ENTREPRENEURSHIP AND UNCERTAINTY

The emergence of a private sector in China

Barbara Krug and László Pólos

Introduction

The study of entrepreneurship offers a paradox.[1] On one side it is claimed that the emergence of entrepreneurship depends on a hospitable environment provided by private property rights, and liability laws (supported by legislation and state enforcement), as well as free trade, competition, and factor mobility. This is the static view that invites cross-country comparisons (Whitley 1990; 1999). In most of the literature it is implicitly assumed that functioning capital markets exist or private property rights are enforced, leaving the impression that entrepreneurship is a phenomenon of the developed, industrialized world. On the other hand it is argued that without entrepreneurs constantly exploring new ways to fight off scarcity of resources, or political constraints that inhibit voluntary exchange, functioning markets would not emerge. Such a dynamic view has for a long time been the domain of economic history, recently followed by the management science literature (Nelson 1995; Nooteboom 2000, O'Sullivan 2000; Shane and Venkataraman 2000). This state of affairs has changed in the last twenty years. First, new approaches that can be broadly summarized as New Institutional Economics, evolutionary economics, and organizational ecology provided the tools by which the interdependency between institutional/organizational structures and the appearance/disappearance of firms, industries, and even business systems can be analysed (Williamson 1993a; North 1984; Nelson 1996; Carroll and Teece 1999; Carroll and Hannan 2000; Hannan and Freeman 1984; 1989). Second, internationalization and the collapse of socialism helped to remind us that without new entrepreneurs, new firms and a new private business sector there would be no 'transformation' of emerging markets and transition economies.

In what follows it is argued that the dominating model, which assumes that entrepreneurs are constrained by technical and competitive uncertainty, needs to be modified to catch the reality of transition economies. Undoubtedly entrepreneurs in transition economies do not know how successful technical innovations will be, or whether and how many competitors will be in the market at the time when they start production. Yet, what distinguishes them from entrepreneurs in developed economies is a third form of uncertainty, which can be called *process uncertainty* (Krug and Pólos 2000; Qian 2000; Tan 2002; Lukas *et al.* 2001). As will be argued presently two factors cause this kind of uncertainty, *weak institutions* and the *liability of newness*. Both factors define the threshold of entrepreneurship, i.e. limit (or facilitate) the number of private firms in transition economies. Moreover, both factors also shape those entrepreneurial activities that precede the 'start' of new firms, define the mortality hazard, and eventually steer the strategic decisions of expanding firms. In short, the general assumption is that in transition economies *technical, competitive and process uncertainty independently shape the dynamics and direction of entrepreneurship but also reinforce each other.*

The following draws on our research in China. The fieldwork needs to be seen as the database against which our line of reasoning is checked. The Chinese case serves this purpose for three reasons. First, it provides a striking example of entrepreneurship in what at first sight looks like 'adverse' circumstances. As long as the Communist Party does not relinquish power and sticks to its notion of a socialist market economy entrepreneurship has to compete with a still heavily protected state sector. Second, entrepreneurship in China shows that second-best technology and the production of conventional goods can become profitable and trigger off economic development in transition economies due to changes in the organization of firms and in the way firms co-ordinate activities, in short if they find ways to reduce transaction costs. Third, in transition economies the entrepreneurs' endeavour to fight off external constraints often enough implies bending if not violating existing laws. The need to create an environment that allows long-term business relations often leads to personal bonding and the establishment of networks that can provide contractual security to all its members. However, networking in the new private sector is frowned upon, if not criticized as nepotism, cronyism, the Mafia, or patronage systems (Flap 1990; Gambetta 1993) by most economists if not the general public (Cheung 1996; Shleifer and Vishny 1993; Krug and Hendrischke 2002), with one notable exception. Chinese *guanxi* networks are not to be dismissed as a Mafia-kind of organization but rather to be seen as assets. Chinese networks regarded as exogenously given, or a remnant of Chinese tradition, are claimed to lie at the core of China's booming private sector and subsequently China's economic development (Boisot and Child 1999; Kiong 1991; Wong 1985; Yoshira 1988;

Redding 1996). This contradiction points to the need to strive for a more rigorous analysis. In our case this led to the assumption that social capital should not be *a priori* dismissed as cronyism but as an asset that can be as crucial for establishing and operating firms as other forms of capital.

How Chinese entrepreneurs cope with process uncertainty describes the starting point of the fieldwork. The interviews concentrated on the core of entrepreneurial activities: first, the founding of a company and the search for an organizational form that allows the co-ordination of resources effectively enough to ensure profit (and survival); second, the search for ways to establish long-term business relations with other firms (or stake-holders) that might facilitate a flexible response to changes in the environment. While the information about the founding and development of the firm relies on life histories as recalled by the respondents, the configuration around the new firms and their strategic choice relied on a questionnaire that reflects some conventional assumptions from the literature.[2] The answers show that

- process uncertainty matters
- the models on entrepreneurship need to be modified when the business environment is a transition economy.

These conclusions are not meant to represent a better model. Instead, the following analysis ends with a set of hypotheses, which can and should be empirically tested in order to gain further insights into both the functioning of the Chinese firm, and the problem of entrepreneurship in an environment that is shaped by process uncertainty.

Process uncertainty: weak institution and the liability of newness

According to an evolutionary perspective the development of a new private sector is the outcome of individual attempts to find an organizational form for firms and sectors that fit best the environment. Intensifying competition serves as the selection mechanism that ensures that those entrepreneurial activities which do not conform to the situational requirements will lose out.

Uncertainty

Uncertainty may come from market competition when one firms does not know, for example, how many others offer the same product or a close substitute. Uncertainty may be generated internally by technological change as well. New technology creates uncertainty if the available technology-specific knowledge is not sufficient, if primary processes are not (yet) routinized, if the operation of technology is mainly based on tacit know-ledge, if dominant designs in the organization are not established (Nooteboom, Berger and Noorderhaven 1997). While entrepreneurs in both market and transition economies face these forms of uncertainty, those in the latter are confronted by two additional challenges.

Weak economic institutions

The usual way economies and societies deal with behavioural uncertainty, whether it is caused by natural or moral hazard, by external shocks, by value changes, or by innovation, is to create institutions and/or organi-zations to 'streamline', monitor and sanction behaviour. In the Western market economies, business practices, for example, depend on contracts, private property rights, laws, the notion of liability and compensation as well as on the consensus that innovation will be rewarded. Subsequently, the weaker the institution the greater the variety of possible response and the higher the uncertainty with respect to expected outcomes. As uncer-tainty translates into risk, for which an appropriate premium needs to be calculated, agents have a strong incentive to search for (institutional) solu-tions, which are more advantageous for at least some of them (with the loser being compensated). While to change the overall frame of institu-tions might be outside the control of individual agents and rather depend on the functioning of the political market, the governance of individual transactions (private exchange) is not. In short:

> Institutional environments that provide general purpose safe-guards relieve the need for added transaction-specific support. Accordingly, transactions that are viable in an institutional envi-ronment that provides strong safeguards may be non-viable in institutional environments that are weak – because it is not cost-effective for parties to craft transaction-specific governance in the latter circumstances.
>
> (Williamson 1993b)

In order to function institutions should not be in conflict with each other, and they should offer a 'code' connected to a specific sanctioning mech-anism that does not tolerate observed code violations (Pólos, Hannan and Carroll 2002). They are effective if the costs of code violations work as a deterrent (Hannan and Freeman 1984). The less economic agents violate the code, the higher the level of regularity and predictability.

In transition economies, codes work as occasional blueprints only, as they are rarely sanctioned effectively but rather assumed to be one step in on-going reforms or on-going changes. Monitoring is infrequent, and irregular, so that economic agents and firms can easily afford not to pay attention to the codes if they are not convenient for them. The result is that behaviour can easily deviate from what is expected, i.e. their default behaviour. Weak economic institutions, in other words, do not contribute much to the problem of reducing high uncertainty. It is worth mentioning that the problem of China and her entrepreneurs is not that there are still socialist institutions working; it is rather that both the remains of the socialist past and the newly introduced market mechanism are weak (Qian 2000). Moreover, if as in China, such institutional weaknesses lead to the (oligopolistic) competition between the few producers of institutions, such as the Communist Party, local government or a strong social network, then the costs for 'acquiring' a predictable and accountable business environment will increase progressively. In this case bribing oneself into a useful business network is the cost one has to pay for securing a relatively more predictable business environment.

So far the analysis suggests that there would be more entrepreneurship in transition economies, i.e. more private firms and higher growth rates, if the co-existence of the two economic regimes could be brought to an end by getting rid of socialist institutions, or inherited power broking networks. If no resources were to be employed for establishing and maintaining the aforementioned 'transaction-specific governance', start-up costs for entrepreneurship would be lower. The analysis also suggests that the European former socialist economies where socialist institutions were quickly replaced by 'markets' should enjoy a comparative advantage leading to more entrepreneurship when compared to China. Yet, this is not the case. The Chinese must therefore have found a way to (over-) compensate for their comparative disadvantage. In what follows it is proposed that the 'weakly enforced codes' caused by the co-existence of market and socialist institutions explain only one part of the process uncertainty. The newness of a private sector creates another kind of uncertainty, and one all former socialist economies have in common. Thus, it can be assumed that the Chinese found an effective way to deal with the latter kind of uncertainty, obviously effective enough to outrace the European former socialist economies.

Liability of newness

To borrow a term coined by Stinchcombe[3] with respect to individual firms, it is the 'liability of newness' of the *whole private sector*, which causes the following characteristics. First, new organizations, i.e. private firms, lack the technical and social requirements for smooth functioning, such as appropriate skills of members, appropriate decision criteria, sensible division of responsibilities, development of loyalty, and learning 'what can go wrong'. In such a situation the new organization needs to rely on general skills produced outside the organization such as formal education, or it has to invest in organization specific training. Second, new firms need to invent roles and role relations, rewards and sanctions, which rely on a learning-by-doing process rather than on easy blueprints. Third, new firms need to build up business and social relations among strangers. Finally new firms might lack strong ties to external constituencies, in particular the political environment. This makes it harder to mobilize resources or fight off 'hold-up' on profit. All in all, the need to compensate for such uncertainties takes away vital resources from young organizational forms of private entrepreneurship, which in turn lowers their survival chances. Thus, entrepreneurs in transition economies can be expected to face the following problems:

- First, there is no routine of business practice upon which an economic agent can rely. The changes in the society at large, which accompany the transition process, make it hard to locate expertise, agents or procedures, which can be imitated or copied. Neither can expertise be bought or learned with the help of formal or informal education. In short: *It is the newness of an organizational form that poses the challenge for entrepreneurs.*
- Second, there is no 'template' for success or failure as there is no collective memory about what may go wrong, and no past experience on which to rely.
- Third, there is no general knowledge about (excess) demand, price or income elasticity of demand, let alone systematic research that would help entrepreneurs or industries to calculate the risk of his venture.

Hypothesis 1: In modelling Chinese firms and sectors, next to technological and competitive uncertainty transactions costs considerations account for process uncertainty. The costs for detecting, establishing, and enforcing behavioural patterns need to be identified, and integrated into the analysis (Macauley 1963).

This has to be seen in contrast to models built on the assumption that private property rights and voluntary contracting are the single most crucial factors defining transaction costs. As already argued by Williamson, that would imply that all future outcomes can be captured and transacted in present days contracts (Williamson 1993). This is already difficult in a world of well-established business practices, and the more so in a world of high uncertainty.

The insights gained from the hypothesis function as the foundation of the empirical study presented in the next section, in which an attempt is made to single out factors by which Chinese entrepreneurs and firms try to organize, manage, and sustain business practices. The analysis is summarized in Figure 4.1.

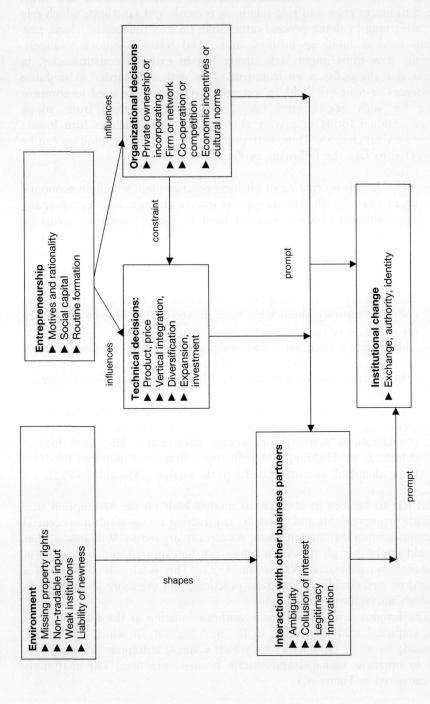

Organizational decisions
- ▲ Private ownership or incorporating
- ▲ Firm or network
- ▲ Co-operation or competition
- ▲ Economic incentives or cultural norms

Entrepreneurship
- ▲ Motives and rationality
- ▲ Social capital
- ▲ Routine formation

influences

constraint

Technical decisions:
- ▲ Product, price
- ▲ Vertical integration,
- ▲ Diversification
- ▲ Expansion, investment

influences

prompt

Institutional change
- ▲ Exchange, authority, identity

Environment
- ▲ Missing property rights
- ▲ Non-tradable input
- ▲ Weak institutions
- ▲ Liability of newness

shapes

Interaction with other business partners
- ▲ Ambiguity
- ▲ Collusion of interest
- ▲ Legitimacy
- ▲ Innovation

prompt

Figure 4.1 Factors involved in establishing business relations in China

The empirical study

The analysis uses the database described in Chapter 1 plus around one hundred interviews undertaken in the years 1996–8 in Shanxi that preceded the more structured questionnaire. The aims of the analysis presented are: first, to identify common features in the development of the new private business sector in China; second, to search for similarities in entrepreneurship irrespective of the location of new firms; third and foremost, to screen the analytical toolkit and search for models that promise high (or better) explanatory value in explaining the specific features of the new private firms and the new private sector.[4]

The open interviews executed in Shanxi between 1996 and 1998 proved to be indispensable for the final database[5] as they highlighted both the limitations of the 'Western' economic vocabulary and also a problem that might be called *conceptual equivalence*. To start with the former, it was quickly learned that an analysis of Chinese firms must include the impressive display of entrepreneurship that *precedes* the establishment of a firm. The interviews revealed a specific feature, not often found outside China and not systematically reflected in the literature. While the pooling of resources in (Western) economies goes via the market, the pooling of resources in China is based on *personal connections and networks*. So questions asking how entrepreneurs make use of markets miss Chinese reality. Instead it is crucial to ask how entrepreneurs establish property rights, secure access to suppliers and customers, and negotiate the scope of 'autonomy' necessary for a professional management. In other words in the Chinese context the analysis must search for systematic factors that can explain how China's entrepreneurs make use of personal contacts in order to acquire the necessary *initial endowment* of a firm. For that reason the interviews needed to include questions about the activities that eventually led to the establishment of a firm.

Moreover, the open interviews also revealed that over the years Chinese firms experience *frequent ownership changes irrespective of their performance*. That failing businesses will be sold or see their assets transferred to other ventures is hardly a surprise, but why the original owners of a successful profit making firm should change ownership and/or line of production deserves attention. In this case too, it was essential to let the *founders* of the company give their account of why they changed the organizational form of the firm.

The interviews also showed the limitations of an analysis that does not strive for conceptual equivalence but assumes that statistics are concept-free. The State Statistical Yearbook is based on the concept of a planned economy where for planning purposes to distinguish between firms that are owned by a province, as opposed to a ministry or county, serves a purpose. These data would therefore already be useless, regardless of the problem of misleading registrations of firms for political reasons. Thus for example during the 1980s the statistics listed only three categories of firms: 'owned by the people' (quanmin suoyou), 'owned by a collective' (jiti suoyou), and 'other forms of industry' (qita leixing gongye). Needless to say the third category was the one with the best performance and the one that anyone researching into the emergence of a private sector was most interested in. Only in the 1990s were other categories invented which distinguished between a 'public' (gongyou) and a 'non-public' (fei gongyou) sector, the latter of which listed private companies, those funded by investment from Hong Kong, Taiwan and Macao, and finally foreign direct investment.[6]

For analysing the emergence of private firms, therefore, data need to be generated that reveal control over material and immaterial resources including the right to transfer these resources. An economic definition was used in the sense that the calculation of net (residual) profit and the competition in the respective sector decided whether a firm was regarded as a private firm, or a socialist firm. Questions about the distribution of net profit helped to identify owners and ownership changes over the years preceding the interview. Knowing the history of the economic reforms, it was not surprising that most firms have both private and institutional owners, the latter being mostly the former collective units, such as villages or former departments of ministries. We included those 'joint' ventures in our study as long as no individual state agency controlled more than 30 per cent, and as long as the management did not have to 'report' to a superior state agency, or were forced to transfer all profit. In the end, the data set included seventy-four 'private' firms that met the requirements.

The interviews explicitly covered two separate time periods: a pre-sample period concentrating on the life history of the respondent's firm in which the respondents were asked to recall how the present firm came into being, and the sample period concentrating on a description of the governance structure within and around the firm. The study presented here relies basically on the retrospective data as collected in the open questions.

The database and legitimization of the procedure: the life history of a firm

Each interview started with general questions, such as position, title, age, background of the respondent, and of the firm, such as founding year, production, output, employees and turnover. The result is an overview of the development of seventy-four 'private' enterprises as briefly set out in the Appendix.[7]

The advantages of the open questions about the life history are:

- They offer a frame for the respondents to express their own understanding in their own terms to the effect that the interviewer and the respondent can establish a joint vocabulary, which allows unambiguous communication (Patton 1980).

- They offer a means to gather information in cases or situations in which established concepts cannot be put to test on technical grounds or because some innovation had taken place that is not yet integrated into the theory (Madhok 1996; Eisenhardt 1989). One example is social capital, which in China is generated within trust-based social relations. This needs to be seen in contrast to social capital in market economies, which is generated in contract-based social relations. As trust is to a great part unobservable from the outside, and even left unscrutinized by partners involved, only specific questions and direct communication can help to 'dig out' the scope and content of trust-based social capital.

The following section presents a summary extracted from all the life histories, and offers some suggestions how to modify established concepts. The modifications reflect the insights gained from the interviews, more precisely from the life histories of the firms. Our suggested modifications do not presume to offer a superior model for explaining China. Indeed there may well be others of similar explanatory value. The modifications have to be seen rather as an invitation for further empirical research, if not for further attempts to model Chinese firms.

The founding of a firm: initial endowment and trusted management

Questions like who were the initial founder(s), who came up with the idea to start a company, how was the financial capital provided, or how was the work force recruited show that, indeed, institutional weakness and the liability of newness clearly shaped the ways in which Chinese entrepreneurs started a company. The interviews revealed that two decisions were crucial for the subsequent success: how to get the initial endowment together, and how to find a competent manager who knew how to best use the resources trusted to him. At the general level, weak institutions in China imply low private savings, lack of private property rights, non-transferable production factors and *ad hoc* intervention by state agencies at the different levels of the state bureaucracy. From the point of view of the respondents, this weakness translates into the need to: first, pool complementary assets by forming partnerships with the owners of those assets; and second, form an alliance with local jurisdictions or economic agencies that could offer property rights protection as well as 'contractual security'.[8] The newness of a private firm as seen from the point of view of the respondents made the selection of partners and the manager crucial. It is worth mentioning that the decision on what to produce was in no case regarded as a crucial one. With almost everything in short supply, the output decision was almost completely resource-driven. For example one entrepreneur (in Shanxi), though a graduate from a prestigious university, started as a restaurant owner only later investing in coal production and pig-iron, both sectors having been state monopolies before. The lack of knowledge of technology was overcompensated by the good relations with politicians in charge of the villages around the production sites and bureaucrats in the coal ministry.[9]

In contrast to the gambling feature in deciding to produce, the selection of partners and managers was seen as crucial.[10] The interviews showed to what extent asymmetric information, competence and *trust* were the dominant features in the selection of managers leading to another work profile. While managers in market economies are described as in control of resources, technology, and personnel, in China managers are also expected to control external relations with potential market partners and local politicians. In short they need to command social capital based on personal relations with economically valuable partners and political capital, i.e. personal relations with (local) politicians. The case studies in the following chapters provide illustrative evidence for the variety and importance of social capital 'with Chinese characteristics'.

The respondents argued that trust was a necessary but not sufficient requirement for the selection of partners or managers. Trust was not seen as a substitute for contracts, but complementary. For example, in the villages, auctions for lease contracts were organized so that each potential manager could bring forward his concepts about the future of the firm. The lease contract then offered the manager a fixed salary plus a share on net profit, and by doing so asked him to accept part of any profit or losses plus a share on the innovation rent.[11] This procedure was the beginning of *privatization* in China. As the interviews also show, most private companies started by transferring managerial control to an individual manager who, depending on performance and risk-taking, was later allowed (and able) to buy larger shares in the company till he became the majority shareholder or single owner. As will be elaborated on below over the years managers succeeded in incrementally increasing their share in the firms' total capital, replacing, mostly, villages or local state agencies while at the same time paying back loans received from family or friends.

The cases where no state-controlled physical assets were concerned but which relied exclusively on private savings (or, beginning in the 1990s, bank loans) were not much different. Here too, competence was seen as the single most crucial factor in the decision to start up a company. In short, irrespective of the source of fixed assets (private savings or state transferred assets), the initial endowment of the firm shows a distinct feature. Capital and technology, or a 'superior' product seem to have played a relatively small role in the decision to start a company. Instead, access to knowledge about organizing production, steady supply of input, and how to take a product to the market was stressed as the most essential component in the original endowment.

The interviews also show that it would be wrong to assume that this expertise can be modelled as human capital, i.e. knowledge of the entrepreneur himself, and that therefore Chinese entrepreneurship is basically nothing but Schumpeterian entrepreneurship where the initial endowment depends on physical, financial and innovative human capital. In the context of uncertainty and weak institutions, social capital needs to include the ability to gather marked relevant information, detect (with the help of others) new business opportunities, and, foremost, form alliances with local jurisdictions, or establish long-term business relations with suppliers and customers within and outside the state controlled sector. Social and political capital in China is generated by groups with certain identifiable characteristics such as politicians, i.e. people in certain positions, or business partners, i.e. people controlling certain assets. Unlike Western firms where such social capital sometimes plays also a role at the starting phase of a company, in China this social capital remains a constant feature the management of the firm relies on. Changes in legislation, new competitors, but also keeping good relations with those state agencies that hand out or withdraw licenses, make 'socialising' a permanent feature of a firm's management. The interviews showed that the costs for maintaining the social/political capital can be exorbitant, as they imply a drain of the firm's cash flow in form of social invitations and other favours paid by the company (see for example Case 3.1 in the contribution by Krug and Mehta, Chapter 3). To sum up:

Hypothesis 2: Entrepreneurship in China starts with the formation of a partnership (social capital) or alliance[12] (political capital) by which owners of assets, and information, plus those with access to state controlled input or supplier contracts with bigger (state or foreign) firms form a partnership in order to ensure control over resources transferred to the newly registered firm.

This has to be seen in contrast to the models of entrepreneurship that assume that new firms result from start-ups by entrepreneurs with good ideas but lacking capital.

Hypothesis 3: The selection of a manager depends on the assessment of organizational competence, individual social capital and his/her willingness to bear part of the business risk. It is worth mentioning that the relative scarcity of managerial skill allows individual managers to exchange their capabilities for generous rewards, if not options on the firm.

This has to be seen in contrast to models in which the manager is not an entrepreneur but an agent implementing the design and strategies defined by others.

The strategic decisions of a Chinese firm

Questions concerning the expansion of the firm, investment, location, or concerning the construction of distributional channels revealed that our respondents were only too aware that the output decisions by which they started a company were blind shots. Moreover, entrepreneurship in China does not stop or calm down once a company is established or starts selling. The strategic decisions involve the growth path of firms, and its governance structure.

The growth path of the firm

The life histories of the firms distinguish two stages in the growth path of a firm. Establishing a company in non-state controlled sectors and keeping the firm afloat posed not much of a problem apparently so long as the general shortage of goods and lack of competition protected the business in the 1980s, and so long as the firm produced for the local market only. Information impactedness, i.e. knowing each other well, frequent economic and social interaction plus efficient arbitration procedures provided by neighbourhoods or the village, ensured low transaction costs leading to rising total factor productivity. In some places, such as Shanxi, entrepreneurs could even rely on a political environment where local, i.e. Shanxi, entrepreneurship was seen as part of the local culture and therefore supported by the political leadership.[13]

The picture changes drastically when market liberalization and competition start to play a role, forcing firms to expand beyond the local nexus.[14] From then onwards, the problem of differences in business practices, or behavioural patterns add to uncertainty and ambiguity to the effect that the original alliances lose their value. First, the resource base provided by the different members of the original network or alliance becomes too small and restrictive. Second, the alliance proves to be of limited help only if it comes to monitoring and enforcing behavioural patterns of business practices in other locations (or provinces). As the life histories and the different case studies in the following chapters indicate, the growth path of a firm depends crucially on the ability to switch networks. For the establishment of a firm a small number of strong ties with local administrators and business partners were essential, but expansion was dependent on broader and weaker ties with a more heterogeneous group of business partners and politicians.[15]

From the perspective of the respondents, a firm's growth path is severely hampered by the non-transferability of assets, the need to accumulate entitlements to invest in other localities or other sectors, and the confiscation risk, i.e. *ad hoc* taxation by state agencies. The respondents' solution to this problem is to diversify risk by diversifying revenue sources. Therefore, they invest in *unrelated* business sectors and/or other jurisdictions, to:

- keep the confiscation risk low (Seagrave 1995)
- better exploit the accumulated stock of assets
- get access to additional assets or skills.

While these three factors indicate the influence of the uncertainty based on weak institutions the following factor shows to which extent the entrepreneurs respond to the liability of newness problem. Most respondents insist that they use something that would be called in the literature the 'Real Options' approach (Trigeorgis 1993; McGrath 1999). Whenever they receive trustworthy information about market chances or meet another trustworthy business partner willing to embark on long-term commitment, they take the chance, even if they cannot immediately exploit the new entitlements, or assets. The reason given is that on one side an entrepreneur cannot be sure that his first output choice will offer long-term survival, and that second a 'fishing' strategy works better in a situation in which relative prices and values are (not yet) known, when compared for example with Western (vertical) integration strategies.

Some informal talks with entrepreneurs revealed that to expand and invest is not always welcomed by the political authorities, who fear loss of control, and the loss of a rather safe tax base within their jurisdiction. Local authorities will either design all kinds of 'trade barriers' or they will blatantly ask to get a share in the subsidiary in another county. Moreover growth and size is still regarded as the most crucial indicator for success. The bigger the firm the more often they are expected to organize dinners and other forms of entertainment for the local authorities. This drain on the cash flow of new firms needs to be interpreted as the new 'confiscation risk' that can be observed not only in China but in all transition economies (Shleifer and Vishny 1993).

Hypothesis 4: New firms are threatened by the liability of success. Whenever a business volume exhausts local resources and local jurisdiction, then weak institutions, and the liability of newness, cause transaction costs to increase progressively. Yet firms face the following trade-off: the size (scale) effect of expansion needs to be compared with an increasing confiscation risk plus increasing transaction costs that emerge from moving in an unknown territory. Whenever the combined costs (confiscation *cum* transaction costs) exceed expected returns, firms will rather invest in unrelated sectors.[16]

This has to be interpreted in contrast with the economies of scale, or vertical integration argument, which expects high concentration of industries. It is worth mentioning that our analysis so far expects a future business environment where large firms will be the residual state firms, while private entrepreneurs will attempt to exploit economies of scope instead. By diversifying production and investing in quasi-independent firms they can considerably lower both the confiscation risk and the risk associated with differences in business practices and expectations.

Organizational forms of firms

The life histories of firms revealed how often a firm changed its official registration between, for example, an individual firm, a collective firm, and a corporation.[17] Though undoubtedly some of the changes were forced by changing legislation, some changes reflect a learning process of the owners and managers. The general picture shows that the expansion of Chinese firms is accompanied by frequent changes in both the property rights structure and the organizational form. Depending on the relative weight of each component in the initial endowment – financial/physical assets, human or social capital – at this moment (2000) three different forms of firms can be distinguished according to the composition of the initial endowment:

1 *Private entrepreneurs* are basically Schumpeterian entrepreneurs, i.e. they have an idea and social capital, but are in dire need of finding partners who control access to capital, machinery, land or potential customers. Organizational change in this case reflects the need to widen the resource base. To this purpose partnerships with mainly local state agencies willing to give up control rights are formed.[18]

2 In contrast, *private companies established by state firms* start with machinery, land, buildings and a work force but need innovative managers, and increasingly more connections to private domestic and foreign firms. The intention here is to safeguard the resource base by better employing the firm's assets. To assume that a firm owned by a state agency must be managed in a bureaucratic style, i.e. by fiat, is short sighted. As the cases in the contribution by Duckett and Goodman show, such an analysis does not take into account successful examples of state entrepreneurialism (Duckett 1998; Liu 1992; Nee 2000; Rozelle and Lee 1998; Rozelle *et al.* 2000). While state entrepreneurialism generally confines itself to the business area of the original state sector, state corporations can also act like private firms when they have to offer monetary returns for co-operative behaviour, compete for managerial professionalism, try to maximize profit by expansion into new business areas or new partnerships. With on-going reforms, in particular the

implementation of the Company Law since 1994, their ability to coerce economic agents into co-operation diminishes. Instead, one or a group of successful managers are offered the opportunity to buy shares, sometimes up to the point that they become the major shareholder while the founding state agency, or for example the village, turn into *rentiers*, being satisfied with dividends shared. In this case the organizational change refers to a *management buy-out*. Whereas in the 'West' managers swap their informational advantage and competence for shares, in Chinese management buy-outs the competence of a manager is not restricted to the operational side of a firm but explicitly honours his/her social capital and the ability to form alliances.

3   The most intriguing type of firms are *private/public corporations* where one or several private investors and some state agencies establish a new firm, usually with the private shareowners in control of the management (Davies *et al.* 1995; Oi and Walder 1999). In this case too the private shareowners are the Schumpeterian entrepreneurs who bring in new product ideas, new technology, and access to new networks while the state firms provide the complementary assets and/or contractual security. The intention in this case is to search for new market opportunities. When to exploit such opportunities needs changes in the initial endowment and/or changes in the supplier or distribution channels for which the state firms have no expertise, then a 'joint venture' with the private sector seems an attractive alternative. Subsequently, spinning off subsidiaries provided with the necessary assets and *mergers* with other private companies that can provide the complementary knowledge seem attractive ways to move into new markets. The interviews show that the (main) motivation (of the state firms) for doing so is to buy in expertise in the new private sector, an expertise that cannot easily (at low costs) build up in-house.[19]

The formation of industries and sectors

Will China's economy remain one in which a few big state firms control most economic assets, as claimed for example by some academics (for instance Nolan 2002) and as intended by the Chinese government, while small and middle scale firms fulfil complementary functions only? What else can be predicted with the analytical tools developed for explaining the size distribution of firms in different industries?

In the literature, most explicitly the 'Transformation literature',[20] the introduction of private ownership and subsequently privatizing the inherited state monopolies is seen as the decisive policy without which no private sector could emerge. For this reason all fixed assets of the big state firms needed to be divided up and re-assembled at the smallest size that would (still) allow the exploiting of technical scale economies. Such a procedure got stuck in most Central European countries such as Hungary (see for instance Whitley *et al.* 1996) or Poland, where a government tried to implement this policy. Resistance at local level often proved too strong, or, if that was overcome, only a few (mostly foreign) investors could be found who were willing to pay a positive price for these newly carved out firms.[21]

Leaving aside for the moment the political aspect of privatization, theories tested and proved for Western economies, and also the theory of resource partitioning in organizational ecology, would argue that over time big firms will concentrate on the 'market centre' of an industry while small firms will occupy the periphery which big firms are unwillingly or unable to cover. It is market competition that forces the big firms to move toward the market centre while the periphery offers a market niche that can be profitably exploited by smaller firms.[22] Subsequently, it is expected that the most vulnerable firms are middle scale industries that are exposed to competition in the market for resources. They cannot compete with big firms in the factor market and do not enjoy the comfortable market niche in the product market as small firms do.

At first sight, this reasoning seems to support the claim that big state firms in China will go on dominating the new industries irrespective of ownership due to their broader resource base, and the fact that a broad range of input is still state controlled, while the new private firms will be kept at the periphery irrespective of economic legislation. And indeed, so far the analysis has also argued that confiscation risk, the liability of success, and non-tradability of input generate a pretty similar size distribution: the proliferation of numerous small and few large (surviving, state owned) organizations; and discontinuity, with a hiatus in between. The question that remains to be tackled is whether the large state firms will occupy the market centre.

Yet the theoretical considerations presented above and the interviews point to another scenario if ownership and uncertainty are taken into account. Uncertainty, often enough accompanied by markets where due to excess demand almost everything sells, makes it empirically hard to define what a market centre is. Even without sophisticated tools that help to isolate and define a market centre, firms in China are aware that the 'market moves'. Thus, for example, consumers demand higher quality of products, and products that not so long ago were unavailable in the domestic market, while on the other hand, fashion is allowed to play a role. Unlike new private firms, which know that their survival depends on producing goods for which there is positive demand, state firms facing no competition have neither the management tolls nor the incentive to adjust to such an environmental drift (Shleifer 1998).[23]

The interviews and cases in the following chapter illuminate this feature of the new private sector. On the one hand some respondents in Zhejiang

(Appendix) managing private silk companies had established successful contracts with European companies providing them with designs that were at the centre of the world fashion market and had acquired sophisticated textile machinery on lease contracts that allowed them to produce at world standard quality. On the other hand there was a state firm (for this reason not included in the sample) that insisted on producing the old designs, despite a sharp drop in demand, while complaining that they had not got enough money to buy modern equipment.

In other words in contrast to the findings for market economies it is claimed the following modification is needed.

> *Hypothesis 5:* Due to uncertainty and (state) ownership large firms will be driven to the still (resource rich) periphery while the market centre will be occupied by numerous small firms.

Aside from uncertainty and lack of incentive for state firms to search for a market centre, the interviews showed another factor that can explain why private firms, inevitably starting small, might not expand around one core business with the result that large firms now in private hands will occupy the centre. The analysis showed that as long as diversification and investment in other sectors or regions (by establishing independent new and small companies) provide a way to escape over-taxation or indirect confiscation of profits and cash flow, even successful firms have an incentive to remain small, forgoing scale and scope economies around a core business. To invest in other lines of production or other jurisdictions is to be seen as a response that actually exploits the institutional weakness, one that attempts to spread resources across different unrelated businesses so that each remains smaller than the threshold at which political action can be expected. This tactic explains the rapid growth of relatively small companies in the Chinese private business sector. It is worth emphasizing that this feature distinguishes Chinese entrepreneurship from European transition economies where large foreign or domestic firms set the pace. The large number of (relatively) small companies seems to reflect the necessity to safeguard profit and capital accumulation of existing firms and preceding entrepreneurship rather than a greater pool of potential entrepreneurs as often is argued in cultural explanations.

The data set suggests that the weak institutional context seems to have different consequences for private companies founded by state firms. In their case the need to reduce the enormous overhead costs and to fight off state legislation (and intervention) makes a breaking up of the conglomerates into several smaller firms crucial. Yet by doing so these firms weaken their asset base. A way out here is to establish several small companies that can be coerced to use the initial resource base. As the interviews show many of these spin-offs got the initial endowment for free, can rely on state subsidized prices for input, and keep part of the work force on the payroll of the founding company. At the same time they have access to the market and market prices for their output. In other words, these companies, i.e. their size and profit, reflect the arbitrage between the socialist and market sector rather than performance in a competitive market.

All in all, these strategic decisions must lead to segregation in the future business sector in China. Large firms will dominate the old state sector, where size will not reflect vertical integration but rather the arbitrage between the socialist and market sector, plus the ability of inherited networks to entrench their functions, such as safeguarding local monopolies, (large) size, and old business practices, depending on their lobby effort and national policy aiming at protecting state industry and/or the workplaces maintained there. In a second sector small and middle scale firms will dominate, while size here is reflecting risk diversification and the need to connect with 'strangers' as business partners. With respect to industries, the small private firms will occupy the market centre, in particular in new and fashion-driven industries, while large state firms will dominate industries that are controlled by state legislation and relatively protected from international competition.

Conclusion

Our research suggests that process uncertainty matters. Entrepreneurs behave differently in transition economies, and these differences can be explained by the two factors isolated at the beginning, namely weak institutions and the liability of newness. This result of our research should not be seen as a strong enough proof, for the database is too weak. Yet the results suggest that it might be a fruitful endeavour to start where our analysis ends, namely by basing the analysis of Chinese firms on the following assumptions, which we suggest to better reflect the economic environment in China (see Table 4.1):

1   In addition to technological and competitive uncertainty, entrepreneurship in China faces process uncertainty.
2   New firms result from collective entrepreneurship by which owners of assets, political capital or information form a partnership in order to secure control rights for the newly registered firm.
3   In return for having taken over part of the business risk, managers get an option on the firm, eventually becoming entrepreneurs.
4   New firms are threatened by a liability of success due to a considerable confiscation risk, and the need to move to unknown territories.
5   Firms diversify in order to prevent state agencies or other stakeholders appropriating rents.

Table 4.1 Summary

Hypotheses	General assumptions	Modified assumptions: in transition economies/in China
1	Entrepreneurship faces technological and competitive uncertainty	Entrepreneurship faces process uncertainty in addition to techno-logical and competitive uncertainty.
2	New firms result from start-ups by entrepreneurs with good ideas but lacking capital, making use of (capital) markets.	New firms result from collective entrepreneurship by which owners of assets, political capital, and information form a partnership in order to see control rights secured for the newly registered firm.
3	Managers are not entrepreneurs	Managers become entrepreneurs: in return for taking over part of the business risk managers 'get an option' on the firm.
4	New firms are threatened by a liability of newness	New firms are threatened by a liability of success due to a higher confiscation risk and the need to move to 'unknown territories'.
5	Firms diversify to economize on resources	Firms diversify in order to prevent state agencies and other stake-holders to appropriate rents.
6	Industries get fragmented according to size and range of operation.	In transition economies industries get fragmented according to size and range of operation and ownership structure.

6 In China industries and sectors can be expected to get fragmented according to size, range of operation, and ownership structure of firms.

Further research might find it fruitful to see whether these modifications can be generalized for all transition economies or to what extent culture-specific, i.e. China-specific, factors play a role. It might also be intriguing to transfer some of these hypotheses to another case of process uncer-tainty, namely when such uncertainty is caused by drastic technological change, as for example in the IT sector.

Notes

1 The classical analysis is by Thuenen, Marshall, Menger, Schumpeter, Hayek, Knight. Useful summaries and critiques can be found in Baumol, W.J. 1993.

2 As for example found in the literature listed in Note 1. The questionnaires can be asked for from Barbara Krug, one of the authors of this chapter.

3 Stinchcombe 1965; the whole subsequent debate can be recalled by the following articles: Bruederl and Schuessler 1990; Henderson 1999; Gimeno *et al.* 1997; Romanelli 1989; Katz and Gartner 1988.

4 The following notes therefore list some key articles from the approaches used and mentioned in the text.

5 And which is described in Chapter 1.

6 For a systematic analysis of the vagaries of the State statistical system see Fischer 2002.

7 See the Appendix, Table A1 and Figures A1–A4.

8 See the contribution by Krug and Mehta in this volume, Chapter 3.

9 See Case 3.2 in the contribution by Krug and Mehta, Chapter 3.

10 Questions 57–88.

11 The technical expression for this kind of contract is 'sharecropping', a contractual form that has been employed in Chinese tenancy for 1,500 years. See Cheung 1969; Stiglitz 1974.

12 It is worth emphasizing that such joint action does not imply the 'collective nature' of Chinese entrepreneurship. On the contrary, the development of a private business sector is accompanied by individualization and personalization of business activities. It is no longer THE Party, or A state firm, or A ministry, but a friend, a schoolmate or a fellow villager (whose names are known) who are quoted as having been the crucial co-investor or the crucial link to suppliers and customers.

13 See the contribution by Goodman, Chapter 7.

14 This phenomenon is not unknown in the 'West'. See Greif 1989; North 1984; Chang 1996.

15 See the contribution by Hendrischke, Chapter 5.

16 The respondents argue that growth of the firm is perceived as reflecting market success, which in turn may attract the attention of state agencies, such as local tax bureaus, state suppliers, or county governments, who can appropriate part of the firm's profit. The Company Law from 1994 legitimizes this. For example Art. 4, Par. 2 stipulates that 'the company enjoys the legal person's whole property rights resulting from the investment of the shareholders', while in clear contrast the next paragraph claims that 'the ownership of the state assets of the company belongs to the state' (Art. 4, Par. 3), and hence is not an asset over which the firm can execute full property rights. See also Guohua 1995.

17 See in particular the contribution by Hendrischke, Chapter 5.

18 See the contribution by Hendrischke, Chapter 5.

19 Another reason should also be mentioned, namely that establishing independent companies is a convenient way to privatize assets for 'private' use by the top management (Ding 2000).

20 The leading journals of this debate are *JITE, Kyklos* and for 'Ordnungspolitik' (the German tradition of constitutional economics) *ORDO* – Jahrbuch fuer die Ordnung von Wirtschaft und Gesellschaft. See in particular Kiwit and Voigt 1995; Streit 1992. See also Denzau and North 1994; Wohlgemuth 1995.

21 The best summary and analysis far exceeding the German case can be found in Sinn and Sinn 1992; and Sinn 2000.

22 The technical term is *resource partitioning* and can be found in Carroll 1985. A fascinating and more contemporary rendering of the theory can be found in Carroll and Swaminathan 2000.

23 Further empirical evidence can be found in Tan 2002; Lukas *et al.* 2001.

References

Baumol, W.J. (1993) *Entrepreneurship, Management and the Structure of Payoffs*, Cambridge, MA: MIT Press.

Boisot, M.H. and Child, J. (1999) 'Organisations as adaptive systems in complex environments: the case of China', *Organisation Science*, 10(3):237–52.

Bruederl J. and Schuessler, R. (1990) 'Organizational mortality: the liabilities of newness and adolescence', *Administrative Science Quarterly*, 35(3):530–47.

Carroll, G. R. (1985) 'Concentration and specialization: dynamics of niche width in populations of organizations', *American Journal of Sociology*, 90:1262–83.

Carroll, G.R. and Hannan, M.T. (2000) *The Demography of Corporations and Industries*, Princeton: Princeton University Press.

Carroll, G. R. and Swaminathan, A. (2000) 'Why the microbrewery movement? organizational dynamics of resource partitioning in the U.S. brewing industry', *American Journal of Sociology*, 106:715–62.

Carroll, G.R. and Teece, D. (eds) (1999) *Firms, Markets, and Hierarchies*, Oxford: Oxford University Press.

Chang, S. (1996) 'An evolutionary perspective on diversification and corporate restructuring: entry, exit, and economic performance during 1981–89', *Strategic Management Journal*, 17:587–611.

Cheung, S. (1969) 'Transaction costs, risk aversion, and the choice of contractual arrangements', *Journal of Law and Economics*, 12:23–42.

—— (1996) 'A simplistic general equilibrium theory of corruption', *Contemporary Economic Policy*, 14(3).

Davies, H., Leung, T.K., Luk, S. and Wong, Y. (1995) 'The benefits of guanxi: the value of relationships in developing the Chinese market', *Industrial Marketing Management*, 24: 207–14.

Denzau, A.T. and North, D.C. (1994) 'Shared mental models: ideologies and institutions', *Kyklos*, 47:3–31.

Ding, X.L. (2000) 'The illicit asset stripping of Chinese state firms', *The China Journal*, 43 (June):1–29.

Duckett, J. (1998) *The Entrepreneurial State in China*, London: Routledge.

Eisenhardt, K.M. (1989) 'Building theories from case study research', *Academy of Management Review*, 14(4):532–50.

Fischer, D. (2002) 'What's in a Number? The Role of Statistics in China's Contemporary Economic Research and Economic Policy', in D. Fischer and A. Oberheitmann (eds) *China im Zeichen von Globalisierung und Entwicklung*, Muenchen: DIW-Sonderheft.

Flap, H.D. (1990) 'Patronage: and Institution in its Own Right', in M. Hechter, K.D. Opp, and R. Wipler (eds) *Social Institutions: Their Emergence, Maintenance, and Effect*, New York: Aldine de Gruyter.

Gambetta, D. (1993) *The Sicilian Mafia: The Business of Protection*, Cambridge, MA: Harvard University Press.

Gimeno, J., Folta, T.B., Cooper, A.C. and Woo, C.Y. (1997) 'Survival of the fittest? Entrepreneurial human capital and the persistence of underperforming firms', *Administrative Science Quarterly*, 42(2):750–83.

Greif, A. (1989) 'Reputation and coalition in medieval trade: evidence on the Maghrabi trades', *Journal of Economic History*, 69(4):857–83.

Guohua, Wang. (1995) 'On Three Important Issues of the Company System of the PRC', in Ersen Gao (ed.) *Symposium On Chinese Economic Law*, Tianjin: Publishing House of Law.

Hannan, M.T. and Freeman, J. (1984) 'Structural inertia and organizational change', *American Sociological Review*, 49:149–64.

—— (1989) *Organization Ecology*, Cambridge: Cambridge University Press.

Henderson, A.D. (1999) 'Firm, strategy and age dependence: a contingent view of the liabilities of newness, adolescence, and obsolescence', *Administrative Science Quarterly*, 44(2):281–314.

Katz, J. and Gartner, W.B. (1988) 'Properties of emerging organizations', *The Academy of Management Review*, 13(3):429–41.

Kiong, T.C. (1991) 'Centripetal Authority, Differentiated Networks: The Social Organization of Chinese Firms in Singapore', in G. Hamilton (ed.) *Business Networks and Economic Development in East and Southeast Asia*, Hong Kong: Centre of Asian Studies, Occasional Papers and Monographs , 99:176–200.

Kiwit, D. and Voigt, S. (1995) 'Ueberlegungen zum institutionellen Wandel unter Beruecksichtigung des Verhaeltnisses interner und externer Institutionen', *Ordo*, 46:117–48.

Krug, B., and Hendrischke, H. (2002) 'The Economics of Corruption and Cronyism – An Institutional Approach', in J. Kids (ed.) *Governance and Corruption*, Oxford: Palgrave.

Krug, B. and Pólos, L. (2000) 'Entrepreneurs, enterprises, and evolution: the case of China', paper presented at the Annual Meeting of the International Society for New Institutional Economics, Tübingen.

Liu, Y-L. (1992) 'Reform from below: the private economy and local politics in the rural industrialization of Wenzhou', *The China Quarterly*, 130 (June):293–316.

Lukas, B.A., Tan, J.J., Thomas, G. and Hult, M. (2001) 'Strategic fit in transitional economies: the case of China's electronics industry', *Journal of Management*, 27:409–29.

MacCauley, S. (1963) 'Non-contractual relations in business: a preliminary study', *American Sociological Review*, 28:55–67.

McGrath, R.G. (1999) 'Falling forward: real options reasoning and entrepreneurial failure', *Academy of Management Review*, 24(1):13–30.

Madhok, A. (1996) 'Know-how, experience- and competition-related considerations in foreign market entry: exploratory investigation', *International Business*, 5:339–66.

Nee, V. (2000) 'The role of the state in making a market economy', *Journal of Institutional and Theoretical Economics*, 156(1):66–88.

Nelson, R.R. (1995) 'Recent evolutionary theorizing about economic change', *Journal of Economic Literature*, 23:48–90.

—— (1996) *The Sources of Economic Growth*, Cambridge, MA: Harvard University Press.

Nolan, Peter. (2000) 'WTO yu guoqi gaige de zhongjie', *Zhengming*, 12:34–6.

Nooteboom, B. (2000) *Learning and Innovation in Organisations and Economies*, Oxford: Oxford University Press:62–74.

Nooteboom, B., Berger, H. and Noorderhaven, N.G. (1997) 'Effects of trust and governance on relational risk', *Academy of Management Journal*, 40(2):308–32.

North, D.C. (1984) 'Transaction costs, institutions, and economic history', *Journal of Institutional and Theoretical Economics*, 140:7–17.

—— (1994) 'Economic performance through time', *American Economic Review*, 84:359–68.

Oi, J.C. and Walder, A.G. (1999) *Property Rights and Economic Reform in China*, Stanford: Stanford University Press.

O'Sullivan, M. (2000) 'The innovative enterprise and corporate governance', *Cambridge Journal of Economics*, 24:393–416.

Patton, M.Q. (1980) *Qualitative Evaluation Methods*, Beverly Hills: Sage.

Pólos, L., Hannan, M.T. and Carroll, G.R. (2002) 'Foundations of the theory of social forms', *Industrial and Corporate Change*, 11:85–115.

Qian, Y. (2000) 'The process of China's market transition (1978–98): the evolutionary, historical, and comparative perspectives', *Journal of Institutional and Theoretical Economics*, 156(1):151–71.

Redding, G.S. (1996) 'Weak Organisations and Strong Linkages: Managerial Ideology and Chinese Family Business Networks', in G. Hamilton (ed.) *Asian Business Networks*, New York: Walter de Gruyter.

Romanelli, E. (1989) 'Environments and strategies of organization start-ups: effects on early survival', *Administrative Science Quarterly*, 34(3):369–87.

Rozelle, S. and Li, G. (1998) 'Village leaders and land-rights formation in China', *American Economic Review*, 82(2):433–38.

Rozelle, S., Park, A., Huang, J. and Jin, H. (2000) 'Bureaucrat to entrepreneur: the changing role of the state in China's grain economy', *Economic Development and Cultural Change*, 48(2):227–52.

Seagrave, S. (1995) *Lords of the Rim*, London: Corgi Books.

Shane, S. and Venkataraman, S. (2000) 'The promise of entrepreneurship as a field of research', *The Academy of Management Review*, 25(1):217–26.

Shleifer, A. (1998) 'State versus private ownership', *Journal of Economic Perspectives*, 12(4):133–50.

Shleifer, A., and Vishny, R. (1993) 'Corruption', Cambridge, MA: National Bureau of Economic Research (NBER Working Paper 4372).

Sinn, H.W. (2000) *Germany's Unification: An Assessment after Ten Years*, Cambridge, MA: National Bureau of Economic Research (NBER Working Paper W7586).

Sinn, H.W. and Sinn, G. (1992) *Jumpstart: The Economic Unification of Germany*, Cambridge, MA: MIT Press.

Stiglitz J.E. (1974) 'Incentives and risk sharing in sharecropping', *Review of Economic Studies*, April:219–55.

Stinchcombe, A.L. (1965) 'Social Structure of Organisations', in J.G. March (ed.) *Handbook of Organisations*, Chicago: Rand McNall.

Streit, M. (1992) 'Wissen, Wettbewerb und Wirtschaftsordnung', *Ordo*, 43:1–30.

Tan, J. (2002) 'Impact of ownership type on environment-strategy linkage and performance: evidence from a transitional economy', *Journal of Management Studies*, 39(3):333–55.

Trigeorgis, L. (1993) 'Real options and interactions with financial flexibility', *Financial Management*, autumn.

Whitley, R. D. (1990) 'Eastern Asian enterprise structures and the comparative analysis of forms of business organization', *Organization Studies*, 11(1):47–74.

—— (1999) *Divergent Capitalism: The Social Construction and Change of Business Systems,* Oxford: Oxford University Press.

Whitley, R., J., Henderson, Czaban, L. and Lengyel, G. (1996) 'Trust and contractual relations in an emerging capitalist economy: the changing trading relationships of ten large Hungarian enterprises', *Organisation Studies,* 17(3):397–420.

Williamson, O. (1993a) 'The evolving science of organization', *Journal of Institutional and Theoretical Economics,* 149:36–63.

—— (1993b) 'Calculativeness, trust and economic organisation', *Journal of Law and Economics,* 36:453–86.

Wohlgemuth, M. (1995) 'Economic and political competition in neoclassical and evolutionary perspective', *Constitutional Political Economy,* 6:71–96.

Wong, S.L. (1985) 'The Chinese family firm: a model', *British Journal of Sociology,* 36:58–72.

Yoshira, K. (1988) *The Rise of Ersatz Capitalism in South-east Asia,* Oxford: Oxford University Press.

5

THE ROLE OF SOCIAL CAPITAL, NETWORKS AND PROPERTY RIGHTS IN CHINA'S PRIVATIZATION PROCESS

Hans Hendrischke

Introduction

The aim of this chapter is to apply insights from institutional economics to explore the economic nexus between social capital, networks and property rights in the economic transformation and privatization process in the People's Republic of China (PRC).

The chapter proposes a reassessment of the traditional understanding of personal relations (*guanxi*) and networks in Chinese business by interpreting them as economic and not primarily as social phenomena.[1] Traditionally, personal relations and networks are seen as extensions of family values and structures into the economic sphere, where the consensus between business partners is one between family members or personal acquaintances of similar backgrounds who form groups or, more broadly, networks of business partners. Through their shared social background, members of these networks are committed to co-operating on a long-term basis and to maintaining reciprocity in their dealings. On the basis of this collective commitment and the trust that it creates, the members of these networks are able to operate and survive in an adverse economic environment. Adversity can mean a political, hostile or discriminatory environment for overseas Chinese or an environment of weak economic institutions and legal insecurity for private entrepreneurs in the PRC (Seagrave 1995; Chan 1982; Chen and Hamilton 1996; Davies *et al.* 1995; Hobday 1995; Kao 1993; Kiong and Kee 1998; Lever-Tracy 1996; Lukas *et al.* 2001; Luo and Chen 1996; McVey 1992; Park and Luo 2001; Redding 1996; Xin and Pearce 1996; Yoshira 1988). From this perspective, networks are a response to and substitute for weak state and economic institutions.

Their function is to provide patronage for entrepreneurs and create a clientelist relationship between local officials and business people.

An alternative approach proposed below is to focus on the economic role of networks. While accepting the view that both overseas Chinese businesses in the diaspora and private entrepreneurs in the PRC form networks in order to be able to operate in a weak institutional environment, the primary question here is to ask *what demand for institutional support there is in this environment and how networks can fulfil it, irrespective of their form or origin.* Put differently, does the gradual strengthening of state-based economic institutions in China's reform process imply a demise of network structures (patron–client hypothesis) or can there be demand for strong economic institutions and for networks at the same time? An obvious answer is that enterprises require networks to supply what the weak state and economic institutions cannot provide: security, trust, business procedures, conflict resolution, but also, more broadly, access to non-tradable input, such as assets, finance, know-how, personnel, business opportunities. Obviously, this list cannot be static, as it depends on the dynamic process of institutional development that is taking place parallel to the unfolding of business activities, particularly in the PRC under its reform policies. Research through interviews with private entrepreneurs in Zhejiang and Jiangsu suggests that for them the benefits of networks and strengthening state institutions are closely intertwined and mutually dependent. The interviews were conducted over two years and concentrated on small and medium-sized enterprises that fulfilled the economic criteria for private enterprise, irrespective of their current legal status.[2] These small and medium-sized enterprises initially depended on networks with local state institutions to secure business opportunities and property rights for which there was as yet no legal basis. However, by the late 1990s, when national policies and legislation had created a much more secure institutional environment, these networks showed a surprising resilience and in many cases had taken on new functions more akin to an economically motivated partnership than to political patronage.

This aspect of reinterpretation of the role of networks has important theoretical and practical consequences. If, as is usual for China, networks are seen as starting from a family or social group basis, their intention and reach is predetermined; they are confined in size and expansion, as they serve the core or extended family unit and their expansion is ultimately restricted by the need to professionalize, either because of size or complexity, or because of personal and generational changes after the founding generation; in brief, we are dealing with comparatively static structures. If, on the other hand, networks can be explained as a form of social institution that is created for the purpose of entrepreneurial activity in response according to the needs of the market, we can assume that they will be highly flexible and dynamic, as their development will be intertwined with the development of state and market institutions. An indication that networks are set up according to demand and adapted to a changing institutional environment would create a new perspective on their emergence, their durability, and their role as economic actors. The two core points that need to be proved in order to maintain this hypothesis are, first, that personal relations (*guanxi*) are not restricted by the borders of family or narrowly defined social groups, but rather are open and flexible and in fact a means to create networks that are able to take on market functions or substitute markets. Second, in order to prove that networks can be economic actors in their own right, it must be shown that they are able to hold and deal in property rights and that there is a reason for allowing networks to hold property rights, i.e. an economic rationale to the persistence of 'fuzzy' property rights. They are able to hold and deal in property rights. If there is empirical evidence to support these points, this institutional economic analysis of networks would shed new light on the whole transformation process in the PRC.

Guanxi and networks

There is still no generally accepted economically based definition for *guanxi* and networks. Most authors accept the Chinese cultural explanation, which is based on a simple Confucian family ideology that propagates filial piety, loyalty, harmony, and reciprocity as the core values in personal relations between relatives and close friends (Brook 1990; Eastman 1988; Freedman 1970; Mann 1987; Menkhof 1992; Myers 1982; Rozman 1993; Wong 1985). It is argued that in a Chinese cultural environment and Chinese influenced East Asian and South East Asian countries, these values and the related rules for personal conduct can be extended beyond the immediate family (the core of the network) to the extended family (family networks), to other related or befriended families (inter-family networks) and partners beyond who share the common (Chinese) cultural identity and feel bound by its rules for personal business conduct.

The vast business literature on Chinese *guanxi* and networks emphasizes their instrumental role in facilitating business activities and the ease with which they can be produced and used to overcome the lack of procedures and institutions, or alternatively to circumvent institutional procedures (Carney 1998; Davies *et al.* 1995, Lukas *et al.* 2001; Tan 2002; Tsang 1998). *Guanxi* as a mode of operation enables business partners to find communalities and create the mutual trust necessary to share information and to enter into business relations. The use of *guanxi* involves the common commitment to reciprocity and to the social sanctions that will apply if a partner deviates from the established norms of behaviour.[3]

Redding has identified insecurity and weak institutions as the two primary forces at the root of the need for networks in a situation where 'governments are still perceived as interfering, lawyers and contract are not natural parts of Chinese business behaviour, and institutions are not yet depersonalized'.[4] In response, overseas Chinese business people have used their family networks and broader social networks to create trust and dependability.

For the PRC, Victor Nee (1992) decribes a similar situation for private firms. This situation is generally seen as the reason for the predominance of family enterprises and family networks in the PRC. Faced with legal insecurity, private entrepreneurs primarily rely on their immediate kin and, only if their requirements go beyond, on patronage relationships with local authorities. The family as an entrepreneurial core for the development of small enterprises and the self-reliance of these small enterprises were the core elements of the propaganda for the Wenzhou model (Liu 1992). Wenzhou in Zhejiang became a much-celebrated city on a national scale for its success in allowing small private enterprises, in particular family-based enterprises, to flourish. The Wenzhou model still dominates the literature on private enterprises and the official propaganda of Zhejiang province.

The exclusion of family members from management

From the interviews with private entrepreneurs in the more central regions of Zhejiang (and Jiangsu) a different picture emerges. Family enterprises were confined to small enterprises in the hospitality industry, such as small restaurants and guesthouses, while larger enterprises operated much more complex support networks. Most respondents stated that the family was of little use for their entrepreneurial success and in many cases had explicitly taken precautions to exclude family members from participation in their enterprises' activities and enterprise related networks. This was an unexpected observation, as established knowledge about Chinese enterprises would rather have indicated the opposite trend. Admittedly, shareholding by family members during the establishment of enterprises was a common occurrence for many respondents. However, with the exception of smaller enterprises, such as restaurants, this alone would not suffice to define these enterprises as family enterprises.[5] First, in the case of all larger enterprises, capital contributions from family members were generally not given as long-term equity capital, but rather on a short-term basis of two to three years, and at interest rates of twice or three times the level of the going bank rate. As a source of equity and enterprise finance, family members thus offered little advantage over business partners or friends. Another avenue for family members to become shareholders was through the legal requirement in the Company Law of a minimum number of two shareholders. Respondents agreed that these positions were generally filled by trustworthy members of the core family. However, these family members, irrespective of their status in the family, would only receive a minimum share to ensure that they remained at arm's length from enterprise management. In the view of respondents, the involvement of family members bore the risk that on the basis of their capital contribution they might demand a say in the management of the enterprise. The formal aspects alone of family members having made some initial investment or taking on a role, as a silent shareholder or even a low-level employee, do not constitute these firms as family enterprises (Pistrui *et al.* 2001). Some respondents explained that they had taken additional measures to ensure that other family members remained excluded from management functions even after their own retirement. The reason given was that family members were generally not qualified for management tasks. The collective memory of the many failed family enterprises that had to be taken over by functioning enterprises during the recession of 1989 to 1991 in order to secure employment might have served as a lesson for those entrepreneurs who survived the crisis. The important point to note here is that the Company Law, while encouraging family involvement through the stipulation of a minimum number of shareholders, also enabled private entrepreneurs to effectively secure their private interests and exclude family members from enterprise management.

This points to the limitations of family networks in fulfilling the requirements of private enterprises. Where family members or traditional network partners such as people from the same village were able to provide input, they would be approached with priority, but the indication is that entrepreneurs would not rely on these links, but rather build up their own networks. This is borne out by the diversity of networks encountered. To argue that they evolved from family and social groups would be to overlook their emergence around functional needs, such as securing of land, finance, clarification of property rights, institutional protection, as well as business input, such as technical and management expertise, and business opportunities among others. Another point to bear in mind is that these networks developed in response to institutional changes.

From clientelist to functional networks

In Zhejiang there was clearly a dynamic process in which enterprises relied on different networks at different times and for different issues.[6] Land was one of the first issues for private enterprises. Entrepreneurs had to create liaisons with local governments or village administrations to secure land for their factories. Villages in return obtained shares in enterprises, or justified management fees and levies by pointing to their contribution to firms.[7] Land is also an example of the effects that the strengthening of institutions had on the need for networks. Several entrepreneurs mentioned that the changes in land policies made a major difference for them. Such changes included a policy introduced in Hangzhou in 1999 to require any land sales (or sales of land use rights) to go through public bidding. Another, earlier policy was for local governments to set up industrial zones, which increased predictability in the industrial real estate market and even induced inter-local competition in attracting industrial investment. Industrial investors consequently became less dependent on networks able to secure land.

Networks to secure access to scarce investment funds have been a constant concern. In the early 1990s, funds could still be secured through contacts with state firms and large collectives.[8] Initially, clientelist networks were important to gain official support from government or bank officials. After 1995, as a result of the banking reforms, the situation changed. Clientelist networks diminished in importance, as banking supervision was strengthened. For private enterprises their legal status became crucial as banks had different lending policies for collectives and limited liability corporations. Large private enterprises able to provide collateral in fact became preferred customers for local banks as they could base their links with their banks on a commercial footing. Enterprises without this advantage turned to networks to locate venture capital and had to build up new contacts able to provide links and information in this area.

More frequent than the use of networks to find and engage financial partners was the use of networks to locate and utilize technical expertise. In fact, technical know-how was one of the most frequent examples of the exploratory use of networks. Private entrepreneurs who owned land and investment facilities went out to seek products and markets. One frequently encountered standard example was the story of engineers from Shanghai SOEs (State Owned Enterprises) who over years had spent their weekends in the adjoining provinces transferring technological know-how to private enterprises. Over time, these links could expand and some of the private enterprises which had been built around the transferred know-how later acted as suppliers to the SOEs, others became competitors or substituted their products. Clarification of property rights was another major requirement of networks that changed with institutional developments. For example in Zhejiang, incorporation under the Company Law brought an improvement in defining property rights, but did not necessarily lead to full privatization. The enforcement of the incorporation under the Company Law differed locally depending on local network structures. For example, respondents in Huzhou City, one of the localities visited, stated that while their local government supported incorporation, private shares in their locality were generally not allowed to exceed 35 per cent. This limit was enforced by intra-enterprise networks between entrepreneurs and local government officials (as shareholders) who on both sides agreed that privatization would be the eventual outcome of their co-operation.[9] A further move towards privatization and confirmation of private property rights was made in 2000, when provincial authorities propagated a 'deepened system reform' (*shenhua gaizhi*) for the years 2000 and 2001. This reform was intended to reduce all public shares in enterprises of mixed ownership to below 50 per cent. In other words, provincial government policy required private entrepreneurs to become the majority shareholders in local enterprises. At the time of the interviews in October 2000, the related reforms had not been concluded. For example, in Huzhou, a number of smaller enterprises still retained their SOE label, although they were already controlled and operated by private managers. These enterprises had gone through a state corporatist phase when local governments had gradually instituted private entrepreneurs after the local government's initial reform efforts had failed and budget constraints made it impossible to further subsidize these enterprises. Property rights were, however, not bestowed on private entrepreneurs, but transferred in a process of close co-operation and co-ordination of interests with an on-going stake by the local government, i.e. in a network.

In Jiangsu this process followed a different pattern. Jiangsu is the home of a different model of enterprise reform that was often portrayed as an alternative to the Wenzhou model (see Jacobs 1999). The 'Sunan Model' emphasized greater enterprise autonomy, but it was based on the predominance of small state-owned enterprises and local collectives that did not follow the radical privatization path of the Wenzhou model. This created different institutional constraints and reform incentives for local governments. Of practical relevance for respondents was the provincial policy to encourage the formation of collective shareholding enterprises in 1995, which required co-ordination with local governments at a time when disengagement and general privatization was already propagated in Zhejiang. From 1999 onwards, local governments were required to reduce their control over, or shares in, collective enterprises and small state-owned enterprises by 2002. This happened in the form of a phased disengagement of administrators from enterprises with widely varying forms of networks. In some cases, enterprises were allowed to privatize; in others, local administrations forced their will on enterprises, for example by determining shareholder networks and governance structures under which these would be run. Networks here included local governments, but also outside partners. Sometimes the local governments made use of their position in the corporate network to bring in outside partners for mergers, such as in Case 5.1.

Case 5.1 The take-over of a power tool factory

This enterprise was established in 1971 as a state-owned enterprise under the county's Electronic Office to produce semi-conductors. It later diversified its production to small electric motors for fans. By 1980, it had reached an annual turnover of between 1 and 2 million RMB and made a small profit with a staff of 200 people. The local Electronic Office actively managed the enterprise until it was closed in early 1980. By 1985, the enterprise came under the leadership of the local Economic Commission. Not much changed until 1992, when the enterprise became one of the early entrants into the power tools market. This was a co-ordinated activity with a network of ten local suppliers to which the enterprise outsourced part of its production requirements. The enterprise was able to upgrade its own facilities through access to bank funding and within a short time became highly profitable. Its turnover multiplied from year to year and reached 250 million RMB by 1997.

Yet at this stage, changes in the power tool market began to catch up with the enterprise. It was a bundle of factors that included strong domestic competition, higher technical demands, and environmental concerns, in particular noise reduction, that led to a sudden decline in fortune. After initial losses in 1997, it faced bankruptcy in 1998, when the county government was unable to support its debt. For the county government the only alternative to bankruptcy was to privatize the enterprise or to sell it off. Interest in the enterprise came from a Shanghai based company, which had entered the power tool market in 1998 and could make use of the production facilities. The Shanghai company was owned by a Xinjiang funded corporation (75 per cent) and a Hong Kong investor (25 per cent). The Shanghai company shared ownership of the power tool enterprise with a local technology firm, which held a minority share of 7.5 per cent.

The price they paid for the enterprise was meant to guarantee an asset value of 30 million RMB for the enterprise. In fact, the actual payment was only half of that value. The actual amount had been negotiated with the local Labour Office, The Labour Office argued that the work force had to be compensated for the loss of their status as SOE workers. The money was paid directly into Labour Office funds, and served to dissociate the workers from the enterprise and from their previous entitlements under state ownership. The entitlements of retired and retiring workers were extinguished and 'socialized', i.e. transferred from the enterprise to a state institution. An additional condition, also requested by the Labour Office, was that the existing work force would be kept employed for at least one year. In actual terms, the Shanghai corporation changed the status of all workers to contract workers after one year. Manual workers could sign a one-year contract, middle management were offered 2–3 year contracts. Workers who were unwilling to accept contract status were forced to resign and offered minimal compensation.

Aside from labour issues, the Shanghai company had a free hand in managing the assets. There was a verbal agreement that the Shanghai company would invest 2 to 3 million RMB into the enterprise. Between 1999 and 2001, the new owners invested around 40 million RMB into the enterprise. More importantly, they overhauled management and commercial practices. Of the top managers, only the new CEO who had arrived in 1998 in preparation for the take-over, was allowed to stay. He did not receive any share in the enterprise he was managing, but was compensated with shares in the mother company. The new board of directors included five representatives from the Shanghai company, with only two members of the original board.

Institutional security is closely linked but not confined to property rights. Many entrepreneurs, irrespective of their property rights, were concerned about political influence at various scales of local government and forged long-term links with local political institutions. One way was to have local government included, generally through shareholding; another was to have the local Party included by allocating positions in human resources management departments to Party members seconded to the enterprise. Yet another way that opened avenues to influence was to become a member of the local Political Consultative Conference (PCC).

Networks as market substitutes

Businesses do not necessarily only have one network but they can have different networks for different purposes. Even for specific purposes, such as finance, there is not necessarily only one network. Instead there can be independent or intertwined networks that all contribute in various ways. However, the point to stress is that these networks are generally not mutually exclusive, but can be linked for exploratory and other purposes. Such networks are as much defined by the demand for them as they are by the institutional environment. Consequently, when legal or administrative institutions are strengthened, they may disappear or they may change their function. Land was an issue in the 1990s, when networks with local administrations were needed to secure it. Once a real estate market was established and transparency secured through open bidding and public auctions, the need for these networks diminished or disappeared. This did not necessarily mean that the networks disappeared, they could expand to take on other functions, for example the securing of finance when this became a more urgent issue. At other times, depending on the locality, the securing of property rights required institutional support through networks with local government institutions, but often these networks were kept going through giving local government a small minority sharehold, even though there was no immediate need, as if to store the value contained in the links to local authorities. While the analysis suggests that changes in networks reflect changes in the institutional environment, the observed tendency to maintain networks beyond their immediate visible need gives rise to some additional reflections on the nature of networks.

In order to analyse networks it is necessary to differentiate between the ideology of networks and their economic function. Networks create their own language and ideology, which can be recognizable as euphemisms that soften the impact of the harsh rules under which network members operate and make these rules socially more acceptable. The ideology of networks centres around the notions of reciprocity, loyalty, and face. These notions explain as well as hide an underlying reality. Reciprocity and loyalty are generally assumed to bind the members, but they do not bind the network as a whole. The network does not owe loyalty to individual members beyond what is useful for the network. In this sense, the market rationality of the network is stronger than its social obligations. Social obligations that the networks accept and realize are not contradictory to this, as for example the loyalty towards retired members can be explained as an on-going incentive for existing members, or, as the result of the persisting influence of retired members in the network. If we define networks in this way as an economic institution with the purpose of achieving economic (and social) gain, they acquire an inherent economic rationality that makes them open to competition and efficiency considerations. Social capital can be invested in and withdrawn from business ventures and will strive for return on investment.

If *guanxi* or social capital are as ubiquitous and all-pervasive as is generally recognized, the question arises as to whether there are rules beyond the vague notions of reciprocity and trust that govern their use across a whole economy and by partners that are far too numerous and too differentiated to be bound by family-based codes of conduct. In other words, is it possible to define economic rules for exchange of social capital similarly to those that govern the exchange of financial capital?[10] Can social capital be used to store and transfer value or, more importantly for the argument here, act as a medium for the exchange of property rights? If so, how does social capital relate to formal ownership? Social capital is generally defined in a way that emphasizes its similarity with capital stock rather than similarities with financial capital, although there is no reason why social capital could not be regarded as a means of exchange. Financial capital primarily as a means of exchange provides convertibility as its core function, generally in a market. There is no reason why social capital could not be analysed under this aspect as long as important differences are accounted for. Social capital can be utilized and converted only within or with the involvement of the group that shares it. Unlike financial capital, social capital is neither specific in its form nor particularistic when exchanged. It has to undergo further conversion before it can become an individually owned asset; more specifically, the network has to arrange for social capital to become an economic benefit for its members. In brief, one could argue that networks are the markets for social capital. This argument would presuppose several assumptions which can be tested empirically.

One is that networks are particularistic markets with a limited, albeit flexible, number of participants defined by the options for entry, exit, and voice. A further assumption is that members gain entry on the basis of their willingness to contribute social capital, i.e. their willingness to trade useful contacts within the network. Access to networks is graded. Exit from networks happens by social exclusion that can also be graded. Technically, a member has been excluded when the inability to mobilize network resources is evident. Voice is achieved through constant communication among the active network participants. Finally, one would expect a link between social capital and property rights similar to the one that has long been established for overseas Chinese family enterprises.

Networks and property rights

While the role of networks in business operations has been widely documented, less is known about their role in the formation of property rights. In economic transition studies, the generally held assumption is that the formation of private property rights occurs automatically in the process of privatization once the ideological constraints are removed by the central government and local governments face hard budget constraints (Qian et al. 1999). In this view, demand exists only for institutionally secured property rights. More detailed studies on China similarly describe the emergence of property rights as linked to administrative procedures: 'change has occurred in a cascading pattern, with the reformed type most prominent early on, and then a progressive shift down the continuum toward contracting, leasing, and, finally, the private firm'(Walder and Oi 1999). This implies a hierarchy of property rights that becomes clearer as they are gradually devolved to the private firm from which demand for secure property rights is seen to originate. However, equally noteworthy is the existence of 'intermediate forms, especially the very common partnership contracts ... (that) are the prototypical half-measure, a true "hybrid" form of property' (Walder and Oi 1999). This 'hybridity' of property rights requires economic explanation, in particular, an explanation for the communality of interest between local government and entrepreneurs and managers to leave property rights ill-defined that lies at the root of hybrid property rights. The explanation offered below is that networks as an informal intermediate institution combining local authorities and private actors work better with 'fuzzy' or hybrid property rights than with legally defined clear rights, and that this therefore creates demand for 'hybridity'.

The interviews in Zhejiang and Jiangsu suggest that there is a strong informal side to the definition of property rights where administrative categories, status or partnership contracts matter less to the entrepreneurs than the substantial property rights that can be realized in co-operation with the local state in the form of networks. The willingness and the flexibility of local authorities and entrepreneurs in entering into networks can be explained by what could tentatively be termed 'soft institutional constraints' in the implementation of policies at different levels of government.

The local implementation of privatization policies

One characteristic of policy implementation in China is the inability of the central government to administratively enforce its own policies at local levels, i.e. the lack of 'hard institutional constraints' that force provincial and local governments to fully comply with central policies and central legislation. This is not admitted in official statements which emphasize local compliance with central laws and regulations, but limited recognition is given to the problem by the general rule that policies need to be implemented in line with specific local circumstances, which has given rise to central–local bargaining relations (see studies by Lieberthal and Lampton 1992). From the perspective of interview respondents, central policies and legislation, such as the Standard Regulations or the Company Law, in order to have a practical effect, need to be supported at provincial level and furthermore implemented at local level by the authorities in charge of local enterprises. Local implementation followed by no means automatically from central or provincial policies, but varied considerably from locality to locality to the degree that respondents spoke of 'enlightened villages' or 'enlightened counties' where those localities had shown initiative in early privatization. For example, provincial authorities could recommend to local authorities that they should implement national policies in advance of their national implementation, as was the case with the Company Law in Zhejiang. But provincial governments could also propagandistically support a policy without requiring local authorities to actually implement it, as was the case with some privatization policies in Jiangsu (Hendrischke 2002a). The result was that neither local authorities nor local entrepreneurs had a clear frame of reference for policies above local level.

The interviews with entrepreneurs show a surprising discrepancy between national or provincial policies and the actual implementation at local government level. For the respondents, local government level could range from county government institutions down to village governments, depending on the original affiliation of their enterprises. As mentioned above, Zhejiang province played a leading role in the privatization of enterprises from the early 1980s, when the 'Wenzhou Model' was first propagated (Nolan and Dong Furen 1990), and has kept this lead in the following two decades. For most respondents in Zhejiang, the first stage in securing property rights came with the Standard Regulations for Shareholding, issued at national level in 1988 and locally implemented from the same year. The Standard Regulations provided a basis for the separation of local government and private shares in collective enterprises, but the ratio between them was not prescribed by the province. Agreements had to be reached separately at each local level between entrepreneurs and local authorities. The ratio of private shares could vary from anywhere below 10 to above 90 per cent depending on locality and enterprise. The second stage came with the Company Law which came into force nationwide from 1994, but was implemented in different localities in Zhejiang on a trial basis from 1992. Respondents from these localities in Zhejiang reported that their local authorities requested enterprises under their jurisdiction to convert to limited liability companies as soon as possible, but did not enforce any specific limits on the volume of private or public shares, leaving the decision to agreements between local actors.

In Jiangsu the privatization process followed a slower pace and private enterprises emerged later. Respondents mentioned that the formation of collective shareholding enterprises was encouraged in 1995, but not generally enforced until several years later, when from 1999 onwards local authorities were required to reduce their control over and shares in collective enterprises and small state-owned enterprises. Also, the establishment of private enterprises and limited liability companies was not generally enforced at local government level when the Company Law came into force in 1994, although it was propagated as a provincial policy from 1993 onwards. Similarly, Jiangsu had formulated provincial policies aimed at reducing state ownership to minority shares by 2002, but as late as 2001 local SOE respondents reported that they still had made no preparations for even partial conversion to private ownership. As a result, policies promoted in Jiangsu during the late 1990s were already obsolete in Zhejiang. For example, enterprises were still transformed into shareholding co-operatives in Jiangsu at a time when in Zhejiang incorporation was already the dominant form of property rights transformation.

This situation, in analogy to Kornai's hard and soft budget constraints (Kornai 1986), can be described in terms of 'soft institutional constraints'. In the formation of property rights for enterprises, this process works at two different levels. One set of 'soft institutional constraints' can be observed in the implementation of national policies at provincial and local level. These are well documented in the research literature on government negotiations and bargaining (see studies by Lieberthal and Lampton 1992). Another set of 'soft institutional constraints' operates in the relationship between local administrations and enterprises undergoing privatization. Soft institutional constraints exist when the participants in a network have some institutional basis to back up their economic interests, but cannot fully rely on the enforceability of these institutional claims and instead have to realize their interests through negotiation and compromise. In practical terms, the weakness of local political institutions made it impossible for entrepreneurs or managers to appeal to central or provincial authorities in case they faced conflicts with local authorities over property rights. Under market conditions, where both local government and entrepreneurs depend on the success of local enterprises, they had to find a *modus vivendi* that did not primarily rely on external authorities. In theory, if institutional regulations and customary economic exchange were completely separated and unmediated, this could lead to institutional breakdown. The reason why this did not occur is that networks created an alternative and informal forum of exchange between the social and the government sphere. Their main function was to mediate demand for business input and for property rights.

Demand for property rights varied according to the markets for property rights that were created in the transition process. The two main types of property rights are alienability and exclusivity. During the first stage of the reform process, local governments were more likely to be interested in the right to benefit from assets, i.e. in the right of exclusivity. While with the devolution of authority over enterprises, this right excluded higher or competing authorities, it was shared between local authorities and local entrepreneurs (managers or a management team) whose services were required because of their technical and commercial competence. Local authorities, having obtained the right to benefit from assets under their control, co-opted managers for these assets by granting them partial rights to benefit (see for instance Oi and Walder 1999). While respondents entered into various forms of agreements (from verbal agreement to written contracts) for this co-operation, they emphasized their network arrangements with local authorities, as this type of co-operation was for the longer term and required trust to solve issues such as remuneration, operational decisions, institutional support and so on. Initially, sharing the right to benefit from assets did not require specification of the second major property right, alienability, although demand for this right arose as managers consolidated their position and required greater security.

Demand for the right of alienability was related to the emergence of a market for enterprise assets. Its first manifestations were the local markets for land use rights, but once demand for managerial skills had become strong enough, managers or entrepreneurs could demand majority owner-ship shares either informally within the network or by demanding their rights on the basis of local and provincial policies. In Zhejiang, this was a gradual process that accelerated from 1992, after many small enter-prises had failed during the preceding recession years. Respondents stated that in the early stages of reform, they depended on support from local authorities both in securing their rights and also generally agreeing infor-mally on ownership shares, before codifying them either under the Standard Regulations or later under the Company Law. Only when institutional constraints were hardened, for example, when provincial authorities forced local authorities to reduce their involvement in enterprises, did the situation change. Hardening institutional constraints strengthened the bargaining position of private entrepreneurs in their demands for prop-erty rights, because they could now appeal to higher authorities. However, as this process was a gradual one, the resulting demand for clear prop-erty rights also increased only gradually in line with institutional change. Demand for the involvement of local authorities also persisted because the protection of property rights was not only an internal local issue, but also related to external business links with other localities. This process resulted in locally specific development paths for the formation of private property rights (Hendrischke 2002b).

The implication is that the 'fuzziness' of property rights can be inter-preted as much the sign of failing formal institutions as the result of the interplay of rational actors operating in a dynamic institutional environ-ment who are better off dealing with each other than relying on recourse to external authorities. In other words, depending on the institutional environment, demand for 'fuzzy' property rights in an operating network structure could be stronger than demand for clearly defined property rights under the law that was locally unenforceable.

This process did not only bring benefit to managers or entrepreneurs who face transaction costs for the involvement of local authorities.[11] As networks maintain their influence even under harder constraints and in the presence of defined property rights, the fact that there is a limited market for assets and private property rights does not mean that private entrepreneurs can fully enjoy their rights. The implementation of the same national policy at local level, for example, the introduction of the Company Law, might serve an entrepreneur in one locality to gain legal security for private ownership, but under different circumstances, as in Case 5.2, might also prevent a manager from acquiring full control, as an existing net-work can enforce *de facto* collective ownership even after the status of an enterprise has changed to become a private company.

Case 5.2 The chocolate machinery factory

Mr Wang could well be the prototype of an entrepreneur. Engineer by profession and president of the company whose fate he has directed since 1979, he is proud of his flourishing enterprise and sees its future with confidence. Yet, he is also the typical manager who has always played the role of an agent. Even now, as the president and major shareholder of a company that has a unique position as the country's first manufacturer of machinery for making chocolate, he owns only 25 per cent of the company's shares and still has to listen to various principals. His professional career and the development, organizational structure, and business strategies of his company are all the result of local township policies which in turn depended on policies and decisions by higher levels within Jiangsu province.

The enterprise Mr Wang is now heading was set up in 1969 as a township and village enterprise (TVE) to produce simple agricultural machinery, in particular pumps and harvesting equipment. What differentiated this enterprise from hundreds and thousands of similar ones was that in 1979 at the very beginning of the reform period, it linked up with two engineers from Shanghai who were keen to use their free weekends to transfer their technical know-how in return for some additional income. Mr Wang recognized the commercial potential of their skills in designing machinery that could be used to produce chocolate for the emerging consumer markets. Unlike many other types of equipment and capital goods, the production of this type of machinery was under no government restrictions, as it was not included in economic planning and would therefore not compete with similar products of state-owned enterprises which at that stage enjoyed protected markets. There were also no technical standards for this machinery, giving the enterprise free reign in developing new products and expanding its business scope. In 1986, the Ministry for Light Industry restricted the import of competing machinery by recognizing the machinery for import substitution. This secured an ongoing market position for Mr Wang. He now employs ninety staff, among them seven senior management personnel. As a relatively young enterprise, there are no retirees to look after. One tenth of their products is exported to countries such as Malaysia and Pakistan.

Under the ownership of the local township, the corporate structure of the TVE changed very little for more than a decade, in spite of business development. The first restructuring occurred in 1993, when the TVE adopted the Co-operative Shareholding System which required a definition of the various shares. The township's share was fixed at 70 per cent, based on its previous investment of land, buildings, and machinery. The remainder of 30 per cent was allocated to the management and staff and split into relatively small individual shares. Mr Wang obtained the largest individual share of 3 per cent for which he had to pay in 10 thousand RMB. His co-managers were allowed to acquire slightly smaller shares and most of the core staff obtained shares of up to 1 per cent. This initial restructuring was the result of a politically induced reform imposed on the township government by provincial authorities. This arrangement was limited to three years after which the distribution of shares was to be reconsidered. In 1996, the township government as a matter of policy was not allowed to hold a majority in the enterprise and had to reduce its shares to 30 per cent. This was done in a more formal process on the basis of an asset evaluation. Mr Wang's share was now raised to 7.8 per cent. However, unlike three years before, he did not have to make a payment for this increased share. The village authorities decided that he should be allowed to use his share of enterprise profits for payment. The remaining shares were evenly allocated to management and core staff with most shares around 1 per cent.

In 1999, in response to a local policy initiative, the township had to divest itself of all its remaining state shares and convert the enterprise into a limited liability company. Mr Wang's share now rose to 25 per cent, giving him a more distinct majority. The next largest share was 15.7 per cent, held by Mr Wang's deputy. The combined shares of the management team of six people under Mr Wang amounted to 55 per cent, still surpassing his individual share by a considerable margin. Of the remaining shares of 20 per cent, fourteen technical and core staff held 1 per cent each. The remaining 6 per cent were spread among other staff. The township has no formal ownership in the enterprise. It derives a management fee of 1 per cent of turnover from the enterprise. One of the Shanghai engineers who had provided the original technology to the enterprise is still alive and maintains informal relations with the enterprise.

Mr Wang does not consider himself to be the owner of the enterprise, although he feels that he has led it for more than a decade. His plans are humble. The enterprise continues to compete on price and its strategy for the future is to expand into machinery for dried fruit.

As Case 5.1 showed, under 'hybrid' or 'fuzzy' property rights, government owners can equally assert their rights of alienability by selling assets or agreeing to take-overs. Case 5.2 demonstrates that local authorities were able to assign their property rights in a privatization process to private shareholders, but hold on to some of their network rights by determining the future composition of shareholders and depriving a manager of majority ownership in favour of a collective group of managers who were part of an original network.

'Soft institutional constraints' have thus created a specific dilemma for China's gradual transition environment, as local administrations and private entrepreneurs are bound together in networks by common interests and at the same time compete for the use of assets. Central government policies have gradually hardened the constraints on local, primarily provincial, authorities to respect and protect the interests of private entrepreneurs. These policies are implemented in the form of flexible guidelines issued at provincial level and cannot be enforced against the will of local authorities, but local authorities are also not able to disregard them. Local authorities, to which authority over enterprises was devolved in the transition process, can no longer claim or enforce exclusive control of property rights on the basis of the bureaucratic and customary practices that protected their interests during the pre-reform era. At enterprise level, neither local authorities nor private entrepreneurs can appeal to external authorities for protection of their property rights, nor would they in fact want to, as the unstable transitional institutional situation will not allow them to predict in whose favour any external decision would turn out to be. In this situation, the interest of both sides is rather to have undefined property rights and rely on a negotiated outcome within local networks. While this is a sub-optimal solution from a theoretical perspective, it creates most security and predictability in practical terms.

Conclusion

The general statement repeated in all economic literature on China that property rights in China are generally fuzzy and ill-defined is an adequate description of reality, but generally the purpose of this observation is to argue that the lack or weakness of defined property rights is a severe hindrance for privatization, the emergence of firms, and business activities in general. While this is a valid argument in the long run, the point argued above is that, under China's transitional regime, change in ownership does not automatically ensure an efficient use of enterprise assets. In order to better employ assets, aside from ownership, managerial competence, technical and market know-how and enforceability of rules and regulations are needed. As there is no functioning market for assets and a high level of uncertainty with respect to political and market risks, the next best institutions (to functioning capital markets) are networks which are driven by the need to seek full employment of all resources under their control, and have an incentive to expand to the degree that they are able to absorb know-how, business opportunities, and technical as well as human resources.

Once an asset is owned by a network, it can be assigned either to network members or to a group of different stakeholders where the network maintains some influence or share. If such a network asset performs satisfactorily, the network has the option to assign it to a private entrepreneur or to a network member able to manage it. The network can maintain its claim on property rights by assigning them to members, or else assign property rights, inclusive legal ownership, to persons who have the ability to manage the assets. It is the constellation of interests within the networks that determines the way in which assets are privatized. For example, privatization is an option when a local bureaucracy sees its main benefit in increased tax revenue and cannot itself provide the management for a successful operation of assets. It is also an option when a local network comes under hardened political constraints to privatize. The network as a 'quasi-market' for assets helps to explain the low 'exit' threshold that characterizes the Chinese economy. Assets that do not perform well are quickly disassembled and returned to the network exchange to be integrated in more promising constellations: a new firm, or a similar firm under another management.

Notes

1 For a contrary view, see the contribution by Jacobs, Belschak and Krug, Chapter 8.
2 For the details of the empirical research, see Chapter 1.
3 For examples of sanctioning mechanisms see Wank 1999.
4 Redding 1990; see also the contributions by Krug and Mehta, and Krug and Pólos, Chapters 3 and 4.
5 For details see Jacobs, Belschak and Krug, Chapter 8, Tables 8.3–8.8.
6 As the life histories of the firms interviewed revealed.
7 See for example Case 3.2 in Krug and Mehta, Chapter 3. The contribution by Duckett shows how quickly local authorities responded to the increasing demand for land; see Cases 6.1 and 6.2.
8 See for example Case 7.3 in Goodman, Chapter 7 and Case 3.3 in Krug and Mehta, Chapter 3.
9 As the interviews in Huzhou revealed.
10 For a general discussion of other 'modes' of social capital, see the different contributions in Leenders and Gabbay 1999.
11 See the contributions by Krug and Mehta, Duckett, and Goodman, Chapters 3, 6 and 7.

References

Brook, T. (1990) 'Family Continuity and Cultural Hegemony: The Gentry of Ningbo, 1368–1911', in J.W. Esherick, and M. Backes Rankin (eds) *Chinese Local Elites and Patterns of Dominance*, Berkeley: University of California Press:27–50.

Carney, M. (1998) 'A management capacity constraint? Obstacles to the development of the overseas Chinese family business', *Asia Pacific Journal of Management*, 15:137–62.

Chan, W. K. K. (1982) 'The organisational structure of the traditional Chinese firm and its modern reform', *Business History Review*, 56:218–35.

Chen, E. and Hamilton, G.G. (1996) 'Introduction: Business Groups and Economic Development', in G.G. Hamilton (ed.) *Asian Business Networks*, Berlin: Walter de Gruyter:1–6.

Davies, H., Leung, T.K., Luk, S. and Wong, Y. (1995) 'The benefits of guanxi: the value of relationships in developing the Chinese market', *Industrial Marketing Management*, 24:207–14.

Eastman, L.E. (1988) *Family, Fields and Ancestors*, Oxford: Oxford University Press.

Freedman, F. (1970) *Family and Kinship in Chinese Society*, Stanford: Stanford University Press.

Hendrischke, H. (2002a) 'East China – private enterprises in Zhejiang and Jiangsu', paper presented at the Workshop on the Rise of Private Business in China: The Nexus of Corporate Governance and Business-Government Relations, East-West Center, University of Hawaii.

—— (2002b) 'How local are local enterprises? Translocal enterprise networks of small private enterprises in Zhejiang and Jiangsu', paper presented at the Workshop on Translocal China: Place-Identity and Mobile Subjectivity, UTS-UNSW Centre for Research on Provincial China, Haikou/Hainan.

Hobday, M. (1995) 'East Asian latecomer firms: learning the technology of electronics', *World Development*, 23(7):1171–93.

Jacobs, J. B. (1999) 'Uneven Development: Prosperity and Poverty in Jiangsu', in H. Hendrischke, and C. Feng (eds) *The Political Economy of China's Provinces: Comparative and Competitive Advantage*, London: Routledge:113–50.

Kao, J. (1993) 'The worldwide web of Chinese business', *Harvard Business Review*, 71(2):24–36.

Kiong, T.C. and Kee, Y.P. (1998) 'Guanxi bases, Xinyong and Chinese business networks', *British Journal of Sociology*, 49(1):75–96.

Kornai, J. (1980) *Economics of Shortage, Vols. I and II*, Amsterdam: North-Holland.

—— (1986) 'The soft budget constraint', *Kyklos*, 39(1):3–50.

Leenders, R. and Gabbay, S.M. (eds) (1999) *Corporate Social Capital and Liability*, Dordrecht: Kluwer.

Lever-Tracy, C. (1996) 'Diaspora capitalism and the homeland: Australian Chinese networks into China', *Diaspora*, 5(2):239–73.

Lieberthal K.G. and Lampton, D.M. (1992) *Bureaucracy, Politics, and Decision Making in Post-Mao China*, Berkeley: University of California Press.

Liu, Yia-Ling. (1992) 'Reform from below: the private economy and local politics in the rural industrialization of Wenzhou', *The China Quarterly*, 130:293–316.

Lukas, B.A., Tan, J.J., Thomas, G. and Hult, M. (2001) 'Strategic fit in transitional economies: the case of China's electronics industry', *Journal of Management*, 27:409–29.

Luo, Y. and Chen, M. (1996) 'Managerial implications of guanxi-based strategies', *Journal of International Management*, 2:193–216.

McVey, R. (1992) 'The Materialization of the Southeast Asian Entrepreneur', in R. McVey (ed.) *Southeast Asian Capitalism*, Ithaca, New York: Cornell University Press:7–34.

Mann, S. (1987) *Local Merchants and the Chinese Bureaucracy, 1750–1950*, Stanford: Stanford University Press.

Menkhoff, T. (1992) 'Xinyong or how to trust trust. Chinese non-contractual business relations and socialstructure', *Internationales Asienforum*, 23:262–88.

Myers, R.H. (1982) 'Customary law, markets, and resource transactions in late imperial China', *Explorations in the New Economic History*:273–99.

Nee, V. (1992) 'Organizational dynamics of market transition: hybrid forms, property rights, and mixed economy in China', *Administrative Science Quarterly*, 31(1):1–27.

Nolan, P. and Dong Furen (eds) (1990) *Market Forces in China: Competition and Small Business – The Wenzhou Debate*, London: Zed Books.

Oi, J.C. and Walder, A.G. (eds) (1999) *Property Rights and Economic Reform in China*, Stanford: Stanford University Press.

Park, S.H. and Luo, Y.D. (2001) 'Guanxi and organizational dynamics: organizational networking in Chinese firms', *Strategic Management Journal*, 22:455–77.

Pistrui, D., Huang, W., Oksoy, D., Zhao Jing, and Welsch, H. (2001) 'Entrepreneurship in China: characteristics, attributes, and family forces shaping the emerging private factors', *Family Business Review*, XIV(2):141–58.

Qian, Y., Cao, Y. and Weingast, B. (1999) 'From federalism, Chinese style, to privatization, Chinese style', *Economics of Transition*, March (7):103–31.

Redding, S.G. (1996) 'Weak Organizations and Strong Linkages: Managerial Ideology and Chinese Family Business Networks', in G. Hamilton (ed.) *Asian Business Networks*, New York: de Gruyter:64–73.

Rozman, G. (ed.) (1993) *Confucian Heritage and its Modern Adaptation*, Princeton: Princeton University Press.

Seagrave, S. (1995) *Lords of the Rim*, London: Corgi Books.

Tan, J. (2002) 'Impact of ownership type on environment-strategy linkage and performance: evidence from a transitional economy', *Journal of Management Studies*, 39(3):333–55.

Tsang, W.K. (1998) 'Can guanxi be a source of sustained competitive advantage for doing business in China?', *Academy of Management Executive*, 12:64–73.

Walder, A.G. and Oi, J.C. (1999) 'Property rights in the Chinese economy: contours of the process of change', in J.C. Oi and A.G. Walder (eds) *Property Rights and Economic Reform in China*, Stanford: Stanford University Press:10.

Wank, D. (1999) 'Producing Property Rights: Strategies, Networks, and Efficiency in Urban China's Nonstate Firms', in J.C. Oi, and A.G. Walder (eds) *Property Rights and Economic Reform in China*, Stanford: Stanford University Press: 264–67.

Wong, S.L. (1985) 'The Chinese family firm: a model', *British Journal of Sociology*, 36:58–72.

Xin, K.R. and Pearce, J.L. (1996) 'Guanxi: connections as substitutes for formal institutional support', *Academy of Management Journal*, 39:1641–58.

Yoshira, K. (1988) *The Rise of Ersatz Capitalism in South-east Asia*, Oxford: Oxford University Press.

6

THE EVOLVING INSTITUTIONAL ENVIRONMENT AND CHINA'S STATE ENTREPRENEURSHIP

Jane Duckett

The institutional environment and entrepreneurship in China

Other contributors to this book argue that in post-Mao China private businesses are led to form alliances with other actors by the institutional environment.[1] Markets for capital, labour, and information are underdeveloped, liability laws, property rights, and contracts are weak, state regulation is negotiable, certain resources remain bureaucratically controlled, and private entrepreneurs are vulnerable to political persecution. Because a private sector emerged only in the 1980s, after almost 30 years of state planning, would-be business people face the 'liability of newness': they have few models of entrepreneurship to imitate or adopt and little understanding of how markets work. In this environment, it is rational for them to form two kinds of alliances. They ally with state officials to make the environment more predictable and reduce risk,[2] and they ally with other entrepreneurs both to promote 'a stable set of expectations of "good" business behaviour' and to learn about doing business in a market economy.[3]

This chapter looks not at private enterprises, but at semi-legitimate businesses created in the early 1990s by officials in the Chinese state bureaucracy.[4] It argues that some features of the institutional environment that explain the tendency of private businesses to form alliances can also help explain the creation of these new state businesses. State entrepreneurship was fostered most notably by new and underdeveloped markets, the political vulnerability of private entrepreneurs, a weak legal system, a legacy of bureaucratic involvement in micro-economic activity, and poorly defined property rights. Entrepreneurial officials were also able to overcome some of the 'liability of newness' by drawing on practices and networks developed from running state enterprises under the command economy.

119

Since the businesses were created, however, the institutional environment has evolved: not only have markets developed and private entrepreneurs become more politically acceptable, rules on officials' business activities have been clarified and new corporate legislation has been promulgated. The second part of the chapter discusses this changing environment, focusing in particular on property rights relating to the new state businesses. It argues that the institutionalization of property rights has been driven by central state regulations and legislation that local governments have incentives to implement. The result is that while the loss of some state assets has been prevented, new state businesses still exist, though many should no longer be seen as 'state entrepreneurship'.

The chapter is organized as follows. The next section sets out briefly the main features of the new state businesses and the following section examines the influence of the institutional environment and the liability of newness on the formation and operations of these businesses, focusing particularly on property rights. The three case studies in the next section show how property rights have been strengthened over the 1990s. The final section considers what developments in property rights show about the nature of institutional change in China today and the implications of those developments for state entrepreneurship.

New state businesses in the 1990s

New state businesses are set up by officials to earn profits for central government ministries or municipal, district, and county government bureaux (hereafter 'departments') and to create jobs for their underemployed staff.[5] Although some pay taxes, profits do not accrue to central or local governments, but to individual departments within them.[6] These are not, then, private businesses, but neither are they conventional state or collective enterprises.[7] They tend to have simpler internal management structures (Duckett 1998). Although initially registered as state or collectively owned, they are not set up with budgetary investment to help the state, and the departments that constitute them carry out their work (Blecher 1991).[8] A department's leading official usually invests state assets, but these are often in the form of extrabudgetary funds, and the businesses' sphere of operations can be quite different from their parent departments' government work.[9] Moreover, their main objective is to make profit: officials create them in the expectation that business profits will be transferred to the department, again constituting part of extrabudgetary revenues or going into departmental slush funds.[10]

The businesses are best described as semi-legitimate because in the early 1990s there was no legislation that forbade them. Indeed, they were permitted, and perhaps encouraged, by some local governments because they generated income that supplemented budgets and because they provided employment for officials at a time when there was pressure from the centre to cut back the bureaucracy. Yet at the same time the central government has tried, if rather feebly at first, to close them down because they conflict with the central policy to reduce government's micro-economic involvement in state and collective enterprises and raised fears that they might provide opportunities for corruption. During the 1990s therefore there were several central initiatives to close them down or separate them from their parent bureaux.[11] However, central government directives sometimes permitted profitable or beneficial businesses to continue, allowing departments and local governments an excuse for not forcing closures (Duckett 1998). Thus at the end of the decade, official sources continued to make reference to closures, separations from parent departments, and the transfer of such businesses to 'state assets' departments.[12] Following another push in 1999 to close central government departments' businesses, an official report that claimed success at that level noted only that there had been 'some progress' in the localities.[13]

Given their close relationship with the state and central leaders' concerns about opportunities for corruption, is it appropriate to treat these businesses as a form of entrepreneurship? Some scholars would say no, that they involve not entrepreneurship but rent seeking, the abuse of power, arbitrage, profiteering, speculation, exploitation of monopoly, or preferential access to resources (Ding 2002b; Lin and Zhang 1999; Lü 2000; Wong 1994; Zweig 2000). And others have argued that they allow state assets to be stripped in a process of informal privatization (Lin and Zhang 1999). On the other hand, some portray them as profit-seeking businesses that involve the risk that is associated with entrepreneurship, produce and trade real goods, and even have beneficial outcomes in terms of assisting local economic growth, providing employment, or supplementing state spending on welfare (Blecher 1991; Cook 1999; Duckett 1998; Francis 1999; White 1996).[14] These opposing views reflect the fact that there are many state firms involved in a wide range of business, and they vary in their relationship with their parent department and the existence and extent of any unfair advantage.[15] While many officials are no doubt involved in mere profiteering, others have behaved entrepreneurially by investing assets in profit-seeking businesses that sell goods or services in a market environment. It is this latter kind of activity, and what has encouraged and shaped it that is our interest here. The fact that the businesses have close relations with the state – as do many of the private entrepreneurs discussed in other papers in this volume – should not deflect attention from their entrepreneurial features.

How significant are the new state businesses? Because they are only semi-legitimate, they may be excluded from official statistics or hidden among those for state and collective enterprises. As a result, there are neither figures on their distribution across the country nor on their performance individually or in terms of overall contribution to the economy. However, a number of accounts indicate that they were set up in large numbers from 1992 at a time when China's central leadership made a bid to encourage entrepreneurship and stimulate economic growth.[16] Since they, they have been reported across China, from Tianjin and Beijing in north China to Sichuan, Shenzhen and Hainan in the west and south.[17] From these accounts, by the early to middle 1990s the businesses appeared to be numerous and to employ significant numbers of people. John Wong cites reports of as many as 70,000 across seven provinces in the early 1990s (Wong 1994). Others have estimated that at around the same time in some areas of China as many as 70 per cent of state and party departments had set up such businesses, and that in Hunan province alone there were over 10,000 of them, employing 40,000 people (Li 1992). Lin and Zhang have reported that such businesses in Beijing in 1995 employed over 15,000 people (Lin and Zhang 1999). Despite the reports of closures, separations, and transfers, they have been a significant phenomenon in the 1990s and no doubt still exist in substantial numbers.

The institutional environment and state entrepreneurship

What do we mean by the institutional environment of entrepreneurship? Davis and North define it as: 'the set of fundamental political, social and legal ground rules that establishes the basis for production, exchange and distribution. Rules governing elections, property rights, and the right of contract are examples. . . .' (Williamson 1993: 453–86).

In China in the 1990s the institutional environment in which the new state businesses emerged was defined most fundamentally by the political, social and legal ground rules of a modernizing, marketizing Communist Party-dominated state.[18] Continuity in the Chinese Communist Party (CCP, the Party) rule meant that despite the turn to market-led growth, several decades of anti-capitalist politics, which had included the persecution of 'capitalists', made those going into business still vulnerable and socially stigmatized. This vulnerability was enhanced by the poor legal foundations for entrepreneurship in China. Although in the 1980s the CCP centre strove to build the legal system by re-establishing judicial–legal organs and promulgating new legislation, that system remained subject to political interference.[19] Institutions such as property rights and the right of contract were poorly understood, and little used, but in any case, were not assured backing in the courts. Private businesses could be appropriated or closed down upon a change of political direction at the centre.[20] This was demonstrated from mid-1989 to 1991 when after almost a decade of growing acceptance, many private businesses disappeared. Although the political and social environment became more favourable again from 1992, only in 2001 did Party General Secretary Jiang Zemin announce that private entrepreneurs could join the party.[21] As other contributions to this volume have argued, this created a high level of risk for private entrepreneurs above and beyond the usual risks of economic activity in industrialized market economies (see also Young 1991). For state officials, particularly lower level ones transferred to work in the new state businesses who retained their bureaucratic position, this was a safer option.[22]

For entrepreneurial officials, whether those in leading positions who set up and managed the businesses, or their subordinates who worked in them, additional security was provided by a combination of poor legislation and a legacy of bureaucratic involvement in the economy. There were neither laws nor regulations to clarify the limits of official connections with business, and this was in turn due to the legacy of bureaucratic involvement in the command economy: officials had administered state and collective enterprises in line with central and local plans and these practices were still being eradicated in the 1990s. Although the new state businesses at this time were unlike 'traditional' state or collective enterprises in terms of their internal structure, purpose, and sources of investment, the fact that the state administration had long controlled enterprises meant that they were not clearly irregular or problematic (Lü 1997).[23] Despite the changing economic environment and the business opportunities it provided for officials, separation of departments and their businesses over the last decade has been ordered by decree, rather than founded on legislation. Moreover, loopholes in those central government decrees allowed many of the businesses to continue (Duckett 1998).[24]

The institutional environment that created some security for state entrepreneurship also gave officials incentives to go into business. Most notably, imprecise property rights made it possible for officials to register their businesses as state or collective enterprises and yet expect profits to flow into departmental coffers. This is because although both state and collective enterprises are controlled by the state,[25] it is unclear which parts of that state have the rights to profits and liability for losses. As Corinna-Barbara Francis has noted:

> official ownership categories do not recognise individual public agencies and institutions as a distinct category of owner, in contrast to private individuals ... no differentiation is made between the property rights of individual subunits of the state and 'the state' more broadly.
>
> (Francis 1999)

Moreover, departments in charge of state and collective enterprises had had access to profits under the command economy.[26] Officials in the market reform period could therefore register firms using conventional ownership forms, such as state and collective, while expecting to have *de facto* rights to business profits. This is what has led some to predict that the companies will allow assets to be stripped.

The legacy of bureaucratic involvement in micro-economic activities not only provided ambiguity over the limits of officials' business activities and access to profits, it also created an environment conducive to new state business ventures by furnishing officials with the social capital necessary for entrepreneurship. Some officials, through their work administering the command economy, had gained experience of running enterprises and knowledge about producers, suppliers, retailers, and emerging markets. They therefore suffered less than many other potential entrepreneurs from the 'liability of newness'. Although the workings of the market system were new to them, they had some of the professional or trade networks that facilitated successful business. They also, of course, had the networks within the state administration itself that many private entrepreneurs seek because they help negotiate the various bureaucratic procedures involved in running a business.[27] For officials, like private entrepreneurs, networks also provided a measure of protection in the wider institutional environment of political uncertainty and an underdeveloped legal system.

Finally, the social environment within which officials operate have influenced their decisions to create new businesses. First, a widespread business fever in 1992–3 may have encouraged officials to follow others and 'take the plunge' into business.[28] Second, social networks, enhanced by stable, long-term work unit employment practices and an imperfect legal system, make it difficult to effect redundancies in the state sector. Leading officials were, in the early 1990s, under considerable pressure to cut back their staff, but attempts to do this would burden leaders with unending pleas for exemptions by staff members and their patrons.[29] The businesses conveniently offered a route out of this problem by providing some staff with alternative and perhaps more attractive and lucrative employment. At the same time, complying with directives to cut back staff by this means would have offered added justification for the businesses and thereby further protection.

In sum, new state businesses emerged in an institutional environment characterized by the political vulnerability of private entrepreneurship, an underdeveloped legal system, ill-defined property rights, and the legacies of bureaucratic involvement in the economy.[30] While private entrepreneurs formed alliances to overcome the problems of this environment, many officials had ready-made the resources and protection that those alliances provide. For them, it was safer to hedge their bets by playing on the ambiguities surrounding official involvement in economic activity than to leave their posts and move into the private sector. Although officials could not legitimately profit as individuals from the businesses, they nevertheless would have considerable discretionary control over any income.[31] Some of these advantages of state entrepreneurship were to evaporate, however, as the institutional environment evolved over the course of the next decade.

Institutional development: strengthening property rights in the 1990s

Developments in the institutional environment of entrepreneurship since the early 1990s have been policy led. The central government has pursued market-oriented reform even through the Asian financial crisis of 1997, and markets have continued to develop. CCP General Secretary Jiang Zemin's July 2001 speech permitting private entrepreneurs to join the party reduced further the already declining stigma surrounding private entrepreneurship. Most importantly in relation to the state businesses, new central government directives and regulations have begun to set the limits of officials' business activities and tighten control over extrabudgetary funds, while legislation has strengthened the legal foundations of business activity. Early exhortations for departments to sever links with their businesses were followed by rules limiting officials' connections with businesses.[32] From the mid-1990s, the rules on extra budgetary income were tightened in order to try to limit officials' controls over discretionary funds (Wang 1997; Ministry of Finance 1997). But most importantly, in 1994, the Company Law was promulgated, providing a basis on which local governments could assert the rights of the state to certain businesses and their assets, and therefore effectively become their owners.[33] These central government regulations and legislation, together with local government incentives to implement them, have clarified property rights and strengthened local government claims over new state businesses, in some cases putting an end to state entrepreneurship.

Central government regulations and legislation were implemented only gradually by local and central governments, so that throughout the decade there were continued reports of closures, separations, and, more recently, 'transfers' of party and government department businesses.[34] Fieldwork in Tianjin in the late 1990s using in-depth interviews with officials and current business managers confirms that while some businesses retained close links with their parent departments,[35] others were either privatized or taken over by local governments.[36] It seems that small or struggling businesses are often closed down or privatized, ending state entrepreneurship by taking the businesses out of departmental control (for further detail see Duckett 2001a).[37] Large, profitable ones have often continued to operate but have had their registered ownership, managerial control, and income flows transferred away from the original parent bureau to the local government in a clarification of property rights. The rest of this section discusses three such successful businesses, and how local governments have asserted their ownership.[38] In each case I discuss the initial ownership of the business, focusing on those features that indicate who had *de facto* management and controls over income. I then show how institutionalizing property rights has changed the locus of managerial control and redirected income flows.[39]

Case 6.1 'Brightness' real estate development company

In 1989, a Tianjin urban district bureau chief set up the 'Brightness' real estate development company.[40] According to the bureau chief, who had managed the business from the start, his aims had been to earn income to assist with the bureau's work, provide work for some of its staff, and make profits. The business was initially staffed with three others from the bureau, and began with a 50,000 RMB bureau loan and a bank loan, both of which, according to the bureau chief, were soon repaid. At this stage, the business submitted its profits to the bureau, and the bureau chief/manager had considerable discretion in using the income it generated. The business was therefore the *de facto* property of the bureau. In formal terms, however, property rights were unclear. As the bureau chief/manager noted with hindsight more than a decade later: 'When I set up the company I did not think in those terms. I did not think about the property rights . . .'[41]

By the mid-1990s, the issue of property rights had become important. In 1996, the district government separated the business from the bureau and took it over. According to the same manager, who still headed the company in 2000,[42] the business, now registered as state-run (*guoying*), had been transferred from the parent bureau to the district government's newly-established State Assets Bureau.[43] Profits were now to be submitted via this bureau to the district government, though the company was not at present making a profit.[44] The manager expressed irritation that the company had been taken over. It was now classed as state-run, he said, because he had been an official when he set it up, because many of its staff were former officials, and because of the initial 50,000 RMB bureau loan. However, he did not agree that the loan constituted bureau investment; it had, he said, been repaid quickly. He noted, perhaps with some regret, that 'I did not invest any money in the company and so it is not mine or classed as privately owned . . . Because the [bureau] loaned 50,000 RMB to start the company the local government says it is state property.'[45]

In this case, rights to the firm have been clarified to the benefit of the district government. Based on the business's links with a government bureau and on its sources of investment, the local government asserted its rights, clarifying the business's formal registration as 'state-run', and placing it beneath a bureau created in 1997 to protect state assets. Although the locus of managerial control was still with the manager, he was no longer an official in the business's parent bureau, and he had reduced control over profits. Moreover, while he ran the business as an independent profit-seeking enterprise, the local government now directed him to undertake infrastructure development projects. The manager noted that the company would become more independent from the local government in the future, because the policy was to separate government and enterprises. However, the process of separation was to be a gradual one.

Case 6.2 'Victory' real estate development company

The 'Victory' real estate development company was created in July 1992 by a bureau in another Tianjin urban district. Again, the aim was to generate profits for the bureau, and in this case the company's manager was a deputy bureau chief. The bureau invested 2 million RMB in the business using its discretionary 'extrabudgetary' finance, and contributed other assets in the form of buildings. The company was registered as state-owned, but according to the managers, was not separate from the bureau.[46]

The bureau did not receive profits as it had planned because in 1994 the company was taken away and placed under district government control.[47] The company now paid taxes rather than submit profits to bureau or district government, and the management[48] had a great deal of autonomy. According to the current managers, they made all the business decisions, and set their own growth targets. The only government-set target was for increases in state assets.[49] They emphasized their business's autonomy from both the bureau and the local government,[50] noting only that they sometimes carried out some housing redevelopment work for the local government at cost. However, such work did not seem onerous, and unlike the manager of 'Brightness', these managers did not appear disgruntled. On the contrary, they said such work was good for their business as it improved its reputation.[51]

127

For 'Victory', like 'Brightness', property rights had been clarified to the benefit of the district government, which wrested the business from the parent bureau's control. 'Victory' was, however, about to undergo another transformation, this time to a joint stock company, that would further clarify and strengthen property rights.[52] The property rights reassignments that this entailed were clearly a concern to the current management. What worried them most was the power that the stock system would give the local government to formally appoint the head of the board of directors and the chair of that board. This would be possible because, as set out in the 1994 Company Law, it is the shareholders who hold the power in joint stock companies, and the management expected the state to become the majority shareholder.[53] At present, although the company had a board of directors, there had been virtually no *de facto* change to the management since the company had begun, and the managers had retained a considerable amount of autonomy despite shifting to local government control. It was now feared, however, that the local government would assert its managerial control over the company and replace the current management.[54]

The current managers were also concerned about how shares would be allocated in the transformation to a stock company. They noted that there were no clear rules on how shares should be divided in cases like this: a committee composed of representatives of the local government's State Assets Bureau, the Commission for Structural Reform, and the district government were to decide on the division of shares. It was expected that the local government would become the majority shareholder but the question for the members of the management team was what their own personal shares would be. The 1994 Company Law (Article 81) stipulates shares shall not be distributed to individuals at low prices or without charge. However, members of the management seemed to expect to be allocated shares, and were concerned about the 'question of how they calculate the value that has been added to the company' by them since it began business.[55] They noted that the company's initial registered capital of 8 million RMB had by 2000 increased over six fold, implying that they had created this added value. They even cast doubt on the original state investment in the business, arguing that the bureau's buildings investment had been overvalued. As with the manager of the 'Brightness' company, they were afraid of losing their perceived stake in the company as the local government clarified property rights in ways that strengthened its claims over them. Once again, the entrepreneurs who had started these businesses were finding that the initial advantage of unclear property rights was working to their disadvantage as those rights evolved and became institutionalized through a combination of central state and local government actions.

Case 6.3 'Riverside' trading company

In 1992 a district bureau had started up the 'Riverside' trading business, registering it as a state-owned enterprise.[56] The bureau chief who initiated the project claimed that investment had been raised from three sources: the bureau had loaned 10 million RMB, and a bank and individual employees had loaned small sums. All the loans, he said, were repaid by 1995.[57] The bureau chief noted that his 'two main reasons for setting up [the business] were to cut back bureau staff and earn money',[58] and he had intended that it should submit profits to the bureau. Between 1992 and 1995, he had managerial control over the business, organizing the investment and making appointments to the company's management from among his own bureau staff.

But in 1996, soon after the loans were repaid, the district government 'took away' the company.[59] The bureau chief had evidently not been willing to relinquish it,[60] but the district had justified the take-over by saying that the company was too large.[61] It was placed beneath a newly created State Assets Bureau, and re-registered as 'state-owned with a single investor' (guoyou duzi), a new type of company registration specified in the 1994 Company Law.[62] Following its take-over in 1996, the business expanded. It merged with another former state enterprise and the resultant company was transformed into a holding company (jituan) in late 1997, with seven subsidiaries handling a diverse range of business. The total value of assets had quadrupled between 1994 and 2000, by which time the company was one of the largest of its kind in the country.[63] It now raised its own investment for expansion, paid taxes, and did not submit profits.[64] Although, according to the current management, the local government did not actually get directly involved in business decisions, it did set broad performance targets for GDP, retail turnover, tax, sales, and net profits, and the district government chief appointed the company's top management.[65]

In this case too, the local government had moved to establish its own stake in 'Riverside' by transforming it from a state-owned enterprise into 'state-owned with a single investor', a category which specifies a single registered investor agency and clarifies sources of investment, distribution of profits, liability, and lines of management. It would now presumably be difficult for any other part of the state to take the company from the local government.[66] However, state entrepreneurs have been quick to take advantage of institutional developments. The entrepreneurial bureau chief who had started the business, undaunted by losing his bureau's first business, had started another. This time, he noted, ownership would be clearer because he would create a stock company:[67] 'The bureau will hold stocks for the state for its share of investment. This way the district government cannot take the business away.'[68]

Property rights, institutionalization, and local government interests

Some aspects of the institutional environment have become less favourable for state entrepreneurship. In all three cases, state entrepreneurs set up businesses at a time when property rights were ill-defined. But this initial advantage soon became a problem. They had expected to receive profits from businesses registered as state-owned enterprises, and had initially had managerial control over them. However, 'state-owned enterprise' registration does not specify individual public agencies' property rights (Francis 1999). The bureaux therefore had no legal basis on which to defend their rights to the businesses, and the local government could lay claim to them. This became evident following the promulgation of the Company Law in 1994, which established the principle that companies should have a named investor and that state-owned enterprises could be transformed into companies with clearer property rights. This law was given further institutional support toward the end of the decade in Tianjin, by an initiative to create 'state assets' departments to handle such property.[69] It was also implemented in an environment of tightening rules on official involvement in businesses, giving, as we saw particularly in the case of Brightness, an added justification for take-over.

These three cases show institutional development in the 1990s, but they also demonstrate that it was gradual. In terms of property rights, even across district governments in a single city development has occurred at different rates and in slightly different ways. All the urban district governments had acted in the late 1990s, following the promulgation of the Company Law, but they had not implemented the new legislation immediately.[70] Victory was taken over in 1994, but Brightness and Riverside only two years later, in 1996. In terms of methods and ownership forms, while Brightness and Victory had initially remained 'state-run' in terms of formal registration, Riverside had been made 'state-owned with a single owner', in line with the Company Law. In 2000 Riverside was only just about to adopt the 'joint stock company' form specified in the Company Law, but this was not at as advanced a stage as with Victory, while there were no such plans yet for Brightness.

These cases also show that although institutionalization has been initiated by central government legislation and directives to establish 'state assets departments', use of legislation and policy implementation has been driven by local government interests. Local governments use the law selectively and gradually: they take over only certain companies and do so when they become successful because then they are useful to them. In the cases of Victory and Riverside, for example, local governments had asserted their rights once the companies had repaid their start-up loans, begun to expand and could play a substantial role in helping them meet their own economic growth targets.[71] As Whiting and Edin have shown, local officials are set targets that induce them to develop their economies (Whiting 2001; Edin 2000). They therefore have an interest in ensuring the success of businesses in their locality by controlling its most important enterprises. Brightness was used apparently not to meet growth targets, but to develop the local infrastructure in support of economic growth. Local governments have strengthened and help institutionalize property rights because this served their own short-term interests.

Conclusion

The Chinese economy has grown rapidly in an institutional environment characterized by underdeveloped markets, a vulnerable private sector, a weak legal system, and ill-defined property rights. This has been possible in part because private entrepreneurs have overcome the problems of that environment by drawing on the networks and alliances available to them. In this same environment, some state officials have been able to draw on similar networks, as well as on resources and experience made possible by strong bureaucratic institutions that are a legacy of the command economy, to go into business on their departments' behalf.

Although China's legal framework is still flawed, economic institutions have evolved since the early 1990s. Legislation has increased, and property rights have begun to be institutionalized. These institutional changes mean that the informal privatization that some predicted is not necessarily the outcome of entrepreneurial state activities, at least in the case of businesses that are important to local governments, whether for developmental purposes, as in the case of Brightness, or for helping local governments achieve economic growth targets, as in the cases of Victory and Riverside.

131

If the individual managers do in fact receive shares as they expect in Riverside, local government take-over may facilitate the formal privatization of some assets (Ding 2000a; Lin and Zhang 1999). However, in the three companies discussed here, at least, it has not been the case that 'nominal public ownership is totally abandoned' (Lin and Zhang 1999:223). Of course, because institutionalization is gradual, there is still scope for asset-stripping in businesses not taken over by local governments.[72]

Do these institutional developments spell the end of state entrepreneurship? For companies like Victory and Riverside, no longer directed by their parent departments, their entrepreneurship now resembles that of large state enterprises, which are not entirely autonomous of the state but have considerable independence in their business activities.[73] For those like Brightness that are taken over and put to work on local infrastructure projects, state entrepreneurship has been reined in and put to the service of the local developmental state).[74] However, local government take-overs, as well as privatization and closure, of new state businesses are still selective. Entrepreneurial state activities therefore continue, as the Riverside entrepreneur's new business reveals, but in an increasingly hazardous environment.

Notes

1 See in particular the contribution by Krug and Mehta, Chapter 3. On other marketizing command economies, see Whitley *et al.* 1996.
2 For similar arguments from a sociological perspective, see Wank 1996. The relationships between state officials and private entrepreneurs in China have been shown by others. See Bruun 1993 and Wank 1996. For an account which sees the same weak institutions across the former command economies of central and eastern Europe and the former Soviet Union, see Peng 2001.
3 Krug and Mehta, Chapter 3.
4 Identified by Blecher 1991; Ding 2000b; Duckett 1998; Francis 1999; Lin and Zhang 1999; Lü 2000; White 1991; Wong 1994. Similar businesses have also been identified in Vietnam by Gainsborough 2001.
5 I have described such municipal and urban district government level businesses in some detail in Duckett 1998. Similar businesses are also run by party organizations and the Communist Youth League, as well as universities and other not-for-profit public institutions, and the army; see Bickford 1994; Francis 1999; Karmel 1997.
6 This will be illustrated in the case studies discussed later in the paper. Sometimes the businesses or their parent departments make donations to their local governments.
7 It is possible that some may, like many rural enterprises, be 'red hat' companies, that is private businesses masquerading as public ones. If so, then as will be shown below, some may have had their ownership registration confirmed as or converted to that of 'state' enterprises (*guoying*) since the mid-1990s in a way that has established a state stake in the businesses.
8 Under the command economy, state-owned and collective enterprises were government controlled, and departments were involved in the micro-economic

management of enterprises related to their administrative work. Thus commerce bureaux ran wholesale and retail enterprises, while different industrial departments ran industrial enterprises in their sphere of industrial production (for example chemical industry, metallurgy industry).

9 There is often investment from a number of sources, including state extra-budgetary funds, bank loans and private individuals.

10 Extrabudgetary revenues and expenditures, now being phased out, were used in the planning system for finance that was difficult to include in plans. They were less monitored, and they have grown in size and significance in the market reform period. See Wong 1996. Leading officials do of course have considerable discretion in the use of such funds, and may use them to their own personal benefit as well as those of their employees. However, as I have discussed elsewhere, such benefits are often passed on in the form of investment in office and dormitory accommodation, technology and employee welfare provisions; see Duckett 2001b. To dismiss the businesses as simply a form of personal corruption would be to miss important features of this phenomenon.

11 Central government calls to end such activities date from August 1988, though there were few mentions of attempts to close such businesses in 1991 and 1992, probably because many were closed in 1991. Calls were renewed again from 1993, after they had begun to spring up again. The focus is usually on the army, armed police, and political and legal agencies (*zhengfa jiguan*).

12 In 1998, 19,241 businesses of the 'army, armed police and political and legal agencies' were reported to have been closed down, 5,557 separated and 6,491 'transferred' (*yijiao*) (*People's Daily*, 14 January 1999). In 1999, 19,458 were closed down, 56 separated, and 6,494 'transferred' (*People's Daily*, 13 January 2000). Reports of closures and separations have continued into 2000, and it is clear that the exhortations have had only incremental effects.

13 *People's Daily*, 13 January 2000.

14 These accounts do agree that the companies are not unambiguously beneficial and entrepreneurial.

15 The differences also arise out of the methodological problems involved in researching such businesses. See Duckett 2001a.

16 In the 1980s many officials set up companies that profiteered using the dual track pricing system. Such practices continue, but many new state businesses in the 1990s are not of this profiteering kind, and do actually produce goods and provide services; see Li 1992. Some of these companies were closed between 1989 and 1991, during the period of economic and political austerity that followed the crackdown on the Tiananmen demonstrations, but they reappeared extremely quickly from mid-1992.

17 See Note 4.

18 As I have argued elsewhere; see Duckett 1998. My earlier account does not discuss property rights, the significance of which, as I shall show in this chapter, has only become evident since.

19 The legal system had been destroyed during the Cultural Revolution but lack of judicial autonomy has meant that despite the massive increase in legislation in the reform period, laws are not reliably enforced.

20 Of course unless some officials have invested their own personal income in the businesses, their personal economic risk is limited because they are investing state assets. Though there are still opportunity costs to these investments, their personal liability is minimal. They were also taking some personal political risks given the 1989–91 clampdown on business activity.

21 Jiang Zemin, speech at a rally in celebration of the 80th anniversary of the founding of the Chinese Communist Party, 1 July 2001.

22 It was common for employees to retain their bureaucratic positions, and sometimes to return to government work, at least in the first years of the businesses.

23 Lü Xiaobo has also shown that there had been practices of administrative departments having productive enterprises to support them back as far as the CCP's Yan'an years. In any case, for added protection officials sometimes set up businesses through their 'not-for-profit' (*shiye danwei*) sub-organizations, which are not, technically, 'state organs' (*guojia jiguan*).

24 Moreover, state entrepreneurialism emerged at a time when although the centre was urging 'separation of government and enterprises' the institutions for doing so had not yet been created. As Wang and Liu (1989) have shown, there was considerable debate over which institutions would best achieve separation deemed necessary to harden budget constraints and create incentives for state enterprises.

25 Ibid.

26 Though this had been prescribed and controlled through state plans.

27 Of course in the case of officials, the fact that they do so may mean that they are open to accusations of rent seeking or unfair competition.

28 'Taking the plunge' (*xiahai*) is used to refer to anyone going into business, including officials who leave their government posts to do so. In the case of many state businesses, however, officials remained in their official posts, at least initially.

29 This was explained to me by an official working in a local government's general office who had seen several attempts to cut back staff. Because personal connections (if patrons are powerful enough) can be used to override mandates to implement policy, staff can draw on influential patrons (if they have them) to pressure for special treatment. This makes policies such as these that involve redundancies for officials, who are likely to have dense *guanxi* networks within the local government, difficult to implement.

30 The same arguments may apply to some rural enterprises, particularly township ones, or ones run by county governments.

31 It is of course difficult to obtain reliable data on the uses of business income. There are anecdotal accounts of it being used not only to support bureaucratic work, but also for building or refurbishing new offices or dormitories, installing computers, buying mobile phones, or supplementing departments' social welfare funds. See *China Civil Affairs (Zhongguo Minzheng)* (1996):2:32. Although this brings personal benefit, it is not clearly corrupt. Undoubtedly some income will have found its way into the pockets of officials.

32 The May 1992 circular directing departments to cut links with businesses was reported in *South China Morning Post*, 16 July 1992; the September one was reported in BBC, *Summary of World Broadcasts, Far East*, 15 October 1992. Lü Xiaobo notes that the 1997 Penal Code tightened up on the activities of 'public units'. See Lü 2000. A Central Discipline Inspection Conference in December 2000 announced that cadres would not be permitted to join private or foreign-invested joint venture enterprises for three years after leaving their official positions. China Central Television news, 27 December 2000.

33 See the revised Company Law (Zhonghua renmin gongheguo gongsi fa), adopted 12 December 1993, and revised 25 December 1999. Text in (*Zhonghua renmin gongheguo fadian* 2000: 2668–734).

34 *People's Daily*, 14 January 1999; *People's Daily*, 13 January 2000.

35 Businesses with close links to departments have become more difficult to research than in the early 1990s. Although some officials acknowledge that they do still have such businesses, they are unwilling to discuss them.

36 Systematic quantitative research is not possible because of the semi-legitimate nature of the businesses, but we can build up a picture from official reports, anecdotal accounts, and interviews with officials and employees. I do not claim that these experiences encompass the whole range of transformations to the state businesses.

37 Based on author's interviews in Tianjin, 2000 and 2001.

38 The identity of my interviewees and their businesses have been obscured so as to ensure anonymity. Interviews are given an identifying code as follows: the first two digits refer to the year of the interview, the letter indicates where it took place (T, for Tianjin), and the final digits show the interview's chronological number that year.

39 I follow the convention of seeing ownership, or property, rights as the rights to utilize, derive income (and liability) from, and transfer, an asset or piece of property (see Putterman 1995).

40 Names have been changed to protect the identity of interviewees.

41 Interview 00T10.

42 The bureau chief had left his post to become full-time manager of the business when the local government took it over. Since then, his salary, and those of the company's employees, had been paid by the company.

43 A central government State Assets Bureau (*guojia zichan ju*) was created in 1988, but in Tianjin, district governments reported such bureaux being created in the late 1990s.

44 It is not clear what investment there had been in the main company's subsidiaries or their share of the total stocks. It is also unclear whether as the new 'owner' of the main company, the local government would now be the recipient of any income from the subsidiaries. Given the tightening up on the bureau's assets, this is likely.

45 Interview 00T10.

46 They use the term 'one institution with two nameplates' (*yige jigou, liangkuai paizi*). Interview 01T1.

47 Managers of the company used the term 'department in charge' (*zhuguan danwei*) to indicate the district government's relationship with the company. They indicated that they retained a professional (*yewu*) relationship with the parent department. Interview 01T1.

48 The manager of the company had remained the same since the beginning, and like the other bureau staff who had gone to work in it, had fully left the bureau in 1994.

49 The government had established, probably through its State Assets Bureau, that in order to protect state assets, they should grow at an annual rate of 2.5 per cent per year.

50 In the sense that they could not return to the bureau to work now after they made the decision to leave in 1994, and also in terms of the hardening of the budget constraint: there would be no subsidies or further state investment.

51 Interview 01T1.

52 According to the Victory managers, this had been decided at the city level, and all companies in the real estate and construction sector were to be similarly transformed over the next few years. Interview 01T1.

53 The Company Law is the basis on which the stock system is promoted, according to Interview 00T27.

54 Interview 01T01.

55 Interview 01T01.

56 A current manager used the term 'owned by the whole people' (*quanmin suoyou*), saying that it was synonymous with 'state-run' (*guoying*) and 'state-owned' (*guoyou*). Interview 00T30.

57 Interview 00T11. The employees' loans were paid back with 'over 10 per cent interest', while the bureau's loan was paid back without interest. Note that a member of the company's current management team in 2000 denied that there had been any actual initial bureau investment. According to him, the bureau had organized their employees to raise investment and taken out a bank loan. Interview 00T30. The bureau would have had access to significant capital because (without revealing its identity) the nature of its work meant it had access to large amounts of extrabudgetary income.
58 Interview 00T11, with the bureau chief.
59 Interview 00T11.
60 Confirmed by a member of the firm's management in 2000. Interview 00T30.
61 Interviews 00T11 and 00T30.
62 See Section 3 of the Company Law. The law specifies (Article 64) that such 'wholly state-owned companies' are to be limited liability companies.
63 Details of the expansion of the company from an interview with the current management. It has not been possible to verify these, but the bureau chief who initiated the business did note that the company has continued to expand at a rapid rate.
64 Interview 00T30. Profit submission is a planned economy practice that is being replaced by a corporate taxation system.
65 The company had a board of directors. The government appointed the head and deputy head of the board of directors, as well as the managers and deputy managers of the subsidiaries. Interview 00T30.
66 Article 7 of the 1994 Company Law notes that state-owned enterprises that restructure to form these and other companies (*gongsi*) 'must transform their operating mechanism, gradually produce an inventory of their assets and verify their funds, delimit their property rights, clear off their claims and debts, evaluate their assets and establish a standard internal management mechanism in accordance with the conditions and requirements set by laws, administrative rules and regulations'.
67 The Company Law established the legal principles of joint stock and limited liability companies. See Article 1.
68 Interview 00T11.
69 See for example, *People's Daily*, 15 August 2000, where it is noted that some areas have done this since the late 1990s.
70 The Law specified only that state-owned enterprises *could* become 'companies', not that they must. See Article 7.
71 Interview 00T30, with a member of the current management.
72 And as I have noted some smaller businesses are certainly privatized, though apparently formally. Further research is needed to understand these processes of privatization.
73 Though companies work with bureaux and local governments and still have some preferential treatment.
74 Local developmental state activity includes local government support and promotion of development through practices that improve the environment for local businesses (see Blecher 1991).

References

Bickford, T.J. (1994) 'The Chinese military and its business operations: the PLA as entrepreneur', *Asian Survey*, 34(5):460–74.
Blecher, M. (1991) 'Development State, Entrepreneurial State: the Political Economy of Socialist Reform in Xinji Municipality and Guanghan County', in

G. White (ed.) *The Chinese State in The Era of Economic Reform*, Basingstoke: Macmillan.

Bruun, O. (1993) *Business and Bureaucracy in a Chinese City: An Ethnography of Private Business Households in Contemporary China*, Berkeley: University of California, Institute of East Asian Studies.

Cook, S. (1999) 'Creating wealth and welfare: entrepreneurship and the developmental state in rural China', *IDS Bulletin*, 30(4):60–70.

Ding, X.L. (2000a) 'The illicit asset-stripping of Chinese state firms', *The China Journal*, 43:1–28.

—— (2000b) 'Systemic irregularity and spontaneous property transformation in the Chinese financial system', *The China Quarterly*, 163:655–76.

Duckett, J. (1998) *The Entrepreneurial State in China*, London: Routledge.

—— (2001a) 'Between developmentalism and corruption: understanding China's new state businesses', paper delivered at the American Association for Asian Studies Annual Conference, Chicago.

—— (2001b) 'Bureaucrats in business, Chinese style: market reform and state entrepreneurialism in the PRC', *World Development*, 29(1):23–37.

Edin, M. (2000) 'Market forces and Communist power: local political institutions and economic development in China', Ph.D. dissertation, Uppsala: Department of Government, Uppsala University.

Francis, C. (1999) 'Bargained property rights: the case of China's High-Technology Sector', in J.C. Oi and A.G. Walder (eds) *Property Rights and Economic Reform in China*, Stanford: Stanford University Press.

Gainsborough, J. (2001) 'Reconsidering reform: politics and money in Ho Chi Minh City', Ph.D. dissertation, Department of Political Studies, London: SOAS, University of London.

Karmel, S. (1997) 'The Chinese military's hunt for profits', *Foreign Policy*, 107:102–13.

Li, Q. (1992) " 'Shiti re' chu tan (Initial discussion of the 'craze for economic entities')", *Liaowang (Outlook)*, 10:9–11.

Lin, Y. and Zhang, Z. (1999) 'Backyard Profit Centers: The Private Assets of Public Agencies', in J.C. Oi and A.G. Walder (eds) *Property Rights and Economic Reform in China*, Stanford, CA: Stanford University Press.

Lü, X. (1997) 'Minor Public Economy: The Revolutionary Origins of the Danwei', in X. Lü and E. J. Perry (eds) *Danwei: the changing Chinese workplace in historical and comparative perspective*, New York: M.E. Sharpe.

—— (2000) 'Booty socialism, bureau-preneurs, and the state in transition: organizational corruption in China', *Comparative Politics*, 32(2):273–94.

Ministry of Finance, State Planning Commission, People's Bank of China Audit Office, and Ministry of Supervision (1997) 'Opinions on Cleaning up and Inspecting Extrabudgetary Funds (11 March 1996)', in Ministry of Finance Social Security Division (ed.) *Selected Documents on the Social Security Finance System, 1995–6*, Beijing: Zhongguo caizheng jingji chubanshe.

Oi, J. and Walder, A.G. (eds) (1999) *Property Rights and Economic Reform in China*, Stanford: Stanford University Press.

Peng, M. (2001) 'How entrepreneurs create wealth in transition economies', *The Academy of Management Executive*, 15(1):95–110.

Putterman, L. (1995) 'The role of ownership and property rights in China's economic transition', *The China Quarterly*, 144:1045–64.

Wang, L. and Liu, Z. (1989) 'On the property-rights system of the state enterprises in China', *Law and Contemporary Problems*, 52(2–3):19–42.

Wang, S. (1997) 'China's 1994 fiscal reform: an initial assessment', *Asian Survey*, XXXVIII(9):801–17.

Wank, D. (1996) 'The institutional process of market clientelism: guanxi and private business in a South China city', *The China Quarterly*, 147:820–38.

White, G. (1991) 'Basic-Level Local Government and Economic Reform in Urban China', in G. White (ed.) *The Chinese State in the Era of Economic Reform: The Road to Crisis*, London: Macmillan.

—— (1996) 'Corruption and market reform in China', *IDS Bulletin*, 27(2):40–7.

Whiting, S. (2001) *Power and Wealth in Rural China*, Cambridge: Cambridge University Press.

Whitley, R., Henderson, J., Czaban, L. and Lengyel, G. (1996) 'Trust and contractual relations in an emerging capitalist economy: the changing trading relationships of ten large Hungarian enterprises', *Organization Studies*, 17(3):397–420.

Williamson, O. (1993) 'Calculativeness, trust, and economic organization', *Journal of Law and Economics*, XXXVI (April):453–86.

Wong, C. (1996) *Financing Local Government in the PRC*, Hong Kong: Oxford University Press for the Asian Development Bank.

Wong, J. (1994) 'Power and market in mainland China: the danger of increasing government involvement in business', *Issues and Studies*, 30(1):1–12.

Young, S. (1991) 'Wealth but not security: attitudes towards private business in China in the 1980s', *Australian Journal of Chinese Affairs*, 25:115–38.

Zhonghua renmin gongheguo fadian (Legal Compendium of the People's Republic of China) (2000), Changchun: Jilin renmin chubanshe.

Zweig, D. (2000) Review of the entrepreneurial state in China: real estate and commerce departments in reform era Tianjin, *American Political Science Review*, 94(1):210–11.

7

LOCALISM AND ENTREPRENEURSHIP

History, identity and solidarity
as factors of production

David S.G. Goodman

The rise of the local entrepreneur has clearly been a key feature of the
rapid economic growth experienced by the People's Republic of China
(PRC) during the last two decades. This reform era has been characterized by the decentralization of economic management, the increasing
growth of the market sector of the economy and the restructuring of the
state sector, as well as the increasing involvement of external economic
influences in the development of the PRC's regional economies (White
1993; Naughton 1994; Keng 2001). Despite the confusing and complex
variety of enterprises to be found in this post-socialist phase of development (Nee 1992), the result of all these influences has been to draw
attention to the firm and the individual entrepreneur. That the entrepreneur
had become central not only to economic but also political development
was recognized in the middle of 2001 when the Chinese Communist Party
(CCP) apparently at President Jiang Zemin's behest, engaged in a relatively public discussion about the extent to which individual capitalists
and entrepreneurs should be permitted to participate in its ranks (Pomfret
2001; Wo Lap Lam 2001; Xu Yufang 2001).

There has been a plethora of studies of this newly emergent social
formation, for the most part derived from fieldwork focusing on the local.
Throughout, little distinction is made between enterprise as ownership
and enterprise as management, not least since the difference is inherently
blurred in the hybrid forms of enterprise to have emerged with reform
(Solinger 1992; 1993; Nee 1996; Nee and Su Sijin 1996). There have
been studies of state-owned enterprise managers who turned themselves
into more market-oriented entrepreneurs (You Ji 1998; Guthrie 1999); of
the managers and entrepreneurs of the newly reconfigured collective, or
local government, sector enterprises (Weixing Chen 1997; Goodman 1995;

Nan Lin 1995; Walder 1995); of private entrepreneurs (Young 1995; Parris 1996); and of entrepreneurs and managers in foreign joint ventures (Pearson 1994; 1997).

Invariably, explanations for the rise of the local entrepreneur are found in the analysis of politics and the economy, placing local developments in their wider policy and economic environments, in particular, the introduction of market forces and the liberalization of the economy in the transition from state socialism. The most usual explanatory model of change concentrates on the role of local government in economic restructuring and management, and the development of local corporatism in various guises (Oi 1999; Whiting 2001), though not all have gone as far as some in identifying the emergence of 'the local state' (Oi 1992; 1995). A minority interpretation emphasizes the initially economic, but then political power of individual peasants, or more accurately rural entrepreneurs, who, independent of the party-state, began to take the initiative once the state, weakened by the Mao-dominated years of China's politics, was no longer able to provide leadership (Xiao Zhou 1996; White III 1998; Weixing Chen 1997).

These various perspectives while not totally misleading do not provide an adequate explanation of the processes of change. They omit almost totally consideration of the role of culture, specifically the creation and development of beliefs and values that encourage the emergence of a strong local entrepreneurialism. An examination of the North China province of Shanxi during the late 1990s, including the results of a survey of local entrepreneurs, emphasizes precisely those non-economic factors of production.[1] In particular, it identifies the emergence of a strong and state sponsored discourse of localism that reminds society in a specific location of its past, pre-state socialist entrepreneurial practices, emphasizes the importance of investing in one's native place, and provides opportunities for local networking.

Local entrepreneurs in Shanxi

Shanxi is a North China province which in 1998 had 31.7 million people, a GDP of 160 million RMB, and a GDP per capita of 5,072 RMB.[2] Although it is, and had been for the previous seventy years, one of the country's major heavy industrial bases, with exceptionally large and high quality resources of coal, its reputation within China is one of peasant radicalism. It was the site of the major front-line base areas against Japanese invasion during the War of Resistance of 1937–45; and the later Mao-era model production brigade of Dazhai is located in its east. Nonetheless, since the 1920s Shanxi has been an established major centre for heavy industry, and it currently produces large proportions of China's coal, coke, aluminium, electricity, and specialist steels. The lack of understanding of Shanxi's local conditions more generally is not too surprising given its mountainous topography and lack of transport links with the rest of China. Other Chinese were effectively hindered from visiting Shanxi, let alone doing business there, until a massive road-building programme made the province more accessible during the mid-1990s.[3]

Until the 1990s, provincial economic development had depended heavily on central government investment, growing fastest during the mid-1950s and mid-1980s: it was only during the mid-1990s that sustained, though still only moderate, above-national-average rates of growth were achieved without that support. In 1999 and 2000 growth rates fell well below the national average. This less spectacular economic profile, and other aspects of its economy, means that Shanxi has more in common with many of China's provinces – particularly those inland – than the more economically advanced coastal provinces of Guangdong, Zhejiang and Jiangsu; as well as the large municipalities of Beijing and Shanghai.

During the 1990s Shanxi's economic structure ceased to be completely determined by the central state sector, though it still played a sizeable role in provincial development. There was relatively little foreign inter-action with the province though there was considerable domestic investment from and trade with other parts of China, particularly in the development of the collective and private sectors of the economy. By 1997, 32 per cent of the province's Gross Value of Industrial Production (GVIO) was produced by the state sector, all of which was in heavy industry, compared to a national average of 25.5 per cent; 37.1 per cent of provin-cial GVIO was derived from the collective (or local government) sector of the economy, based predominantly on coal industry support activities and by-products, compared to a national average of 38.1 per cent; 17.9 per cent; of GVIO was nationally produced by the private sector of the economy, whereas in Shanxi a much higher 26.8 per cent of provincial GVIO came from the private sector, with production based in the new technologies, foodstuffs, and textiles.[4] In 1997, only 4.1 per cent of GVIO was derived from the foreign-funded sector of the economy, compared to a national average of 18.5 per cent.[5] In 1998, industrial production was 47.5 per cent of GDP in Shanxi, agricultural production was 13 per cent of GDP, whilst the retail and other service sectors were (and remain) dominated by private entrepreneurs.[6]

From interviews with 210 local entrepreneurs during 1996–8 it was possible to identify six broad categories of entrepreneur: the senior managers of state owned enterprises, urban collectives, rural collectives, equity-based enterprises, and joint ventures (with foreign companies) as well as owner-operators.[7] All are identifiable as entrepreneurs because they were centrally responsible for the management of an enterprise's economic risk. Defining entrepreneurs only by ownership in this context would not be accurate given the complex transitional nature of the economy. There

141

were individual entrepreneurs who were owner-operators, but for the most part their enterprises were small-scale and concentrated in the retail and service sectors. As their enterprises expanded they were all almost inevitably forced to share their equity with local government in order to ensure further access to land, equipment, finance and local political support.[8]

At the same time, there were entrepreneurs who had emerged through, and to a large extent led the changes in both the state and collective sectors of the economy. These managers had staked their careers on restructuring their enterprises and adjusting to the new demands of a market economy. Moreover, some of these new entrepreneurs were simultaneously both owners and managers in ambiguous ways. Ambiguity was particularly prevalent in the development of rural town and village enterprises (TVEs) to be found among the rural collectives and equity-based enterprises. As already indicated, an owner-operator wishing to expand might be forced to share equity in establishing a TVE but would still regard the enterprise as a personal company. The managing director of a TVE that had emerged from the investment of notional village or township assets might nonetheless also regard the enterprise as a personal company, because of the individual leadership and initiative that had been invested.

As these comments suggest, there were nonetheless differences amongst enterprises, largely related to genesis and operation that might be expected to impact on the social and economic behaviour of their entrepreneurs. One key difference was that of size and scale, as Table 7.1 indicates in terms of assets and profits.

During the late 1990s state owned enterprises remained the dominant form of industrial economic organization in Shanxi largely because of the centrality of heavy industry, and especially the coal industry, in the provincial economy. The managers of state owned enterprises during the late 1990s had emerged from the system of state socialism that preceded reform and were a more technocratic version of their colleagues who were the officials in the political system (Goodman 2000). They were well educated,

Table 7.1 Average annual fixed assets and profits after tax, 1997, by enterprise category (in million RMB)

Category of enterprise	Fixed assets	Net profits
State owned enterprises	1,258.39	24.31
Urban collectives	110.45	27.69
Rural collectives	22.27	3.02
Equity-based enterprises	29.87	8.21
Foreign-funded joint ventures	42.36	1.78
Private enterprises	7.68	0.28

Source: interviews with 210 entrepreneurs in Shanxi 1996–8

and though only a few were not Shanxi natives they tended to move around the province for work. These were characteristics they shared for the most part with the managers of urban collectives:[9] enterprises established for the most part by state owned enterprises and social units in the reform era.

Rural collectives were enterprises established by village, townships and rural districts. Although originally fairly small-scale and village-based, many took advantage of the rural sector's preferential economic regulation to develop sizeable industrial concerns, especially in mining and coal-industry related activities. The growth of rural collectives was particularly spectacular in suburban areas around the larger cities where villages were able to benefit from their rural status as well as access to markets and technical inputs, and where despite their rural designation few continued to engage in agricultural production, and many ceased to grow their own food. The entrepreneurs who led these developments were most likely to have been key local residents who had mobilized the locality behind the particular idea that had led to the development of the enterprise.

As already noted, Shanxi's level of foreign investment was extremely low. The few foreign-funded joint ventures were mostly large and developing versions of either state owned enterprises or rural collectives that had transformed themselves through co-operation with an external investor. The entrepreneur-managers at their head varied with the nature of the enterprise from which the Shanxi side of the joint venture had developed, not least since that was often their immediately previous workplace, though depending on the skills and techniques required some were also professional managers hired for the specific task.

There was quite a variety of equity-based enterprises to have emerged in Shanxi by the late 1990s. There were equity-based enterprises developed by or from state owned or collective enterprises, but by far the largest number were originally private enterprises that had grown through co-operation with local government, and where the original individual entrepreneur remained in the senior management position. Like the leaders of rural collectives, these entrepreneurs were very much people of the locality, but they tended to be much better educated. About half had gone away to university or college and later returned to their home village.

As might be expected, the owner-operators of the private sector tended on the whole to be younger versions of the managing directors (or equivalent) of equity-based enterprises, with enterprises markedly smaller in size and scale. The exceptions were a handful of extremely successful entrepreneurs, whose very success as private entrepreneurs was maintained as a useful role model for other entrepreneurs and would-be entrepreneurs by the provincial leadership. Elsewhere in the PRC owner-operators have been frequently characterized as young and poorly educated (for instance White III 1998:127; Young 1991), but in Shanxi the difference in education levels though still apparent is much less pronounced. Certainly, like the managers of both rural collectives and equity-based enterprises, the owner-operators were almost always locally based entrepreneurs, though unlike the latter they had spent little if any time away from home.

The discourse of localism

The emergence of a state-sponsored discourse of localism, in which the creation of a specifically provincial identity played a central role, was central to Shanxi's development during the 1990s.[10] It was remarkable not only because in the past throughout the PRC discourses of localism had most usually brought immense political problems for their progenitors (Teiwes 1979:366), but also because of its impact on the province's economic development. While the absolute rates of growth achieved during the 1990s were modest, there were significant gains in infrastructural development and integration with other parts of the country; and for the first time since the establishment of the PRC the provincial economy ceased to be dependent on central government.

State-sponsored localism was part of the provincial leadership's response to its realization that the province was falling behind the rest of the PRC in its embrace of the principles of reform. The inherent weaknesses in Shanxi's economic development for 40 years had been its dependence on central government investment, and the lack of infrastructural development. When, as in the late 1970s and early 1980s, central investment in Shanxi rose, so too did the rate of economic growth. In 1984 for example, there was a 24 per cent increase in GDP over the preceding year as a result of increased central investment during 1981–4. However, when central government investment decreased, as with the seventh Five Year Plan in the latter part of the 1980s, then the provincial economy slowed and the rate of growth in GDP not only fell back to single-digit figures, it fell beneath the rate of inflation. In addition, there was an overemphasis on the extraction of Shanxi's natural resources rather than their processing, and the province's infrastructure was almost completely ignored. Coal was mined almost exclusively for transport to other parts of China despite the lack of either adequate road or rail networks linking the province to the rest of the country.

Change came with the emergence of a nativist and technocratic provincial leadership in and after 1992. Led by Hu Fuguo, first as Acting Governor, and then in 1993 as CCP Provincial Secretary (until June 1999) it developed a radical new style of Shanxi politics that was both popular and populist, and that sought explicitly to create strong feelings of community. The emphasis on a new Shanxi identity was designed above all to change previous popular self-conceptions of the province as socially conservative, isolationist and not commercially minded.

144

According to the new provincial leadership, Shanxi needed to become more self-reliant, having contributed greatly to the national cause without necessarily gaining adequate recompense. In part that attitude was derived from an understanding of Shanxi's role in the war years. However, in part it also came from the attitudes of the Shanxi coal administrations who had long felt that the operation of the coal industry benefited the rest of the country more than it benefited the province, a situation that was seen to be exacerbated during the 1980s when price controls for coal and energy appeared to disadvantage a heavy industrial centre such as Shanxi in comparison to the light industrial centres of the south and east.

The essence of the provincial reform agenda was a series of major infra-structural development projects concerned with communications, transport, science and technology, energy, water, and education.[11] The most spectacular were those to solve Shanxi's communication problems by a massive road-building programme, and the attempt to ameliorate the severe water shortages through damming the Yellow River at Wanjiazhai and diverting water through pipelines to Datong and Taiyuan. During the 1990s Shanxi experienced the most intense period of road building ever, including both local and main roads, and Hu Fuguo was frequently referred to within the province as 'the road building secretary' (see for instance Gong Guoqiang 1998). The star turn was the four-lane super-highway from Taiyuan through the Taihang Mountains to Shijiazhuang (in Hebei) – the Tai-Jiu Expressway – which brought the rest of China much closer, and was the first stage in a network of expressways within the province linking Datong in the north of the province with Yuncheng in the south, and Shanxi with neighbouring Hebei, Henan, and Shaanxi (Xu Guangqing 1996; Du Wu'an 1996). The Yellow River diversion project was no less spectacular for having been discussed forty years earlier (Liang Zhihong 1996).

In addition there were equally as important projects to develop industries that would process Shanxi's raw materials within the province: notably the construction of electricity generation capacity, and the processing of bauxite into aluminium. Both the electricity and aluminium industries had been established during the 1980s but were developed greatly during the 1990s. Before the start of the reform era Shanxi had exported coal physically to supply energy to the rest of the country but little attention had been given to the possibility of establishing thermal generation plants in the coalfields and then exporting the electricity. The long-distance supply of electricity became a major feature of reform in Shanxi. Large new power plants were established in Shuozhou and Yangcheng supplying respectively Beijing, Hebei and Tianjin, on the one hand, and Jiangsu on the other. Moreover, China's largest aluminium smelter and major source of supply was built in Shanxi.[12]

The problem with all these projects, and others, including the expansion of educational services and the building of an international airport

145

in Taiyuan, was financial. Foreign direct investment in Shanxi had been extremely low, even for a non-coastal province (Cui Yi 1998). Investment was more likely from within the PRC, as with the development of the Yangcheng Power Station funded by the Jiangsu People's Government, than from foreign investment. By the end of the 1990s foreign investment still accounted for less than 5 per cent of provincial GDP, compared to a national average of about 20 per cent. The Pingshuo Open Cast Mine (in Shuozhou), originally developed in co-operation with Armand Hammer's Occidental Petroleum, was the spectacular exception to this at the start of the decade, but this relationship ended with Hammer's death and the end of the Cold War.

Since the start of the PRC, Shanxi's investment for industrial development and infrastructural projects had almost completely come from central government. Although central government did not completely withdraw all promise of contributions to investment, it also made it very plain that much less would be forthcoming in future. Investment and indeed operational funds would in future have to be locally generated. This was another major determinant of the provincial leadership's decision to emphasize a local, and particularly Shanxi identity. With the national imperative of rapid economic growth, yet starved of external funds, the only realistic option for the provincial leadership was to mobilize whatever resources were available locally.

As a medium- to long-term strategy, the development of a stronger provincial identity and an emphasis on localism might provide a means of encouraging economic opportunities and activism. In the short term, though, the emphasis on provincial identity was also designed to encourage people to donate their savings to the public good. Much of the provincial leadership's infrastructural programme was funded by essentially mandatory public subscription.

The development of the Tai-Jiu Expressway project provides an example of the process that was put in place. Only 40 per cent of the costs of the expressway development had been provided by governments, either national or provincial. The remainder was funded through public contributions and collection. Cadres at different levels in the Shanxi party-state were assigned a level of donation based on their rank. Given that the province had considerably more cadres as a proportion of the population than the national average (1.6 times more) this strategy was possibly more effective here than elsewhere, but nonetheless represented a considerable financial burden (Xu Guosheng 1998). The public at large were also encouraged to contribute, with their labour if not with cash donations (Hu Fuguo 1996; Shiwei 1997).

Economic and commercial traditions

To some extent the emphasis on the local paralleled experiences elsewhere in China with the introduction of reform. However, the leadership of the party-state in Shanxi seems to have promoted its identity on a scale not followed in other provinces, and to greater effect.[13] In part, explanation of these differences may lie with the relative homogeneity of the provincial population, as well as the creation by the former warlord of Shanxi, Yan Xishan, of a distinctive polity and provincial identity during the two decades before the War of Resistance against Japan (Gillin 1967). While neither can provide a total explanation of the relative success of the leadership's strategy, in Shanxi's case there was probably a greater sense of retrieval of traditions within recent memory, and of the reconstruction of the provincial identity, rather than a cynical creation to immediate political purposes.

The rallying call for local development was to produce 'A Prosperous Shanxi and a Wealthy People'. As in other provinces the propaganda system of the provincial government produced a whole series of publications dedicated to the promotion of local culture, though perhaps to a greater extent. A determined encouragement of the reconstructed Shanxi identity was to be found in the regular media – the radio, television and newspapers – which carried stories and items of local content. Where the establishment newspapers and programmes carried stories of strategic interest in terms of economic development, the more popular media concentrated on items of cultural or general interest. Thus not surprisingly the provincial CCP's daily newspaper featured development of the Shanxi coal industry (see for instance Zhao Shurong 1996), as well as the development of other industries (Zhang Xiu and Ji Ping 1996). More popular papers concentrated on issues such as local foods, vinegar consumption, and local history, both ancient and modern (see for instance Zhen Sheng 1996; Qu Shaosheng 1996; Liu Fang 1998; Kang Yuqin 1998).

To support this construction of local and provincial identity, the provincial leadership ensured the development of a whole network of institutes, study groups, and associations dedicated to popularizing the idea of Shanxi. These included a Shanxi Culture Research Association, and a Shanxi Overseas Exchange Committee. The provincial leadership also established a Shanxi Research Institute under its Provincial CCP Committee, with an initial staff of just under a hundred people. Perhaps even more remarkably, it also appointed 165 local historians in different locations around the province. In absolute terms this figure is clearly not large in a population of some 30 million, but given the other challenges that were facing the provincial leadership at the time, and that required funding, these appointments reflect the importance attached to the development of local knowledge. A major feature of the work of these local historians was to supply news stories of various kinds to the official media.

The CCP's pre-reform interpretation of the province had stressed Shanxi's role both as a supplier of national resources, and as a source of Communist traditions. The new provincial identity under reform built on those two elements and added two more. One was a considerable discussion of and emphasis on the distinctive social characteristics of Shanxi people, clearly designed to establish a provincial sense of solidarity. The other was to identify Shanxi as a source, and sometimes the authentic source, of Chinese traditions. Legitimacy was sought in an interpretation of Shanxi's centrality to China's development as much in the past as in the present. Within this account of Shanxi's traditions, emphasis was placed for the first time since the CCP came to power on the province's pre-socialist economic development and commercial culture, as well as on its links with the world outside Shanxi, both within China and beyond.

To some extent an emphasis on Shanxi's historical centrality to the development of Chineseness was the necessary counterweight, from the provincial leadership's perspective, to its emphasis on localism. As well as the practical need to encourage local economic activity, the provincial leadership had a political need to simultaneously emphasize national unity, not least as insurance for their individual careers. In addition though, the emphasis on the pre-socialist past also allowed for the selection and development of aspects of Shanxi's history more concerned with the modernizing causes of the reform era.

One important and obvious example of this use of history was the reference to industrial development under Yan Xishan during the 1920s and 1930s. Although Yan Xishan was not about to be rehabilitated by the CCP[14] the considerable industrial development of the province during the 1920s and 1930s was much celebrated. Yan Xishan had started the development of Taiyuan as a centre of heavy industry, based on coal mining, iron, steel, chemicals, and munitions production. Roads were built throughout the province, with a main highway for the first time connecting Datong (in the north of contemporary Shanxi) through Taiyuan to Yuncheng (in the south), and a start made on a rail network within the province (Jing Diankui and Kong Jinzhu Yan Xishan 1993). Shanxi under Yan Xishan was even credited with having developed the first, albeit limited, native Chinese automobile industry (Jiang Lianbao and Hao Xiaobin 1997).

The provincial leadership was also able to resurrect the tradition of the native Chinese bankers – the Exchange Shops (*piaohao*) – originally based in the Central Shanxi Basin towns of Pingyao, Taigu, and Qixian from the late eighteenth through to the early twentieth centuries. These bankers had rapidly grown to dominate not only the local and provincial economy, but also the national economy. Their banking institutions spread throughout North China and the most prominent underwrote and supported the Qing Government financially. The Exchange Shops eventually provided credit and financial services throughout China, as well as to customers in Japan, Russia, Mongolia and Afghanistan (Mu Yang 1996; Zhang Jihong 1996; Wang Xiaoge 1999; Kong Xiangyi 1998; Huang Jianhui 1992).

This was a ready-made tradition of commercialism that the provincial leadership attempted to mobilize in support of reform. It suggested very firmly not only that there were no apparent cultural impediments to commercial activity in Shanxi, but also that despite a period of isolation – emphasized during the warlord years of Yan Xishan, when he had wanted to exclude external influences – the province had also had significant national and international interactions, especially in economic development. Coincidentally too, the renewal of interest in the province's commercial traditions also proved a boost to tourism. The nineteenth century bankers had been major landowners who had built their own large houses and courtyards. Many remained almost intact, were restored to their original condition and opened to the public, particularly after the success of the film *Raise the Red Lantern* that had been filmed in the house of the former Qiao family in Qixian, just south of the provincial capital, Taiyuan.[15]

Both in general, and where the possibility existed in particular, those of Shanxi's entrepreneurs who were interviewed often located the economic activity for which they had responsibility in the context of provincial or local traditions. There were no questions that asked specifically about tradition or traditions. Yet when asked about their interpretation of the prospects for provincial and local economic development the overwhelming majority of those interviewed referred to the importance of provincial and local traditions of economic and commercial activity. The most commonly mentioned aspects of pre-socialist economic activity were the achievements of the Shanxi bankers, and their roles in national as well as provincial development.

While it would seem likely that these perspectives on provincial and local traditions have played a role in the creation of a climate of opinion that encouraged initiative and out-going, economic activism, it is less certain that they were actively utilized by entrepreneurs in the development of their enterprises. On the other hand, where a specific company had a history of economic success, outreach or national importance this certainly played a role in its reform era development as the entrepreneur sought to manage change within the enterprise and its wider environment. Not all entrepreneurs were able to call on a history going back to the Han Dynasty, as with Case 7.1, but many were able to refer to reputations that pre-dated the PRC, while a large number of reform activities drew on success in enterprises that had been developed between 1949 and 1980 under state socialism.[16]

Case 7.1 Manager, state sector enterprise: Wang Mengfei, Shanxi Nanfeng Chemical Industry Group, Yuncheng

Wang Mengfei was born locally in 1944 into a peasant family.[17] In 1969 he graduated from the China University of Science and Technology, and was assigned back to his native place and the Yuncheng Salt Industry Bureau, becoming Director of the Bureau in 1988. The Bureau had responsibility for Yuncheng Salt Lake, one of the world's largest. In 1996 he led the transformation of the former Yuncheng Salt Chemical Company, under the Bureau, into the Shanxi Nanfeng Chemical Industry Group, which is now a very substantial large-scale state enterprise. The Group attracted investment from Xi'an, Tianjin, and Zhejiang, and its twelve separate enterprises and total work force of more than 10,000 produced substantial proportions of the national output of inorganic salts, fertilizers and daily-use chemicals, such as detergents. Wang was very conscious of the roots of the enterprise, and used this sense of history to engage the work force and management in the process of change. As Wang Mengfei himself pointed out, there were few enterprises in China that could trace their industrial activities back to the Han Dynasty; and he was inordinately proud of being a state sector enterprise manager whose responsibilities included a temple that had been visited by thirty emperors.

Local activism

If one of the goals in the provincial leadership's development of a state sponsored discourse of localism was to encourage entrepreneurs to be locally active, then it was clearly highly successful. The new entrepreneurs and managers who were stimulated by the Shanxi reform agenda were characterized and motivated by an intense localism. Of those interviewed, almost all maintained that they were acting in order to improve their local community, be it urban district, town, village or county. They invested locally, mobilized local populations behind their ideas and initiatives, and brought new technologies and new market knowledge to their homes, sometimes returning after having studied or worked elsewhere.

The strength of localism appears quite clearly through the analysis of the background of entrepreneurs and managers in terms either of native place, or length of working in a specific workplace. Table 7.2 provides information on the localism of entrepreneurs in terms of these two criteria.

Case 7.2   Manager, urban collective: Wang Baoguo, Manager, Taiyuan Trust Stock Exchange, Taiyuan

Wang Baoguo was born in Taiyuan in 1951 and graduated from technical school in accountancy. He had been a long-term member of the CCP who previously worked in the Credit Department of the Bank of Industry and Commerce. He started work at the Taiyuan Trust Stock Exchange when it was established in 1985 by Chen Chuntang, a relatively well-known Taiyuan banker, and became manager on Chen's premature death in 1993.[18] The Taiyuan Trust Stock Exchange was an interesting use of state sector resources to the specific ends of the development of the local economy. Chen Chuntang saw the need for greater specialization in banking at an early stage in the reform era, and particularly the need to separate commercial from political banking. The Stock Exchange was established with a number of state run companies as stock holders: the Coal Management Department of Taiyuan City, the Taiyuan Iron & Steel Company, the Taiyuan Heavy Machinery Factory, the West Shanxi Machinery Factory, the Twentieth Project Department of the Railway Ministry, and the Shanxi Minerals Department. It provided loans to enterprises or individuals looking for investment, and its activities were profit-driven: its only criterion for granting a loan was an assessment of the capacity to repay. Though started in Taiyuan it established its own offices throughout the province.

The first identifies the proportion of those entrepreneurs who were natives of the county in which they were working when interviewed. The second considers the average number of years non-natives had worked in the same enterprise, or a parent company, before starting their current occupation. Taken together these data suggest a high degree of localism and probable local connections for all categories of entrepreneur, even those that had a relatively low proportion of natives in place – such as the managers of state sector enterprises and of urban collective enterprises.

Appointment practices before the reform era ensured few natives had been appointed as managers of either state sector enterprises or urban collectives. All the same it would seem that once appointed to a specific enterprise, they tended to stay there. One result that came through strongly from the interviews conducted during the late 1990s was that these entrepreneurs came to identify strongly with the locality and indeed the province, even when, as was sometimes the case with senior managers

151

Table 7.2 The localism of local entrepreneurs

Entrepreneurs of different categories of enterprise	Native to county workplace (per cent)	Average number of years working in workplace before appointment
State owned enterprises	32	12.8
Urban collectives	27	11.5
Rural collectives	63	12.2
Equity-based enterprises	52	6.7
Foreign-funded joint ventures	64	6.4
Private enterprises	54	6.8

Source: interviews with 210 entrepreneurs in Shanxi 1996–8

and entrepreneurs, they had been allocated to work in Shanxi on gradu-ation from university or college. Surprisingly this identification even extended to food and eating customs – the noodles and pasta, as well as strong tastes of vinegar and lamb favoured in Shanxi – in complete contrast to the more usually quieter tastes of their homes in the south and east of China. In some cases, identification with the local had been facilitated through intermarriage, but even where this was not the case most non-native interviewees expressed a high degree of local identification in a variety of ways, including on many occasions pointing out that this was their children's native place and the family's home.

Case 7.3 Manager, rural collective: Zhang Zhengwu, General Manager, Qianheng Industrial Company, Yangquan

Zhang Zhengwu was the executive of a rural collective in Xiaqian Village, in the suburbs of Yangquan where he was also the village head and CCP branch secretary.[19] Yangquan is a major coal producing city in east Shanxi, and the once famous Dazhai is located just to the south. Zhang was born in 1953 in Xiaqian Village. A middle school graduate, he joined the CCP in 1974. In the 1980s he realised that Xiaqian could develop rapidly by involving itself in zircon-oxide processing and other process industries, with large numbers of its inhabitants abandoning their former agricultural occupations. As village head he led and masterminded its transformation. The village rapidly became completely urbanized: the villagers no longer grew their own food and their productive activities were all organized through the

Qianheng Industrial Company. Its main industrial activities were linked to the coal industry of Yangquan, either supplying its needs or using its by-products for production. Qianheng established a refractory plant, a zinc-oxide plant, and a bauxite processing plant; and it produces aluminium in a number of forms, zinc-oxide related materials, and coal-based chemicals.

As Table 7.2 indicates, the managers of rural collectives were the most local in terms of birthplace and work location. Interviews revealed that they were also the most parochial in their outlook. A few had become village and local leaders after a period away, most commonly in the PRC's armed forces, but most had always lived where they now worked. They were essentially the villages' customary leaders who the local population turned to because of their social status or a perceived expertise – the former local village cadre, the production brigade or production team accountant, the agricultural machinery workshop technician. As the wider political economy started to change during the early 1980s they responded with initiatives to develop the local economy. When asked in retrospect to explain their motivations, all provided a variation of the theme that they wanted to improve the standard of living and life in their village or locality, though as Case 7.4 also demonstrates this did not exclude the possibility of beginning to think of their economic activities in more personal terms.

Case 7.4   Manager, equity-based enterprise:
Hu Jianping, Chairman, Shanxi Zhenzhong Coal
and Coke Company, Zhongyang County

Hu Jianping was a native of Zhongyang County and was born in 1963.[20] His father was a CCP member, a veteran of the Korean War, and a former leader of the local militia. The junior Hu set off on his own in 1985 as a lorry driver, and once he had saved enough, opened a restaurant, and then on its profits established his own transport company. By 1989 he had personal assets of approximately 300,000 RMB and at that stage having put out feelers about the possibility of investing in his home village was invited to become manager of the village enterprise, a coking plant based on the village coal mine. Hu Jianping's personal investment in the village enterprise was combined with a matching grant from the provincial Poverty Relief Fund and this enabled the new enterprise to eventually further obtain bank loans of 600,000 RMB. Further development, though, was to prove more contingent. Hu had found a Taiwanese partner willing to invest, but local government was also interested in co-operation. The compromise was the establishment of an equity-based enterprise, led by Hu Jianping, in which he, his Taiwanese partner, and local government held shares. In return, Hu was mandated to join the CCP and also agreed to become secretary of the party's village branch. All the same according to Hu, this did not stop him regarding the company as his own. The company subsequently expanded to include three additional factories which exploited the local bauxite resources as well as coal, and which bought out the local mine. It also opened a research institute and restaurant in Taiyuan. The company developed relations with business partners in Taiwan, Japan, and Australia, and exported to Brazil, Turkey, UK, Spain, the Netherlands, and Japan.

In general, as Table 7.2 also indicates, the entrepreneurial managers of equity-based enterprises and foreign-funded joint ventures could be regarded as somewhat less local than the managers of rural collectives. Fewer were natives, and the average length of local service was shorter, though this by no means indicates a low level of local identification or development of roots. The majority were still natives or had worked in the same enterprise, or a parent company, for an average of over six years. They shared many of the characteristics observed amongst the managers of rural collectives, and for many of the same reasons. At the start of the reform process the ability to start out on new ventures did not just require an economic motivation and the necessary resources, but in addition the imagination and political courage that came through strong local identification and ties. Developing new forms of enterprise in the emerging market sector of the economy was far easier when sheltered by an established state sector enterprise or urban collective, or when supported by one's own village or township.

Those who were private sector owner-operators when interviewed, or who had been and were now managers of equity-based enterprises that had grown from their earlier endeavours, were similarly more usually local natives than not, or had worked locally for an extended period. While clearly there is less confusion between collective and individual assets for enterprises that remain in the private sector, nonetheless most of those who were either owner-operators or managers of once private enterprises explained their

154

motivation from a collectivist perspective: they wanted to improve their native place, where they worked, or where they lived and called 'home' now. This may not have been either their only or their main motivation, but all the same it is clear that the state sponsored discourse of localism gave them the opportunity to become economically involved locally.

Certainly the emphasis on the local appeared frequently in provincial news stories of individual success. Perhaps the best known entrepreneur in Shanxi during the late 1990s was Li Anmin, of Antai Enterprises, usually regarded as the province's richest person. His wealth was based originally on the industrial development of his native Jiexiu County explicitly on localist grounds. Li Anmin later became nationally well known because his company had its 'own' railway trains and a purpose-built railway line. In 1984 Li Anmin had used 3,000 RMB of his own money to establish a private company, which organized twenty-seven of his neighbours to produce coke. The operation then expanded during a decade into the large-scale and multi-million dollar Antai International Enterprise Group Company, with interests in coking plants, coal-washing, high-grade cement, clothing and various other activities (Liu Liping *et al.* 1989). Though perhaps other examples are less spectacularly successful, nonetheless it is not an uncommon story. In addition to Liang Wenhai (Wang Yonghai *et al.* 1996), the subject of Case 7.6, there is also Qiao Yijian, a Yuncheng native, who after graduation from Central China University of Technology chose to return home to establish a high-technology chemical industry enterprise (Lu Zhifen and Li Hong 1996).

Networks of influence

As the comments on entrepreneurs's local activism indicate, local ties were crucial for the success of a new economic initiative. Local identification might have presented the opportunity for the development of a new enterprise, but it was the ability to tap into local networks that offered the promise of success. Local ties provided not only access to resources such as buildings, labour, equipment and bank loans, but also, of even greater importance, the political insurance that was necessary to facilitate the exercise of initiative. Much of this insurance was derived through associations centring on the party-state. However, the development of a state sponsored discourse of localism by the provincial leadership legitimated its operation at the local, and particularly the county, level.

It is relatively self-evident that the entrepreneurial managers of state owned enterprises and urban collectives had ready access to resources and political connections that assisted them in their responses to the imperatives of reform. State owned enterprises and urban collectives were well-established social communities in most cases long before the advent of reform, and in some cases from even before the establishment of the

PRC. In Taiyuan, for example, the Taiyuan Iron & Steel Works had been the city's largest enterprise for over seventy years, both a mainstay of the local economy and central to local politics. Its reform could not have been contemplated, let alone achieved with any degree of success, without the active support of the party-state at city and provincial levels, not least because of the goals of reducing the work force by almost 80 per cent and hiving off different parts of the original enterprise to establish new and independent companies and enterprises. Whatever the economic gain, there was bound to be a significant impact on the local community in terms of the levels of unemployment, the dislocation of the work force, and the redistribution of centres of economic activity.

Access to resources and political connections locally were also central to all other categories of entrepreneur and for broadly similar reasons. Almost all those entrepreneurs interviewed repeatedly referred in a variety of ways to the importance of local networks of influence in providing local knowledge, resources, and political safety, if not always precisely in those words. As already noted, managers of rural collectives, equity-based enterprises and foreign-funded joint ventures all found it easier to operate in the new market economy when supported by a state sector enterprise or a unit of local government.

Case 7.5 Manager, foreign-funded joint venture: Qiao Jiuchong, Managing Director, Gucheng Dairy Company, Shanyin County

Qiao Jiuchong was born in Shanyin County in 1942, and left school after completing his primary education. He joined the CCP in 1966 and had been a worker in a chemical plant before becoming village CCP branch secretary. Determined to do something for themselves and the village, he and his wife started to raise seven cows in 1976 and from that built a sizeable herd through reinvestment.[21] In 1982 he established the Shanyincheng Milk Powder Factory, with a personal investment of 230,000 RMB and a further bank loan of 400,000 RMB. In 1994 the company was restructured as an equity-based enterprise with a total capital of 30 million RMB between himself, the work force and local government. In 1995 the business developed further through the establishment of the Gucheng Dairy Company, a joint venture with Dutch partners. Its products then became marketed under the KANNY trademark. Throughout the 1990s it regularly upgraded its equipment to produce not only milk powder but also daily fresh milk, liquid milks, and ice creams, and became one of the ten largest dairy factories in China.

Local roots and access to local networks were even more important for those entrepreneurs who went a step further and launched private sector companies, particularly as their enterprises grew and became equity-based co-operatives with local government. The few outsiders – from outside the county and not just the province – with a marketable idea found it necessary to develop a close relationship with a local resident in order to proceed. Many of those interviewed who were or had at some time been private sector owner-operators had been local officials of the party-state when the reform agenda was introduced, and had been able to draw on these associations to develop their business. Those who had not been local officials had mostly been excluded for political reasons – usually connected to their family's class background – from full social and political partic-ipation before the reform era, and saw the opportunity as one of social advancement (see Case 7.6). However, even in their case development and success depended on incorporation into a local political network.

Case 7.6 Private entrepreneur: Liang Wenhai, General Manager, Shanxi Huanhai Group, Yuci

During the 1990s, Liang Wenhai was often referred to in the press as China's 'Boiler King'.[22] Liang was the General Manager of the Shanxi Huanhai Group which not only made industrial boilers but had also diversified into property development, especially supermarkets and shopping malls. Liang had been born in 1963 to working-class parents in Yuci, a city just south of Taiyuan. Apprenticed at the age of 13, in 1984 he established his own boiler factory with capital of 3,000 RMB borrowed from friends. He believed he knew how to make boilers that would operate with less smoke and noise, and with greater efficiency. From six workers, a handcart and an electric welder in 1984 the enter-prise had grown by 1996 to 1,800 workers, fixed assets of 160 million RMB and annual turnover in excess of 100 million RMB. Liang's com-pany owned six subsidiaries, including a boiler manufacturing company, a boiler equipment company, a boiler installation company, a trade and industry company, and a travel agency, and had interests in hotels, dance halls, and shopping malls. It developed a new trade and indus-try centre during 1995–6 just outside Taiyuan. According to Liang his motivation was both to develop his native place and to show the CCP that he was a suitable candidate to join. His father had been denied membership of the CCP because of his parent's poor class background in the judgement of the CCP. Liang was clearly resentful that the CCP had refused to let either his father or himself join. All the same,

> the CCP did promote Liang as a 'model entrepreneur' and the CCP branch in his company had its headquarters next to the General Manager's office.

Not surprisingly, given the transitional nature of the economy from state socialism, local networks seem to have revolved around the organizations of the party-state, and particularly centred on the city and county branches of the CCP. Table 7.3 provides information on CCP membership for all those interviewed, their average age (by category) at the end of 1998, and the date at which entrepreneurs joined the CCP, as between, before, and after the introduction of an ideology of reform. A large proportion of all local entrepreneurs were members of the CCP. Somewhat under half of owner-operators interviewed were members of the CCP, and a little over half of managers of equity-based enterprises. For the rest, though, entrepreneurs of different categories of enterprise were overwhelmingly members of the CCP.

As might be expected, with the exception of managers of equity-based enterprises and owner-operators, many of those entrepreneurs interviewed had been CCP members before the introduction of reform, and substantial numbers had been officials of the party-state. That those who had not previously been members of the CCP were recruited, and were willing to be recruited, to the party later as they became more active entrepreneurs emphasizes the interaction between the political and the economic, rather than a tendency to separation.

Table 7.3 Entrepreneurs' membership of CCP by enterprise category, age, and date of entry

Entrepreneurs of different categories of enterprise	Membership of CCP (per cent)	Average age (end 1998)	Date of entry to CCP	
			Pre-reform (before 1979) (per cent)	Reform era (since 1978) (per cent)
State owned enterprises	100	48	30	70
Urban collectives	75	48	44	56
Rural collectives	77	47	46	54
Equity-based enterprises	58	42	15	85
Foreign-funded joint ventures	76	46	63	37
Private enterprises	39	41	21	79

Source: interviews with 210 entrepreneurs in Shanxi 1996–8

Similarly, in the case of managers of equity-based enterprises and owner-operators – even allowing for their younger average age which might have limited their ability to be recruited to the CCP before the introduction of reform – Table 7.3 indicates that they were incorporated into local political networks with their economic success. However, this is likely to greatly understate the extent to which managers of equity-based enterprises and owner-operators had emerged from and been incorporated into local networks based on the party-state.

In the first place, some of the more successful private sector entrepreneurs in Shanxi had been refused entry to the CCP but nonetheless had been incorporated into the party-state in other ways. Many became 'model entrepreneurs' and were publicized in the province and sometimes nationally too as models for emulation. They attended both provincial and national conferences of 'model entrepreneurs' which were (and still are) organized annually. Some also became delegates elected to the County, Provincial and National People's Congresses (the equivalent of local councils and parliament) and served in government agencies. For example, Li Anmin, the founder of Jiexiu County's Antai Enterprises, had never been a member of the CCP but he served on the Jiexiu County People's Congress and was a member of several provincial government bodies (Liu Liping et al. 1989). Han Changan, the Chairman and General Manager of the Lubao Coking Company in Lucheng County[23] – a medium sized concern that had become a considerable economic success during the mid-1990s, and a major donor to social and infrastructural development projects – was similarly not a member of the CCP, but was a representative to the National People's Congress.

In the second place, there were remarkably few entrepreneurs who either were not themselves members of the CCP or whose parents had not been members of the party, often serving as officials of the party-state, and this includes the managers of equity-based enterprises and owner-operators. Table 7.4 provides information about membership of the CCP for the interviewees and their parents by category of enterprise. Amongst the managers of equity-based enterprises and owner-operators only 23 per cent and 37 per cent respectively of those interviewed were not themselves members of the CCP and had parents who had not been members of the party. Remarkably, 39 per cent of owner-operators interviewed had parents who were members of the CCP, with most in positions of some responsibility within the party-state. There is more than a hint in many of the interviews that the children of officials and party members often did not need to join the CCP, or serve in the party-state, in order to access the networks of influence to which their parents had access, or in some cases had created. Indeed, on a number of occasions this was the explicit response when owner-operators were asked about their party affiliation and lack of membership in the CCP: 'Why should I join the CCP?

Table 7.4 CCP membership of interviewees by parents' membership status (percentages) and enterprise category

Enterprise category	Parent member of CCP Interviewee		Parent not member of CCP Interviewee	
	Not member	Member	Not member	Member
State owned enterprises	0	24	76	0
Urban collectives	8	21	54	17
Rural collectives	10	27	50	13
Equity-based enterprises	7	27	43	23
Foreign-funded joint ventures	13	38	38	13
Private enterprises	23	16	23	37

Source: interviews with 210 entrepreneurs in Shanxi 1996–8

I have grown up locally and my (father, mother, or some other relative) was the (village head, county party secretary, or some other local position of leadership).'

Notes

1 Derived from a project to investigate the emergence of political communities and the negotiation of identity in Shanxi under reform. The project has been supported by a research grant from the Australian Research Council. Professor Tian Youru of the Modern Shanxi Research Institute, and Li Xueqian of Shanxi University provided help and assistance without which this project would not have taken place. Neither they nor indeed anyone else in Shanxi who has contributed to this project, including those interviewed for this study, is in any way responsible for the interpretation or views expressed here.

2 The fieldwork reported here was conducted during 1996–8 and provincial economic indicators are provided for those years rather than the most recently published. 1998 economic development statistics are taken from Editorial Committee on Fifty Years of Shanxi '1949–99 Shanxi wushi nian [1949–99 Fifty Years of Shanxi]' Beijing, Zhongguo tongji chubanshe, 1999, p.160 (GDP) p.168 (population.) A report on Shanxi's development during the 1990s that emphasizes its positive aspects may be found in Governor Sun Wensheng's speech to the 9th Shanxi Provincial People's Congress on 8 January 1998, 'Quanmian guanche dangde shiwuda jingshen baxingjin fuminde hongwei daye duixiang ershiyi shiji' ['Push Forward the Great task of Invigorating and Enriching Shanxi into the 21st Century'] in *Shanxi zhengbao* [*Shanxi Gazette*] February 1998, p.32. A more negative perspective is provided by Acting Governor Liu Zhenghua 'Zhengfu gongzuo baogao [Government Work Report]' in *Shanxi ribao* [*Shanxi Daily*] 30 January 2000, p.1. 8.3 RMB [dollar] RMB [Renminbi or People's Currency] = 1US$. By the national census of 1 November 2000 the provincial population had grown to 32.97 million: Zhang Wei 'Quansheng diwuci renkou pucha zhuyao shuju [The Key Figures of the Fifth National Census for Shanxi]' in *Shanxi wanbao* [*Shanxi Evening News*] 23 May 2001. In 2000 GDP per capita was 5,085 RMB: Shanxi

Statistical Bureau ' "Jiuwu" shiqi wosheng guomin jingji heshehui fazhan huigu [An Overview of National Economic and Social Development in Shanxi during the Ninth Five-year Plan]' in *Shanxi ribao* [*Shanxi Daily*] 10 February 2001.

3 For further information on the development of Shanxi see: Gillin 1967; Breslin 1989; and Goodman 1999.

4 1996 'Shanxi Jianhang xindai zhanlue he zhizhu chanye xuanze [The Shanxi Construction Bank's credit strategy and selection of industries for support]', *Touzi daokan* [*Investment Guide*] (1, February):9.

5 Statistics for 1997 are calculated from Zhonghua renmin gongheguo guojia tongji ju (ed). 1998, *Zhongguo tongji nianjian 1998* [*China Statistical Yearbook 1998*]. Beijing: Zhongguo tongji chubanshe:435. These national figures are used for comparative purposes as provincial and national compilations of statistics are often inconsistent. See Herrmann-Pillath 1995.

6 1998 *Shanxi tongji nianjian 1998* [*Shanxi Statistical Yearbook 1998*]. Beijing: Zhongguo tongji chubanshe:19.

7 Of the interviewees, 50 were managers of state owned enterprises; 31 were managers of urban collectives; 29 were managers of rural collectives; 23 were managers of equity-based enterprises; 14 were managers of joint venture enterprises; and 63 were owner-operators. Greater detail is provided in Goodman 2001.

8 For confirmation of this trend elsewhere, and at an earlier stage of development, see Young 1989.

9 Under the system of state socialism, there were essentially two kinds of enterprise: state owned and collective enterprises, both of whose output was state regulated, but only the former had their inputs provided for within the state plan. The political logic was that state owned enterprises were owned by the society as a whole, whereas collective enterprises belonged to those who worked in them (in the case of urban collectives) or who lived in them (in the case of the rural collectives, based on the commune system). The economic logic was that collectives did not require state financial support.

10 Lan Baoli and Liu Shuxin 1996; and especially the foreword by then Governor Sun Wencheng, 'Wokan Shanxide jinhou shiwunian [My view of Shanxi's next fifteen years]'.

11 The preparatory research reports for the various projects were published as Li Zhenxi 1994. See also Rizhou Lu 1996.

12 See, for example: Shanxi fazhan tuopin zhudao chanye [Shanxi develops core industries to shake off poverty], *Shanxi Daily* [*Shanxi Daily*] 9 October:1. 1996.

13 In Hubei and Jiangxi, for example, the provincial leadership's promotions of discourses of localism resulted in trends to political disintegration and led directly to their failure and loss of office. See, on Hubei, Zhao Ling Yun 1999 and on Jiangxi, Feng Chongyi 1999.

14 Despite an alliance with the CCP during 1936–9, he had acted against the CCP during the early 1930s and sided with the Nationalist Party during the Civil War.

15 *Wu Yiji Zai zhongtang – Qiaojia dayuan* [*In the Great Hall: The Qiao Family Courtyard*] Taiyuan, Shanxi renmin chubanshe, 1993.

16 In addition to the Shanxi Nanfeng Chemical Industry described in Case 7.1, two other enterprises that were covered in the survey had pre-Qing histories: the Yiyuanqin Vinegar Factory (founded 1377) and the Taigu Medical Company (founded 1541). Some 54 enterprises established by Yan Xishan, mainly in heavy industry, were still in operation during the 1990s.

17 Interviewed in Yuncheng, 17 September 1997.

18 Interviewed in Taiyuan, 29 October 1993. Chen Chuntang had been manager of the Taiyuan Bank of Industry and Commerce. His biography (to 1988) may be found in Liu Liping et al. 1989. He died in a traffic accident in Italy.
19 Interviewed in Xiaqian, Yangquan, 11 July 1996.
20 Interviewed at the company's Taiyuan office, 25 September 1997.
21 Interviewed in Shanyin County, 7 October 1996.
22 Interviewed in Yuci, 29 October 1996. See also Wang Yonghai et al. 1996.
23 Near Changzhi in south-east Shanxi, and close to the location of Long Bow Village made famous by William Hinton in Fanshen. Interview, 14 October 1998.

References

Breslin, S. (1989) 'Shanxi: China's Powerhouse', in D.S.G. Goodman (ed.) China's Regional Development, London: Routledge:135.

Cui Yi (1998) 'Zijin weishenme buxiang Shanxi liu? [Why won't capital flow into Shanxi?]', Shanxi fazhan dabao [Shanxi Development Herald], 9 June:2.

Du Wu'an (1996) 'Guanyu TaiJiu gaosu gonglu jianshe qingkuangde baogao [Report on the construction of the Taiyuan-Jiuguan Expressway]', Shanxi ribao [Shanxi Daily], 26 June.

Gillin, D.G. (1967) Warlord Yen Hsi-shan in Shansi Province 1911–1949, Princeton: Princeton University Press.

Gong Guoqiang (1998) 'Wosheng gonglu jianshe xingaochao zaiqi [Another High Tide for Highway Construction in Shanxi]', Shanxi jingji ribao [Shanxi Economic Daily], 25 June:1.

Goodman, D.S.G. (1995) 'Collectives and connectives, capitalism and corporatism: structural change in China', The Journal of Communist Studies and Transition Politics, 11(1):12–32.

—— (1999) 'King Coal and Secretary Hu: Shanxi's Third Modernisation', in Feng Chongyi and H. Hendrischke (eds) The Political Economy of China's Provinces: Competitive and Comparative Advantage, London: Routledge.

—— (2000) 'The localism of local leadership: cadres in reform Shanxi', Journal of Contemporary China, 9(24):159–83.

—— (2001) 'The Interdependence of State and Society: The Political Sociology of Local Leadership', in Chien-min Chao and B.J. Dickson (eds) Remaking the Chinese State: Strategies, Society and Security, London: Routledge:132–56.

Guthrie, D. (1999) Dragon in a Three-Piece Suit: The Emergence of Capitalism in China, Princeton: Princeton University Press.

Hannan, K. (1998) Industrial Change in China: Economic Restructuring and Conflicting Interests, London: Routledge.

Hendrischke, H. and Feng Chongyi (eds) (1999) The Political Economy of China's Provinces: Comparative and Competitive Advantage, London: Routledge:155 and 249.

Herrmann-Pillath, C. (ed.) (1995) Wirtschaftliche Entwicklung in Chinas Provinzen und Regionen, 1978–1992 [The Economic Development of China's Provinces and Regions], Baden-Baden: Nomos: especially p.35.

Huang Jianhui (1992) Shanxi piaohao shi [The History of Shanxi's Exchange Shops], Taiyuan: Shanxi jingji chubanshe.

Hu Fuguo (1996) 'Dalu ru mao xie tengfei [Highways mean flying ahead]', in Shanxi Ribaoshe (ed.) *SanJin tengfei lu* [*Shanxi's roads fly ahead*], Hong Kong: Xiang Gang Zhongguo xinwen cubanshe:15.

Jiang Lianbao and Hao Xiaobin (1997) 'Jinren zhaoche [Shanxi's People-made Automobile]', *Shenghuo chenbao* [*Morning Life*], 25 December:4.

Jing Diankui and Kong Jinzhu Yan Xishan (1993) *Guanliao ziben yanjiu* [*Research on Yan Xishan's bureaucratic capitalism*], Taiyuan: Shanxi jingji chubanshe.

Kang Yuqin (1998) 'Shanxi de gudu [Ancient capitals of Shanxi]', *Taiyuan wanbao* [*Taiyuan Evening News*], 24 December:7.

Keng, K. (2001) 'China's future economic regionalization', *Journal of Contemporary China*, 10(29):587–611.

Kong Xiangyi (1998) *Jinrong maoyi shilun* [*The history of banking and trade*], Beijing: Zhongguo jinrong chubanshe.

Lan Baoli and Liu Shuxin (ed.) (1996) *Shanxi shengqing yu fazhan zhanlüe yanjiu* [*A Study of Shanxi's Provincial Spirit and Development Strategy*], Beijing: Zhonggong zhongyang dangxiao chubanshe.

Liang Zhihong (1996) 'Yinhuangmeng [Dreams of channelling the Yellow River]', *Taiyuan wanbao* [*Taiyuan Evening News*], 14 June:8.

Liu Fang (1998) 'Techan mingchi [Local specialities and famous food]', *Shenghuo chenbao* [*Morning Life*], 7 April:3.

Liu Liping *et al.* (ed.) (1989) *Zhongguo dangdai qiyejia mingdian – Shanxi tao* [*Contemporary Entrepreneurs in China – Shanxi volume*], Beijing: Gongren chubanshe:305.

Li Zhenxi (ed.) (1994) *Xing Jin Fu Min: shida keti yanjiu* [A Prosperous Shanxi and a Wealthy People: Ten important questions for research], Taiyuan: Shanxi renmin chubanshe.

Lu Zhifen and Li Hong (1996) 'Shanxi xiangqi fazhan [Village-run enterprises in Shanxi]', *Shanxi ribao* [*Shanxi Daily*], 5 June:3.

Mu Yang (1996) 'Jinzhong, licai jingshang jiatianxia [Central Shanxi is the tops for business and banking in the world]', *Shanxi jingi ribao* [*Shanxi Economic Daily*], 27 September:3.

Nan Lin (1995) 'Local market socialism: local corporatism in action in rural China', *Theory and Society*, 24:301–54.

Naughton, B. (1994) 'What is distinctive about China's economic transition? State enterprise reform and overall system transformation', *Journal of Comparative Economics*, 18(3):470–90.

Nee, V. (1992) 'Organisational dynamics of market transition: hybrid forms, property rights, and mixed economy in China', *Administrative Science Quarterly*, 32(1):1–27.

—— (1996) 'The emergence of market society: changing mechanisms of stratification in China', *American Journal of Sociology*, 101 (4):908.

Nee, V. and Su Sijin (1996) 'Local Corporatism and Informal Privatization in China's Market Transition', in J. McMillan and B. Naughton (eds) *Reforming Asian Socialism: The Growth of Market Institutions*, Ann Arbor: University of Michigan Press.

Oi, J.C. (1992) 'Fiscal reform and the economic foundations of local state corporatism in China', *World Politics*, 45(1):99.

—— (1995) 'The role of the local state in China's transitional economy', *The China Quarterly*, 144:1132.

—— (1999) *Rural China Takes Off: Institutional Foundations of Economic Reform*, Berkeley: University of California Press.

Parris, K. (1996) 'Private entrepreneurs as citizens: from Leninism to corporatism', *China Information*, 10:1–28.

Pearson, M. (1994) 'The Janus face of business associations in China: socialist corporatism in foreign enterprises', *Australian Journal of Chinese Affairs*, 31:25–48.

—— (1997) *China's New Business Elite: The Political Consequences of Economic Reform*, Berkeley: University of California Press.

Pomfret, J. (2001) 'China allows its capitalists to join party', *Washington Post* 2 July:1.

Qu Shaosheng (1996) 'Yan Xishan tuixingde tuhuo yundong [Yan Xishan's native goods campaign]', *Taiyuan wanbao* [*Taiyuan Evening News*], 14 August:8.

Rizhou Lu (1996) 'Shanxi sheng gaige kaifeng fenxi [The analysis of Shanxi's reform and openness]', *Shanxi ribao* [*Shanxi Daily*], 2 May:1 and 3.

Shiwei, Du (ed.) (1997) *Sanjin tengfei zhilu – shisida yilai Shanxi shixian Deng Xiaoping lilun diaoyan baogao* [*Shanxi's Roads Fly Ahead – a Report into the implementation of Deng Xiaoping's ideas since the 14th Congress of the CCP*], Beijing: Zhonggong zhongyang dangxiao chubanshe.

Solinger, D.J. (1992) 'Urban Entrepreneurs and the State: The Merger of State and Society', in A.L. Rosenbaum (ed.) *State and Society in China: The Consequences of Reform*, Boulder: Westview.

—— (1993) *China's Transition from Socialism: Statist Legacies and Market Reforms 1980–1990*, New York: M.E. Sharpe.

Teiwes, F.C. (1979) *Politics and Purges in China*, New York: M.E. Sharpe:366.

Walder, A.G. (1995) 'Local governments as industrial firms: an organizational analysis of China's transitional economy', *American Journal of Sociology*, 10(2):263–301.

Wang Xiaoge (1999) 'Qiongze sibian [Poverty gives rise to a dream for change: how Shanxi was lifted out of poverty based on Shanxi's businessmen in the Ming and Qing Dynasties]', *Gaige xiansheng* [*Reform Herald*], July:37.

Wang Yonghai, Liu Yaoming, Wang Jikang and Zhang Guilong (1996) 'Shanxi Huanhai jituan yougongsi zhongshizhang Liang Wenhai yu tade Huanhai shiye he huanbao zhanlüe [General manager of the Shanxi Huanhai Group Company, Liang Wenhai, his Huanhai business and environmental strategy]', *Shanxi Ribao* [*Shanxi Daily*], 22 September:4.

Weixing Chen (1997) 'Peasant challenge in post-Communist China', *Journal of Contemporary China*, 6(14):101.

—— (1998) 'The political economy of rural industrialization in China: village conglomerates in Shandong province', *Modern China*, 24(1):73.

White, G. (1993) *White Riding the Tiger: The Politics of Economic Reform in Post-Mao China*, London: Macmillan.

White III, L.T. (1998) *Unstately Power, Vol.1: Local Causes of China's Economic Reforms*, New York: M.E. Sharpe.

Whiting, S.H. (2001) *Power and Wealth in Rural China: The Political Economy of Institutional Change*, Cambridge: Cambridge University Press.

Wo Lap Lam, W. (2001) 'China's struggle for "democracy"', *CNN.com*, 7 August.

Xiao Zhou, K. (1996) *How the Farmers Changed China: Power of the People*, Boulder: Westview.

Xu Guanqing (1996) 'TaiJiulu quanxian tongchele [Taiyuan-Jiuguan Expressway open to traffic]', *Shanxi ribao* [*Shanxi Daily*], 26 June:1.

Xu Guosheng (1998) 'Shanxi jingji luohou shei zhiguo? [Who bears responsibility for Shanxi's economic backwardness?]', *Shanxi fazhan dabao* [*Shanxi Development Herald*], 2 January:4.

Xu Yufang (2001) 'Party slams its door on Jiang's plans', *Asia Times*, 23 October.

You Ji (1998) *China's Enterprise Reform: Changing State/Society Relations after Mao*, London: Routledge.

Young, S. (1989) 'Policy, practice and the private sector in China', *Australian Journal of Chinese Affairs*, 21:57–86.

—— (1991) 'Wealth but not security: attitudes towards private business in China in the 1980s', *Australian Journal of Chinese Affairs*, 25.

—— (1995) *Private Business and Economic Reform in China*, New York: M.E. Sharpe.

Zhang Jihong (1996) 'Jinshang piaozhuang sandabang [The three major exchange shops founded by Shanxi merchants]', *Cang Sang* [*Viccissitudes*], 6:12.

Zhang Xiu and Ji Ping (1996) 'Zhaidi guzhong fuzhong bashe [The development of the food industry is important during recession]', *Shanxi ribao* [*Shanxi Daily*], 8 August:6.

Zhao Shurong (1996) 'Shanxi meitan gongye chengjiu huihuang [Shanxi's coal industry has splendid achievements]', *Shanxi ribao* [*Shanxi Daily*], 15 November: 4.

Zheng Sheng (1996) 'Guanchang [Guanchang (A traditional Shanxi snack)]', *Shenghuo chenbao* [*Morning Life*], 2 August:6.

8

SOCIAL CAPITAL IN CHINA

The meaning of *guanxi* in Chinese business

Gabriele Jacobs, Frank Belschak and Barbara Krug

Introduction

The importance of personal and interpersonal connections in the business world is nowhere disputed. Yet in China these personal connections are supposed to be the most dominant single factor in any (business) activity if the popular Confucianist saying is believed: 'Whom you know is more important than what you know.' In contrast to the West where business relations and ultimately business success are shaped by 'what you know', i.e. technical expertise but also market data such as prices or quality, for the Chinese the notion of *guanxi* in the form of personal relations seems to be all decisive for success.

Usually, the term '*guanxi*' is translated as 'relationship', 'networking', or 'connection', meaning that individuals connect with each other to facilitate the bilateral flow of transaction. It is assumed that *guanxi* implies mutual benefits for both parties. This exchange of favours can be negotiated outside or even in contradiction to formal rules, a feature that makes it tempting to dismiss *guanxi* as a 'particularly corrupt form of neo-feudalism' (Overholt 1993). Though it is hard to evaluate the value of *guanxi* in monetary terms, its use is widespread as surveys from the 1990s show. For example, a survey on 2,000 Chinese from Shanghai and Qingpu (Chu and Ju 1993) showed that 92.4 per cent of the respondents regarded *guanxi* as important for their daily lives. Another survey covering nineteen international companies with stable business relations in China showed that *guanxi* was a necessary condition for a company's financial performance and ultimately long-term business success (Yeung and Tung 1996).

As the following discussion will show, the problem with *guanxi* is not limited to the empirical question of how to operationalize its value. A review of the literature shows that different interpretations of *guanxi* often reflect differences in underlying concepts rather than differences in business environment, let alone differences in behaviour.

166

Guanxi as social capital

One way to put *guanxi* into a theoretical context is to regard it as capital. Some authors start with the Marxian notion of capital as an investment by which a surplus value is produced and captured, a definition no economist would object to (Lin 2001). Later concepts of capital (defined as investment rendering income in the future) include human capital as one component when investment in education, knowledge, and skill is compared to future (life) income (Johnson 1960; Schultz 1961; Becker 1964). The notion of *social capital* follows this line of argument when it is claimed that investment in social relations leads to future returns. Authors such as Bourdieu, Coleman, Erickson, Lin, or Portes argue that individuals engage in networking and social interactions expecting benefits in form of certain favours (Bourdieu 1980; 1986; Coleman 1988; Erickson 1996; Lin 2001; Portes 1998). Membership to a network means, then, having access to and being able to mobilize resources otherwise not, or only at a higher price, available. Generally, four factors can be singled out that explain the asset character of social capital (see Lin 2001):

• *Information*: Networks facilitate the flow of information, in particular on local and tacit knowledge. Knowing people in certain strategic locations and/or positions can provide an individual with useful information s/he otherwise would not have had access to.
• *Influence*: By using their social ties individuals may exert influence on agents who play a crucial role in decision making, thus being able to indirectly influence outcomes instead of being forced to acknowledge any outcome as exogenously given 'constraint'.
• *Social credentials*: Possessing 'social tie' resources in form of reputation, for example, signals that an individual has access to added resources beyond his/her own personal capital, making the individual a much sought-for business partner.
• *Reinforcement*: Finally, social relations reinforce identity and recognition. Being a member of a network is a source of emotional support and social identity and often results in public acknowledgement.

Even though all research on social capital agrees on the points mentioned above, a review of the literature reveals the co-existence of two perspectives (Lin 2001). One stream of literature focuses on the individual level, by treating social capital similar to human capital (for instance Lin and Bian 1991; Burt 1992; 1997). This perspective assumes that individuals make investments in networks and social relations in return for personal benefit. Subsequently, the analysis emphasizes the mechanism that individuals use to invest in social relations, or appropriate the benefits from the resources embedded in social relations. The second perspective regards social capital as a collective asset focusing on the accumulation and employ-ment of social capital by the group in order to achieve better survival chances (for instance Bourdieu 1980; 1986; Coleman 1988; Putnam 1993). The differences in the literature are illustrated in Table 8.1.

The second approach will be used in what follows when it is asked how groups such as potential entrepreneurs/investors or firms invest in and make use of social capital that is assumed to take on a specific feature referred to as *guanxi*. To better understand the Chinese concept of *guanxi* as social capital and its significance in Chinese society the cultural background of *guanxi* – as described in the different approaches – will be shortly summarized. The two (partially) competing models used in empirical studies will be discussed as they form the conceptual base of our analysis that explicitly asked for data by which the relative signifi-cance of the two models can be assessed. The results summarized in the final section show that Chinese entrepreneurs and firms indeed revi-talized *guanxi*, building up a form of *network capitalism* in which, however, networks are assessed by their instrumental value and need to compete.

Cultural foundations of *guanxi*

Culture can be loosely defined as a system of shared values that guides behaviour and helps to construct and attribute meaning. Thus, culture can be expected to at least partly shape the perception and development of social phenomena such as *guanxi*. It is for this reason that Chinese traditional thinking is expected to form the base for social relations when it is for example argued that even Maoist attempts to 'wipe out' remnants

Table 8.1 Theories of capital compared

	Capital	Level of analysis
I Classical Theory of Capital (Ricardo, Marx)	Economic: physical and financial assets	Structural (classes)
II Human Capital (Schultz, Becker)	Human: investment in technical skills and knowledge	Individual
III a. Social Capital (Lin, Burt)	Social: investment in networks	Individual
III b. Social Capital (Bourdieu, Putnam)	Social: joint resources, investment in mutual recognition and acknowledgement	Group/Individual

Source: based on Lin 2001 Chapters 1 and 2

of Confucianism, Buddhism or Taoism were futile (Cheng 1986). The following presents Confucianism as found in the management literature. It is worth emphasizing that by doing so it is not claimed to give a correct overview. On the contrary, any attempt to single out certain patterns of behaviour as being Confucianist carries a strong element of arbitrariness. Whether some cultural elements are Confucianist or not depends first on a consensus of following generations (or academics) to describe them as such, and second on the extent to which (economic) agents behave as predicted. It is to the second claim that the following discussion tries to contribute by systematically searching for evidence for Confucianist behaviour *as defined in the management literature.*

In the literature on *guanxi* Confucius – rather, Kong Fu Ze – who lived around 500 BC plays a dominating role. As in the case of Greek philosophy, his teachings are lessons in practical ethics rather than offering transcendental (religious) explanations. Among the main tenets of Confucian philosophy is the principle of good conduct and correct social relations. Respect for one's elders (and superiors) and loyalty to another form cardinal virtues. Thus, if *guanxi* is a specific form of networking then these factors should form the backbone institutions that can explain the differences between *guanxi* networks and other forms of networks in other cultures.

Nonetheless, because of the difficulty of constructing a direct link between a certain script and actual behaviour, cross-cultural studies[1] attempt to isolate China-specific cultural patterns by developing scales of 'dimensions' which exist in all cultures, yet are differently defined, as for example the dimension 'collectivism–individualism'.

Collectivism

Confucianism sees the family as the core of all social organizations. Moreover, it is claimed that individuals are indistinctly connected with and embedded in a family, a clan, or other social groups so that they do not exist as a separate entity. Children learn at an early age to do nothing that could disturb the harmony within the family to the effect that individual wishes need to be suppressed. Such an understanding of an individual 'self' is in striking contrast to Western individualism, which propagates the 'autonomous self' defined by personal choice or personal achievement. And indeed the empirical studies contrasting these two concepts found that China scores high in terms of collectivism defined as described above (Bond and Hwang 1986; Chinese Cultural Connection 1987; Hofstede 1980; Javidan and House 2001).

The picture needs to be modified however when factors are introduced that allow for explaining the variance within different societies of Confucianist origin such as China and Japan. The Project GLOBE research group around House (House *et al.* 1999; House and Javidan 2001) for example separates an institutional emphasis on collectivism from in-group collectivism. The former refers to the degree by which social institutions such as the state encourage collective action and reward shared use of resources. The latter, in-group collectivism, measures the degree to which individuals take pride in membership of small groups and develop loyalty for the group. This concept allowed the empirical illustration of some of the differences between Japan and China. While Japan, for example, scores high whenever institutions emphasize collectivism, China scores high on the in-group collectivism dimension (House *et al.* 1999; Chinese Cultural Connection 1987).

The dimension of collectivism helps to explain the predominance of *guanxi* in the business sector. Yet, the notion of collectivism must also shape the codes and governance structure by which *guanxi* networks organize themselves.[2] It can be expected for example that in contrast to Western business networks, which need to take into account individual expectations and opportunistic behaviour,[3] Chinese *guanxi*-networks reflect overall group expectations while relying more on loyalty, moral obligation, and norms of reciprocity. The empirical study presented below will discuss some findings which show how *guanxi* in the new business sector is working, i.e. how collectivist (in the sense of cross-cultural studies) the new managers and entrepreneurs are.

Power distance

Confucianist ethics insist on respect, and therefore power, for elders and superiors in return for benevolence, promotion, and protection. As age, gender, formal position, or seniority constitute a hierarchy in Confucianism the idea of social relations between 'equals' must remain alien. To capture the difference in understanding cross-cultural studies employ the dimension of power distance, which measures the degree to which members of groups accept and expect power to be unequally allocated (for instance Hofstede 2001; 1991; House *et al.* 1999). Subsequent empirical studies found evidence in the form of China scoring highly on the power distance dimension (Chinese Cultural Connection 1987; Westwood and Everett 1987; House *et al.* 1999; Javidan and House 2001) meaning they assume (or leave unquestioned) that the old, the senior, or those positioned in higher ranks can command more authority.

For the development of *guanxi* in the business sector it can therefore be assumed that network activities are co-ordinated by individuals 'of authority' rather than by contracts, statutes or laws. To put it polemically, while personal power is accepted institutionalized power remains an empty concept.

Long-term orientation

In order to catch the Confucianist emphasis on patience, perseverance, and thrift in obtaining long-term goals differences in time preferences need to be conceptualized (Hofstede 1991; Hofstede and Bond 1988). The literature developed the dimension of monochronical and polychronical cultures (see Redding 1980; Hall 1983). This distinction allows claiming that Confucianism leads to a polychronic view of time in which the emphasis is laid on a flexible use of time in order to adjust actions and keep in line with changes in the environment. Such a concept of time has to be seen in contrast to the Western monochronic concept that looks for the smallest time unit that (still) allows fulfilling separate tasks by separate individuals. The specialization gain (or division of labour) argument is not seen as being able to contribute to the long-term survival of a group in the Chinese view.

The long-term orientation implies a future-oriented mentality, which needs to be contrasted with a static, tradition-oriented view. One research group therefore designed a questionnaire that explicitly focused on future orientation and 'work dynamics' (Chinese Cultural Connection 1987). The studies found China to score high on a dimension of long-term perspective and future orientation to the surprise of those who regarded China as a prominent example for a stagnant society (Hofstede 1991; 1993; House *et al.* 1999; Javidan and House 2001).

The long-term orientation can explain why *guanxi* relations are built and maintained by continuous, long-term associations and interactions in China. As said before *guanxi* is regarded as a 'stock' from which the group and its member can expect monetary and non-monetary income flows in the long run. The long-term orientation also explains why the internal debit–credit ratio between individual members is rarely balanced as individual members accept a long delay of gratification. This is in contrast to the Western concepts where business networks are built around short-term notions of reciprocity and overall benefits more reflecting spot markets than the build up of a joint capital stock.[4]

Performance orientation

The literature attempts to capture the Confucianist emphasis on scholarship, hard work, and education by the dimension of Confucian dynamism (Hofstede and Bond 1988). This concept is closely related to Western capitalist concepts of performance and achievement orientation; or, in psychology, to the concept of a *need for achievement* (McClelland 1961) where it is shown that the need to achieve is related to job success on the individual level and to economic growth on the collective (societal) level. Integrating these latter approaches, recent cross-cultural studies

171

introduced, therefore, the dimension of performance orientation in cross-cultural comparisons.[5] In empirical studies Confucian societies score high on the dimension of performance orientation, meaning that these societies encourage and reward performance and excellence (Javidan and House 2001).

Nonetheless, these findings led to the formulation of a second competing model for *guanxi*. If performance matters then *guanxi* networks can be explained by their instrumental value. In this case *guanxi* networks are exchange networks whose existence and maintenance depend on gains, sufficiently high to make the continuation of the relationship worthwhile for all, or most, participants. As good personal relations, or even family ties, cannot substitute indefinitely for poor product quality for instance, relationships are not sacrosanct and will be given up should the returns prove to be too small: 'In other words, no *guanxi* connection can exist in the absence of utilitarian gains to the Chinese business partner' (Yeung and Tung 1996). As the following empirical results will show, it is the performance orientation which explains why in Chinese business life *guanxi* relations are only a necessary, but not a sufficient condition for business success (see for instance Lever-Tracy 1996).

Reciprocity

'The Chinese believe that reciprocity of actions (favour and hatred, reward and punishment) between man and man, and indeed between man and supernatural beings, should be as certain as a cause-and-effect relationship' (Yang 1957). In contrast to Western countries, though, this reciprocity does not need to be immediate; rather, favours are regarded as (social) capital and are saved and activated in times of need. The Chinese concept of reciprocity therefore is highly influenced by and should be understood in the light of the long-term time orientation as described above.

As argued elsewhere (for instance Yang 1994; Bian 2001) this concept of reciprocity determines both the start of personal relations as well as the functioning of networks. One common way to establish relations is by tendering favours like gift-giving, lavish banquets, overseas trips, or sponsoring. When a favour has been granted – and accepted by the invitee (e.g. a gift or an invitation to a banquet has been received) – boundaries between the persons are symbolically broken down and *guanxi* connections are established. This has to be seen in contrast to Western customs where joint dinners do not establish obligations, and where reciprocity refers to rather short-term exchange of favours.

The findings of the cultural and cross-cultural studies with respect to China are summarized in Table 8.2. The organization and governance of business relations in the emerging private sector should reflect at least some of these features. For example, while it was argued in some preceding

Table 8.2 Empirical findings of Chinese cultural patterns

Dimension	Empirical findings for China
Collectivism	• individual interest subjugated to group interest • loyalty to groups rather than institutions
Power distance	• co-ordination by individuals rather than institutions • acknowledgement of inequality in power
Long-term orientation	• flexible use of time to adjust for changes in the environment • networks as 'stock of capital' rather than spot markets
Performance orientation	• social rewards for performance and excellence
Reciprocity	• gift-giving as dominant form for establishing contact • mutual moral obligations to be balanced in the long run

chapters[6] that scarcity of resources forces individuals to form groups, partnerships, or alliances for establishing firms, this argument cannot be used for supporting the claim that collectivist norms form the base for the industrial structure of the private sector. What is needed is rather to show that individual agents want (or demand) groups to form the core of private firms and private business relations independent from the availability of resources. Moreover, if Chinese entrepreneurs are willing to spend resources in order to form *guanxi* then they can do so either because they cherish sentimental ties, or because they expect groups to perform better when compared to acting alone within the frame of markets, laws, or political bureaucracies. Which motivation dominates the individuals in the nascent private sector was at the core of the following empirical analysis.

Models of *guanxi*

The existing literature distinguishes two models of *guanxi*: *guanxi* as a form of extended familial ties, and *guanxi* as a form of instrumental ties.

Guanxi as the web of extended family connections

Based on the Confucianist notion of the family as the core of individual and social life, one group of authors define *guanxi* as the web of extended familial ties and obligations (see for instance Liang 1986; Fried 1969; Yang 1965). The basic argument of this model is that in China family relations are ethical in nature, thus combining both sentiment and obligation. These two elements complement and reinforce each other, encouraging co-operation while inhibiting confrontation. It is further assumed that certain groups where people are connected by sentiments work 'as if' families, thus employing the same form of sentiments and moral obligation. As Fei has already argued in his theory of structural differentiation, 'face' is based on sentiments and closeness, and therefore mostly earned in circles of people close to each other (Fei 1992). It is for this reason that the Chinese use the standards and codes of familial sentiments and obligations in interaction with persons they want to have a deeper/closer relationship with, or whom they want to give face.

Empirical support to this theory can be found in studies using historical data. One example demonstrates that the organization of county seats before the 1949 Communist revolution was based on familial and kinship obligations (Fried 1969), another could prove that this feature prevailed also in the period after the agricultural collectivization campaign (Yang 1965). As the contribution by Goodman in this book illustrates,[7] familial obligations and sentiments still or once more shape Chinese communities and villages, while the extended literature on overseas Chinese businesses shows that the family was (and is) at the core of private entrepreneurship.[8]

Fulfilling the moral and ethical obligations to 'pseudofamilies' such as groups of friends or *guanxi* networks improves one's reputation, or 'face' (Lin 1989; King 1985; 1988). It can therefore be regarded as social capital when it grants a person the capacity to mobilize social resources accumulated and stored by the *guanxi* networks. As studies on the 1980s show, it is common in Chinese business circles to work to gain a high reputation (Cheng and Rosett 1989).

To sum up, this group of authors suggests that *guanxi* is based on familial obligations and sentiments. These ties can be extended to other social relations when to achieve a high reputation implies fulfilling the moral obligations known from familial relationships. In turn, a high reputation within a group offers access to social resources.

Guanxi as instrumental exchange networks

The second model assumes *guanxi* to be an exchange network defined by its functional value and the specific mode of reciprocity employed for co-ordinating individual actions (see for instance Jacobs 1979; Hwang 1987; Yang 1994).

The relational base of *guanxi* in this model is not limited to the family or close friends. Instead the network can use any range of social and work-related connections, most commonly a shared past at the base of the personal relation. Thus, for example, partnerships in which people who had gone to the same school, served in the Army together, or are known from the work unit, form the core of entrepreneurship in the private business sector.[9]

As the contribution of Goodman and Duckett in the preceding chapters show, the models are not mutually exclusive.[10] They partially overlap when sentimental ties help to increase the functional value of networks. According to Redding the two models did not always co-exist but rather indicate a shift (from familial to particular instrumental ties), a point that deserves further attention (Redding 1990). One interpretation would be to see the shift as the result of the egalitarian concept of Communist ideology. Furthermore, the policy of the Cultural Revolution where some family members were exposed to public humiliation and the subsequent conflicts within Chinese families might also have contributed to an erosion of the 'trust' base within families and close social groups to the effect that friends are trusted more than cousins. Ironically, seen in this light, the Cultural Revolution might have contributed to the development of *guanxi* networks based on instrumental value.[11] The shift from using familial (sentimental) ties networks to instrumental ties networks was also confirmed in one study that looked into the ways that the Chinese search for jobs (Bian 1997) in the last years.

In contrast to the first model, reputation is earned by keeping promises and by returning favours. Likewise, face is not gained by fulfilling moral and ethical obligations but by following the reciprocity norms, while *guanxi* capital is based on mutual trust and loyalty between the favour exchanging parties (Yang 1994; Hwang 1987). The differences between the two models are summarized in Table 8.3.

Empirical implications of the two *guanxi* models

The two models invite the comparison of their different sets of assumptions for explaining the behaviour in the new private sector.

With respect to the establishment and operation of private firms the familial ties model would expect individual entrepreneurs to search and recruit partners from a pool of people bound together by family bonds,

Table 8.3 Comparison of the two *guanxi* models

	Model of extended family ties	Model of particular instrumental ties
Relational orientation	Sentimental ties	Instrumental ties
Relational base	Pseudo-family	Any group but mostly one of people sharing a 'past'
Source of *guanxi* capital	Closeness and sentiments	Mutual trust and loyalty
Social mechanism	Fulfilling moral obligations	Adhering to reciprocity norms

or close friendship. The model also expects that embarking on or maintaining business relations depends on the perceived contribution such a relation offers to the coherence of and the sentimental ties within the group.

In contrast the instrumental ties model expects the recruitment of partners following expected returns in form of on-going co-operation. Aside from the relative value of input each partner brings with him/her, trustworthiness is seen as a decisive factor without which no co-operation rent can be appropriated. Reputation defined as reliability in behaviour exhibited in the past is regarded as a close enough proxy for assuming (reciprocity) abiding behaviour in the future 'joint venture'. The model also expects business relations to be evaluated in terms of expected overall returns and the individual share on overall outcome. Unsatisfying overall results will lead to an end of the relationship by one or more partners, without, however, threatening the social coherence of the network.

The following presents an attempt to look for data that allow testing the two sets of assumptions derived from the models. The results must remain preliminary, taking into account the limited size of the data set. Yet the findings are conclusive enough to invite further systematic and empirical research, by warning us of the shortfalls in explaining the notion of *guanxi* by relying on general reflections only.

Data collection and analysis

As the general outline of the data set was already described in the introduction, some reminders and additional remarks will suffice here. To investigate the meaning and significance of *guanxi* in Chinese business relations two hundred interviews were conducted with Chinese entrepreneurs between 1995 and 2001. As described in Chapter 1, exploratory open interviews in the first years were followed by a semi-structured standardized questionnaire developed in 1999 and based on the results of the open interviews. The data were collected in three Chinese provinces, namely, Shanxi in north China, and Zhejiang and Jiangsu in the south from 1999 to 2001. Only private firms were included in the sample as only those are relatively free to choose business partners according to their ideas about business relations and *guanxi*. In the end the final sample consisted of seventy-four private firms that met the requirements and participated in the interviews.

The interviews made use of two different sets of data. First, the life history and the governance structure of the respondent's firm was collected by means of open questions. Second, a questionnaire consisting of closed questions was developed to further investigate the governance structure and configuration around firms.

To ensure that not only urban but also village firms, and not only firms working in traditional sectors but also firms working in modern sectors, were included in the sample, strict selection criteria were introduced. Thus, firms were stratified by size, location, and business sector. Despite these efforts the sample selection seems to be biased to the extent that the respondents' firms were selected with the help of certain institutions, namely, the Party, the academic network, banks (in Shanxi), corporate networks (in Zhejiang), and local tax offices (in Jiangsu), the latter being a fertile source of information as taxes are mainly paid by private firms, and therefore tax registers deliver an extensive overview of the private sector.

The analysis of the data made use of both qualitative and quantitative methods. The open questions focused on a sequence of events, where 'events' referred to qualitative distinctions as defined in the conceptual set-up. Such events were the establishment of a company, i.e. those activities that preceded the registration of the firms or the beginning of production, changes in the ownership structure, expansion beyond the local nexus, diversification, or mergers.[12]

The questionnaire that followed the open interview consisted of a combination of open questions and standardized sets of closed questions. It focused on the configuration of Chinese firms including their business partners, i.e. the existence and composition of *guanxi* networks. On the other hand, it also explored the factors Chinese entrepreneurs considered to be important for establishing and maintaining their business relations. The closed questions were used for quantitative data analyses; the answers to the open questions were categorized for further interpretation and analysis.

Results

Will the future business sector be dominated by the Chinese family firm, will other property rights and organizational structures try to copy the set of norms that govern the family business, or will Chinese firms be organized around networks that promise functional value? To give a preliminary answer the following aspects of business relations in and around firms were singled out for study: the establishment and internal structure of Chinese firms, the establishment and maintaining of business relations, and the resolution of conflicts between firms.

The internal structure of firms

The internal structure of a firm offers some insights about the parties involved in the start-up of the firm and the kind of entrepreneurship that marks the beginning of the new private sector. The familial ties model expects an ownership of a new firm that is based on a family business or groups of similar sentimental ties, such as close friends.

Table 8.4 shows that three-quarters of the firms were established by collective action, yet only in 12.7 per cent of the cases was it a family that co-ordinated collective action. Another 18.3 per cent of firms were established by friends, so that sentimental ties cannot be excluded. However, almost half of the firms (43.6 per cent) were established by private investors, indicating that investment interests rather than sentimental ties prompted entrepreneurship.

Taking into account the limited range of skills within one family in post-socialist China, it cannot come as a surprise that the family is no longer the dominating entrepreneur, as it is severely limited by its small pool of talent and skill. The family traditionally was also the institution where savings were pooled in order to start a business. After all, if all or most resources were in the family hand, the firm would still be regarded a family business even if one family did not occupy major managerial positions. Yet this also is not the case: only 27.1 per cent of the respondents agreed that their family was the source of funds for capital assets when the firm was first set up, whereas 72.9 per cent denied this statement. Thus, the assumption that the family in China functions as a surrogate capital or labour market is not supported by the data.[13]

The conclusion that the family's role as an economic agent has diminished in the new private sector (and is low in comparison to the private sector in Taiwan, Hong Kong or overseas communities) gains significance when the next findings are included: the family also does not function as a risk-mitigating institution on which one could fall back in time of need (see Table 8.5).[14] Only one entrepreneur answered in the affirmative when asked whether he would turn to his family in time of need, merely 16.2 per cent of the respondents relied on help of their friends, i.e. some 'sentimental' ties. On the other hand, 52.9 per cent showed confidence in being

Table 8.4 Ownership of respondents' firms

Answer	Frequency	Percentage
Respondent alone	18	25.4
Respondents' family	9	12.7
Respondent with friends	13	18.3
Group of individual investors	16	22.5
Collective, village	2	2.8
Collective plus private investors	3	4.2
Private/state firm	9	12.7
Confused	1	1.4
Total	71	100.0

Table 8.5 Entrepreneurs' choices of sources of help

Answers to the question:
In the event of a serious problem or an emergency, which individuals or
organizations would you expect to come to your help?

Answer		Frequency	Percentage
Banks		36	52.9
	mentioned first	32	47.0
	mentioned second	4	5.9
Friends		11	16.2
	mentioned first	6	8.8
	mentioned second	5	7.4
Local government, Party, 'state'		5	7.4
	mentioned first	4	5.9
	mentioned second	1	1.5
Industrial & commerce associations		2	2.9
Shareholders		2	2.9
No need		2	2.9
Nobody		2	2.9
Company in same sector		2	2.9
Mother company		2	2.9
Employees		2	2.9
Court		1	1.5
Family (Family members)		1	1.5
Total		**68**	**100.0**

helped by banks, indicating that in this case the market mechanisms have replaced old family or friendship bonds. The last point should be seen as a warning to conclude that friends have become the substitute for the family as the backbone institution of *guanxi*. After all, a partnership with friends can reflect sentimental ties or instrumental ties, a point taken up in the discussion of the results on business relations.

A look at the life history of firms shows that with increasing age and expansion of a firm family ownership and control decline further. As is argued in the contribution by Hendrischke, family firms remain in the traditional small-scale retail or service sector.

In short, the data offer evidence for the instrumental ties model. Supportive evidence can be found in the contributions by Duckett and Goodman, who demonstrate that privatization is dominated by the transfer of control rights from local authorities to a manager, i.e. somebody who can credibly promise to turn the local industrial assets into a profitable company. Successful managers were offered 'management-buy-out' schemes. As further studies confirm, some took complete control, the majority, however, preferred a corporate solution[15] in which the local government, or other state institutions were offered minority shares. By doing so the managers want to ensure future benign treatment of these agencies in the form of favourable taxation, complementary infrastructure around the production site, or access to the information network available within the state bureaucracy.[16] This economic behaviour can clearly be understood as reciprocal and being motivated by instrumental ideas ('tit for tat'). Entrepreneurs choose their partners for the resources they control and the contribution they can make in the operation of firms rather than for sentimental reasons.

The establishment of business relations

Guanxi is claimed to be crucial when it comes to start a business relationship, let's say finding a supplier, manager, or customer. Trust in this case functions as a selection device for economic agents when it leads to the creation of a pool of trustworthy partners that is monitored by a guanxi network (Yeung and Tung 1996; Krug and Hendrischke 2002). Table 8.6 asks for a modified answer with respect to the role of the family.

As Table 8.7 shows, price, quality and the reliability of the business partner are the decisive factor in business relations. Comparing the family and personal connections with other factors in choosing and maintaining business relations shows that family and personal connections score significantly lower.

Obviously, managers and entrepreneurs are motivated by economic calculations rather than by sentimental considerations. Paired samples t-tests summarized in Table 8.7 show that all differences between economic and social factors are highly significant at a level of p<0.00.

In this case too, the findings indicate that the guanxi model of instrumental ties offers higher explanatory value. Chinese entrepreneurs regard sentimental value a poor substitute for too high prices, unsatisfying quality

Table 8.6 Entrepreneurs' views on the importance of family connections

Answers to the question:
Family connections with a wide range of people are crucial to the success of the firm

Answer	Frequency	Percentage
Strongly disagree	10	27.8
Disagree	15	41.7
Slightly disagree	2	5.6
Not sure	4	11.1
Slightly agree	3	8.3
Strongly agree	2	5.6
Total	36	100.0

Table 8.7 Factors important for firms in choosing a business relationship

Variables	Mean	Standard deviation	n
Price	2.4	0.66	55
Quality	2.8	0.42	45
Reliability	2.6	0.57	58
Personal recommendation	1.8	0.79	62
Family connection	1.1	0.45	42
Pre-existing contacts	1.5	0.62	61

Differences between economic and social factors

Pairs	t-value	(2-tailed sig.)
Personal recommendation vs. price / quality / reliability	3.9 / 7.6 / 6.3	(0.00)
Family connection vs. price / quality / reliability	8.8 / 13.5 / 13.2	(0.00)
Pre-existing contacts vs. price / quality / reliability	6.3 / 10.4 / 9.5	(0.00)

Note: scales range from 1 = 'not important' to 3 = 'very important'

or unreliability. If the instrumental ties model explains better the configuration of the private sector, then it can be expected that social mechanisms
such as mutual trust and reciprocity will be employed in business relations.

Maintaining business relations

As described above, trust in a business partner's willingness to pay back
favours and acknowledge reciprocity is an essential factor in the model
of instrumental ties. As Table 8.8 shows, Chinese entrepreneurs indeed
consider social factors such as 'mutual trust' and 'mutual co-operation'
to be as important as commercial interests, such as 'prompt delivery and
payment' while once more personal contact and family connections were
dismissed as less crucial.

In particular, 'prompt delivery and payment' supports the assumption
of the instrumental ties model that utilitarian gains are an essential part
of *guanxi* connections, which also claims that mutual trust is the crucial
means to assure reciprocity norms being honoured. Mutual co-operation,
on the other hand, reflects the willingness to invest in joint activities rather
than trying to maximize individual profit to the detriment of the partnership. Thus, unsurprisingly in a further question 77.8 per cent of the
respondents agreed with the statement that they trusted their business
partners not to take unfair advantage should the opportunity arise; only
5.6 per cent disagreed with the statement.

Table 8.8 Requirements for the success of a business relationship

Variables	Mean	Standard deviation	n
Mutual co-operation	6.2	0.7	36
Mutual trust	6.3	0.7	36
Prompt delivery and payment	6.1	1.2	36
Family connections	2.5	1.7	36
Personal contact	4.6	1.5	36

Differences between instrumental and sentimental factors

Pairs	t-value	(2-tailed sig.)
Personal contact vs. co-operation/ trust/delivery and payment	–5.6 / –6.3 / –4.8	(0.00)
Family connection vs. co-operation/ trust/delivery and payment	–11.4 / –11.7 / –10.9	(0.00)

Note: scales range from 1 = strongly disagree to 7 = strongly agree

Abiding by business agreements

Trust is an evasive concept so long as it cannot be operationalized in a way that respondents see their business practices described. The empirical study assumed that trust depends crucially on promises kept and agreements honoured, so the following question was posed: why do Chinese entrepreneurs abide by business agreements? The two models expect firms or business partners to do so for different reasons. In the familial ties model agreements are honoured out of moral obligations; in the instrumental ties model reciprocity serves as the crucial mechanism.

Respondents were also asked whether they would take legal action. There were two reasons for including questions about the use of contracts and courts in the questionnaire. First, part of the economic literature claims that *guanxi* is a transitory phenomenon that will disappear with better functioning markets and courts (see Guthrie 1998). Second, after the Chinese government has made the use of written contracts obligatory, and invested heavily in the legal infrastructure, legal redress offers a viable alternative to the *guanxi*-forms of agreement enforcement. Table 8.9 summarizes the reasons given for abiding by agreements.

The institution on which the honouring of agreements depends in the familial ties model, namely friendship and family, are not the main reason why the respondents abide by agreements. The social mechanism of the instrumental ties model, i.e. trust and reputation, fare better when compared to all other alternatives as Table 8.9 shows.[17]

The results might be seen as a warning to those who claim that 'traditional' institutions will be replaced by court ordering – or that *guanxi* networks will wither away and be replaced by contractual relations.

Table 8.9 Reasons for abiding by agreements with a business partner

Variables	Mean	Standard deviation	n
Threat of legal redress	4.9	2.0	36
Firm's reputation	6.1	1.1	36
Personal reputation	6.1	0.9	36
Honour	5.7	1.5	36
Friendship	4.5	1.2	36
Family connection	2.5	1.5	36
Need for future business	5.6	1.2	36

Differences between various reasons for abiding by agreements

Pairs	t-value	(2-tailed sig.)
Honour vs. family/friendship/ threat of legal redress	9.6 / 4.3 / 2.5	(0.05)
Personal reputation vs. family/ friendship/threat of legal redress	13.0 / 5.4 / 3.5	(0.00)
Firm's reputation vs. family/ friendship/threat of legal redress	12.5 / 5.6 / 3.7	(0.00)

Note: scales range from 1 = 'strongly disagree' to 7 = 'strongly agree'

Conclusion

The aim of this paper was to explore to what extent the concept of Confucianism as found in the management studies literature can help to explain the development of the new private sector in China. It was assumed that success in China as elsewhere depends on the mobilization and use of financial, human *and* social capital. Social capital is shaped by culture, i.e. those inherited institutions, norms and customs by which people interact with each other. According to this literature social capital based on Confucianist norms is called *guanxi*. With Confucianism offering a menu of different norms and values, the challenge is to identify those institutions, which shape *guanxi* in general, and specifically *guanxi* in business relations. A review of the literature and empirical studies shows that compared to other countries the Chinese are collectivist (with respect to groups), performance oriented long-term planners who accept differences in power and authority mitigated by acknowledged obligations as defined by reciprocity norms.

As these findings refer to the general attributes of the Chinese and their interaction, the next step is to 'test' how well these empirical results can be used for explaining business relations in the emerging private sector. Depending on the different weights attached to the different dimensions of culturally shaped behaviour, two competing models dominate the literature, the familial ties model and the instrumental ties model. With the help of the data set available the question was posed: which of the two models fits better – and ultimately, what weight ought to be attached to the five dimensions (collectivism, power distance, long-term orientation, performance orientation and reciprocity) in the case of business relations?

The preliminary empirical results give a warning not to assume that social capital in China is built on family ties or friendship. The empirical results also provide first evidence that private firms working in the new competitive environment will dismiss familial and sentimental ties as a way to co-ordinate individual action. When it is observed that the sentimental ties model does not fit, or fits less and less, to conclude that contractual relations and competition are the 'natural' substitute is premature. As was shown above another form of *guanxi*, as described in the instrumental ties model, might be used instead. In this case the functional value of networking assessed by its long-term performance, i.e. expected survivability, is at the core of network formation. Instead of a *guanxi* model based on sentimental and familial networks, expected outcome decides over size and range of activity. In short networking becomes a business activity. To claim that this indicates a 'crowding out' of Confucianist values is as premature as to claim that the sentimental ties model is thrown into the dustbin of history. To start with the latter, there is enough illustrative evidence to take the assumption seriously that business networks start as networks linked by sentimental ties. It is up to future research to explore whether networks based on familial and sentimental ties offer the 'natural' scaffolding for any form of network, or whether specific situational constraints decide which form of *guanxi* is used in which context.

On the other hand, 'rational' behaviour, or using an economic calculus is not a contradiction of Confucianist values, which as was argued above honour performance and long-term planning. As long as network members judge networks in terms of performance to the extent that networks need to compete for members, overall efficiency is secured. There is no need to switch to unknown contractual relations. On the contrary, as further illustrative evidence suggests, *guanxi* networks might hijack the use of contracts to strengthen internal and external relations. But this again points to another research agenda.

Notes

1 Aside from the seminal work by Hofstede (1980, 1991, 1993), the studies by Javidan and House (2001) and House *et al.* (1999) which developed the Hofstede instrumentarium further, form the base for what follows.
2 See for example the contribution by Krug and Pólos, Chapter 4.
3 A most stimulating analysis of the trade off between co-operation and 'self-interest' can be found in the economic analysis of the 'commons'; see Ostrom 1990.
4 See Hendrischke, Chapter 5.

5 Foremost the Project GLOBE (e.g. House, *et al.* 1999).
6 See Chapters 3 and 4 by Krug and Mehta, and Krug and Pólos. A similar line of argument can be found in Chapter 5 by Hendrischke.
7 See Goodman, Chapter 7.
8 See the literature quoted in Note 4 in Hendrischke, Chapter 5.
9 See Krug and Mehta, Chapter 3, Krug and Pólos, Chapter 4. Other examples that show some of the partners and government officials can be found in Goodman, Chapter 7 and Duckett, Chapter 6.
10 See Duckett, Chapter 6 and Goodman, Chapter 7.
11 And indeed, one study (Walder 1986) identified three kinds of instrumental ties to shape work life in Communist China under Mao. Yang in her defence of *guanxi* as a major agent in the new business sector in China, makes a similar argument (Yang 2002).
12 This procedure is called an event-history design by Carroll and Hannan, who developed it for explaining the changes in the organizational forms of (Western) firms; see for example Carroll and Hannan 2000.
13 See the literature on the Chinese family business in the Introduction, Chapter 1.
14 For all three aspects – the family as an institution for pooling saving, offering different human skills and serving as a risk mitigating institution – see Wong 1985.
15 The different features of this development can be found for example in Ding 2000; Lin and Zhu Tian 2001; Krug 1997; Rozelle *et al.* 2000; or Wank 1995; Wank 1996.
16 Another strong reason for accepting state agencies as shareholders was that by this means the unspecified claims on residual profit could be converted into shares to be compensated by dividends; see Hendrischke, Chapter 5.
17 These findings are in accordance with results of other studies in Confucian societies – China, Japan, South Korea, and Hong Kong – that showed that the establishment of institutional law did not displace the reliance on social institutions like networks (e.g. Yeung and Tung 1996).

References

Becker, G.S. (1964) *Human Capital*, Chicago: University of Chicago Press.

Benedict, R. (1947) *The Chrysanthemum and the Sword*, London: Secker and Warburg.

Bian, Y. (1997) 'Bringing strong ties back in: indirect connection, bridges, and job search in China', *American Sociological Review*, 62:266–85.

—— (2001) 'Guanxi Capital and Social Eating in Chinese Cities: Theoretical Models and Empirical Analyses', in N. Lin, K. Cook, and R.S. Burt (eds) *Social Capital. Theory and Research*, New York: Aldine de Gruyter:275–95.

Bond, M.H. and Hwang, K.K. (1986) 'The Social Psychology of Chinese People', in M.H. Bond (ed.) *The Psychology of the Chinese People*, Hong Kong: Oxford University Press:213–66.

Bourdieu, P. (1980) 'Le capital social: notes provisoires', *Actes de la Recherche en Sciences Sociales*, 3:2–3.

—— (1986) 'The Forms of Capital', in J.G. Richardson (ed.) *Handbook of Theory and Research for the Sociology of Education*, Westport: Greenwood Press: 241–58.

Burt, R.S. (1992) *Structural Holes: The Social Structure of Competition*, Cambridge, MA: Harvard University Press.

—— (1997) 'The contingent value of social capital', *Administrative Science Quarterly*, 42:339–65.

Carroll, G.R. and Hannan, M.T. (2000) *The Demography of Corporations and Industries*, Princeton: Princeton University Press.

Cheng, Y. (1986) 'Characteristics and values of Chinese traditional culture', *Social Sciences in China*, autumn:25–30.

Cheng, L. and Rosett, A. (1989) 'Contract with a Chinese face: socially embedded factors in the transformation from hierarchy to market, 1978–1989', *Journal of Chinese Law*, 5(2):143–244.

Chinese Culture Connection (1987) 'Chinese values and the search for culture-free dimensions of culture', *Journal of Cross-Cultural Psychology*, 18(2): 143–64.

Chu, G.C. and Ju, Y. (1993) *The Great Wall in Ruins*, New York: State University of New York Press.

Coleman, J.S. (1988) 'Social capital in the creation of human capital', *American Journal of Sociology*, 94:95–121.

Ding, X. L. (2000) 'The illicit asset stripping of Chinese state firms', *The China Journal*, 43:1–29.

Erickson, B.H. (1996) 'Culture, class and connections', *American Journal of Sociology*, 102(1):217–51.

Fei, X. (1992) *From the Soil, the Foundations of Chinese Society*, Berkeley: University of California Books.

Fried, M.H. (1969) *Fabric of Chinese Society: A Study of the Social Life in a Chinese County Seat*, New York: Octagon Books.

Guthrie, D. (1998) 'The declining significance of guanxi in China's economic transition', *The China Quarterly*, 154:254–82.

Hall, E.T. (1983) *The Dance of Life*, New York: Doubleday.

Hofstede, G. (1980) *Culture's Consequences: International Differences in Work-related Values*, Beverly Hills: Sage.

—— (1991) *Cultures and Organizations: Software of the Mind*, London: McGraw-Hill.

—— (1993) 'Cultural constraints in management theories', *Academy of Management Executive*, 7(1):81–94.

—— (2001) *Culture's Consequences: International Differences in Work-related Values*, London: Sage.

Hofstede, G. and Bond, M.H. (1988) 'The Confucius connection. From cultural roots to economic growth', *Organizational Dynamics* 16:4–21.

House, R. J., Hanges, P.J., Ruiz-Quintanilla, S.A., Dorfman, P.W., Javidan, M., Dickson, M., Gupta, V. and GLOBE Coordinating Team (1999) 'Cultural Influences on Leadership and Organizations: Project GLOBE', in W.H. Mobley (ed.) *Advances in Global Leadership* (1), Stanford: JAI Press:171–233.

Hwang, K. (1987) 'Face and favor: the Chinese power game', *American Journal of Sociology*, 92(4):944–74.

Jacobs, J.B. (1979) 'A preliminary model of particularistic ties in Chinese political alliances: Kan-Ch'ing and Kuan-Hsi in a rural Taiwanese township', *China Quarterly*, 78:237–73.

Javidan, M. and House, R.J. (2001) 'Cultural acumen for the global manager: lessons from project GLOBE', *Organizational Dynamics*, 29(4):289–305.

Johnson, H.G. (1960) 'The political economy of opulence', *Canadian Journal of Economics and Political Science*, 26:552–64.

King, A.Y.C. (1985) 'The Individual and Group in Confucianism: A Relational Perspective', in D.J. Munro (ed.) *Individualism and Holism: Studies in Confucian and Taoist Values*, Ann Arbor: Center for Chinese Studies, University of Michigan:57–70.

—— (1988) 'Analysis of Renqing in Interpersonal Relations', in K. Yang (ed.) *Psychology of the Chinese*, Taipei, Taiwan: Guihuan Press:319–45.

Krug, B. (1997) 'Privatisation in China: Something to Learn From?', in H. Giersch (ed.) *Privatisation at the Turn of the Century*, Berlin: Springer Verlag:269–93.

Krug, B. and Hendrischke, H. (2002) 'China's new private sector: an evolutionary model', paper for the Conference on New Models on Management and New Mangers in Asia, Fontainebleau: INSEAD Euro-Asia Centre.

Lever-Tracy, C. (1996) 'Diaspora capitalism and the homeland: Australian Chinese networks into China', *Diaspora*, 5(2):239–73.

Liang, S. (1986) *The Essential Meanings of Chinese Culture*, Hong Kong: Zheng Zhong Press.

Lin, N. (1989) 'Chinese family structure and Chinese society', *Bulletin of the Institute of Ethnology*, 65:382–99.

—— (2001) *Social Capital: A Theory of Social Structure and Action*, New York: Cambridge University Press.

Lin, N. and Bian, Y. (1991) 'Getting ahead in urban China', *American Journal of Sociology*, 97(3):657–88.

Lin, Y. and Zhu Tian (2001) 'Ownership restructuring in Chinese state industry: an analysis of evidence on initial organizational changes', *The China Quarterly*, 166:305–41.

McClelland, D.C. (1961) *The Achieving Society*, Princeton: Van Nostrand.

—— (1985) *Human Motivation*, Glenview: Scott, Foresman.

Ostrom, E. (1990) *Governing the Commons*, Cambridge: Cambridge University Press.

Overholt, W. (1993) *China: The Next Economic Superpower*, New York: Norton.

Portes, A. (1998) 'Social capital: its origins and applications in modern sociology', *Annual Review of Sociology*, 22:1–24.

Putnam, R.D. (1993) *Making Democracy Work: Civic Traditions in Modern Italy*, Princeton: Princeton University Press.

Redding, G. (1980) 'Cognitions as an aspect of culture and its relation to management processes: an exploratory view of the Chinese case', *Journal of Management Studies*, 17:127–48.

—— (1990) *The Spirit of Chinese Capitalism*, New York: Walter de Gruyter Press.

Rozelle, S., Park, A., Huang, J. and Xin, H.H. (2000) 'Bureaucrat to entrepreneur: the changing role of the state in China's grain economy', *Economic Development and Cultural Change*, 48(2):227–52.

Schultz, T.W. (1961) 'Investment in human capital', *The American Economic Review*, 1:1–17.

Walder, A.G. (1986) *Communist Neo-Traditionalism: Work and Authority in Chinese Industry*, Berkeley: University of California Press.

Wank, D. (1995) 'Private business, bureaucracy, and political alliance in a Chinese city', *Australian Journal of Chinese Affairs*, 33:55–71.

—— (1996) 'The institutional process of market clientelism: guanxi and private business in a South China city', *The China Quarterly*, 3:820–38.

Westwood, R.I. and Everett, J. (1987) 'Culture's consequences: a methodology for comparative management studies in South East Asia?', *Asia-Pacific Journal of Management*, 4(3):187–202.

Wilson, R.W., Wilson, A.A. and Greenblatt, S.L. (1972) *Value Change in Chinese Society*, New York: Praeger.

Wong, S.L. (1985) 'The Chinese family firm: a model', *British Journal of Sociology*, 36:58–72.

Yang, C.K. (1965) *Chinese Communist Society: The Family and the Village*, Cambridge, MA: MIT Press.

Yang, L. (1957) 'The Concept of Pao as a Basis for Social Relations in China', in J.K. Fairbank (ed.) *Chinese Thought and Institutions*, Chicago: University of Chicago Press:291–309.

Yang, M.M. (1994) *Gifts, Favors, and Banquets: The Art of Social Relationships in China*, Ithaca, New York: Cornell University Press.

—— (2002) 'The resilience of guanxi in its new developments: a critique of some new guanxi scholarship, *The China Quarterly*, 170:459–76.

Yeung, I.Y.M. and Tung, R.L. (1996) 'Achieving business success in Confucian societies: the importance of guanxi (connections)', *Organizational Dynamics*, 25(2):54–65.

9

THE (SOMETIMES) RATIONAL APPROACH TO EMPIRICAL RESEARCH IN CHINA

A personal account

Barbara Krug

Imagine a group of social scientists – half of whom are Chinese, half not – sitting in a hotel lounge with forty minutes to fill before the next interview starts at 2 p.m. Inevitably one of the Chinese colleagues suggests some tea. It might sound innocent enough when the Western female asks for a cup of coffee instead, but only to the inexperienced fieldworker in China, as subsequent events revealed.

The Chinese colleague talks to one or two or three waiters, after which it is suggested that the whole group had better leave the premises and go to one of the coffee shops – of which of course 'there are so many in modern China'. Indeed, there are many such coffee shops in China – albeit they are all concentrated in another part of town. The female, already feeling somewhat embarrassed, is informed that the others will not mind a walk, as the temperature has only reached twenty-seven degrees Celsius, and there is plenty of time. After twenty minutes, during which no coffee shop can be found, and after several pleas by the Western female academic that she is no longer so desperate for a cup of coffee, the party decides to return to the hotel where the tea is served promptly – and where the Chinese hosts disappear in order to 'wash their faces after the hot walk'.

If this should not be enough to teach the inexperienced fieldworker that rule number one is 'never try to deviate from the carefully designed path', the next step certainly ought to do the trick. After the party has gratefully enjoyed its first sip of tea somebody arrives with the news that the interviewee has arrived, is having his tea in an adjacent room and wants to let the Western researchers know that he does not mind being kept waiting for another ten minutes. The message is clear: field research needs to respect a certain etiquette, which is designed by the Chinese colleagues and their collaborators. If the Western research staff want to avoid causing embarrassing situations or spare themselves the necessity of permanently having to apologize for something, then some basic rules need to be acknowledged. Field research in China is a major exercise in cross-cultural understanding and tolerance as the following discussion reinforces.

Of course, all the trouble would be avoided if fieldwork were left to Chinese colleagues or firms, but Western academics insist that fieldwork, based on the much more valuable research input designed in non-Chinese offices and institutions, is the only way to undertake research in China. As the following discussion attempts to illustrate, aside from the implicit arrogance, such a procedure must lead to heavily flawed research outcomes. The problem of cross-cultural research is not limited to its implementation but starts with the selection both of a feasible research methodology and a theoretical paradigm, which is appropriate to the Chinese context and capable of capturing Chinese realities.

Approaching Chinese economic reality I: figures or tales

That the economic reality of a country can best be pictured by figures is a much cherished belief in both socialist and market economics. Unsurprisingly therefore after some adjustments by Chinese authorities to comply with World Bank or IMF standards, economists rushed in, turning China into a 'case' for testing well-established hypotheses and equations. Moreover, economists were not the only ones who based their research in China on the 'figures at hand', and other social scientists followed suit. A great part of this literature has common beliefs that: first, quantitative data can be trusted; second, secondary literature serves only to legitimate selected approaches; and third, personal accounts are regarded as adding flavour, but are otherwise dismissed as 'non-systematic' story-telling. The status of the anecdote is questionable: at worst, the anecdote is regarded as oppositional to the 'truth', and at best as merely an example of some objective fact. But in China, as was learned during the fieldwork, the anecdote may be regarded by the speaker as a valid rhetorical device (or discursive strategy) for describing and explaining reality.

Leaving aside fruitful theoretical discussions about how to model Chinese firms, the nascent private sector, or the interdependence between politics and economic activities in a transition economy, the underlying problem is that the research is driven by the *availability of data*. With remarkable naivety the sources of the data are seldom questioned. Thus, figures quoted in the *China Daily* or released by Chinese authorities are taken at face value with figures appearing in the *State (or provincial) Statistical Yearbook* (*SYB*) regarded as fixed and immutable 'facts'. While once in a while, and mostly to fight off contradicting results from other research, the reliability of the *SYB* is questioned, the underlying conceptual problem is seldom discussed, namely that the *SYB* still uses concepts that reflect the information need of a state-planned economy rather than information that might allow individual firms (and researchers) to calculate demand, supply, scarcity, prices, rentability, risk in production, or investment.

For example, the first interviews in Shanxi during the middle 1990s showed that according to the conventional usage found in most official data, the term capital referred to financial capital, if not liquid capital, only. Unsurprisingly, any (Western) analysis that claimed that lack of capital was a bottleneck of Chinese economic development necessarily found ample evidence. One could make the argument that at the time, with land still state-controlled and physical assets overused, financial capital was indeed the decisive component in the establishment and development of firms and production. However, the longer the boom period lasted, the more foreign and domestic investment changed the 'capital stock' of firms and the economy, and the larger the gap between real capital stock and economic reality as depicted in the official statistics.

Another example is fixed assets as listed in statistics. One wonders what value is attached to resources such as machinery imported from the Soviet Union in the 1950s, let alone the value of land. One part of the China story is that individual managers and in particular local politicians knew better than to rely on the official concepts. As the cases of land speculation and corruption reveal, land became an asset whose value increased rapidly (not reflected in the statistics) and whose use when converted into manufacturing sites, lease contracts, or sales became important, especially in the Chinese countryside. The rapid increase in the value of lease contracts, or the bribes offered, provide a rough indicator of this trend.

In short the capital stock of China has increased and has changed over time, a development that cannot easily be explained by looking at the official (macro-economic) data and press releases. To identify the causes of such developments, in particular the emergence of a private sector, then requires other methods, such as interviews with those economic actors who face the operational side of the economic system, such as managers, or those politicians and bureaucrats in charge of the implementation of the reform.

It follows that one of the differences between analysing, let's say, the Australian or French economy on the one hand, and the Chinese economy on the other, is that in the case of the latter *raw data* need to be generated. Such a method is not exotic. On the contrary, other social sciences such as social psychology, sociology, or anthropology make extensive use of it and have developed sophisticated methodologies for doing so. The advantage of such an approach is that it explores systematic factors behind individual decisions and activities, as compared to the testing of existing hypotheses. In conducting fieldwork one needs to be sensitive to the theoretical paradigm underpinning the hypotheses. Thus, for example hypotheses informed by Western-style concepts and ideas may prove to be irrelevant or untestable where such concepts and ideas are at odds with the realities of Chinese experience. Krug and Mehta (Chapter 3) for example found that entrepreneurs were baffled when questioned about the *core competence* of the firm: this concept proved to be meaningless, at least so long as crucial input and resources remain *non-tradable*.

Moreover, it is easy to claim that the motive behind entrepreneurship in China as elsewhere is income maximization (or at least an increase), while the motive behind the behaviour of firms is profit maximization (or at least an increase), and to find evidence for these phenomena. After all the *SYB* lists only those entrepreneurs and firms that have survived, thus cutting off all those with individual or corporate losses. Such a research design however does not help to explain how individual and institutional actors managed to survive, the differences in successful entrepreneurship, or why China has outperformed other transition economies. There remains a need to search for and isolate factors that account for the growth, direction and speed of development of the private sector.

If an analysis based on quantitative data is so deficient, why is there not more research based on micro-data and interviews? An economic analysis of this phenomenon would point to the opportunity costs: while quantitative data are freely available (and in English) and require not much more than the opening of the *SYB*, creating raw data with the help of interviews (for example) is an expensive undertaking. Aside from the proficiency in Chinese language required by such a procedure, there must also be training in (methodological) skills, as well as a solid knowledge of Chinese history and institutions, all of which must be preceded by investment to establish a network with Chinese colleagues.

Even if all these requirements are met the analysis might not find the attention (in journals or at conferences) it deserves. The most frequently heard objections that need to be taken seriously are given below.

Representativeness

Taking into account the time constraint most academics have to deal with, it cannot come as a surprise that most research based on interviews starts at one place and in one year. Why official documents should offer a higher degree of representativeness remains a secret to those who rely upon them. As mentioned before, the *SYB* is heavily biased toward the inherited classification system. The advantage of having data compiled from all over China has to be weighed against the missing data on property rights, prices, and private investment, let alone the transactions in the shadow economy. One example is the bias in the official data towards the state-controlled sector, i.e. state-owned enterprises (SOEs) or collective enterprises. These data could not explain the economic dynamics of the 1980s and 1990s for the simple reason that the state sector was anything but dynamic. When

the role of small firms as the locomotive of growth, tax revenue, and foreign exchange could no longer be overlooked, despite their lack of everything from up-to-date machinery to access to scarce financial capital, a new
type of firm was discovered, namely the township and village enterprise
(TVE). The classification however was not based on common organizational attributes, such as property rights structure, behavioural patterns, or
risk taking, which would allow an assessment of their impact on economic
development. Instead it reflected once again the level of their administrative control. Unsurprisingly, neither their emergence nor their functioning
could be explained by the available quantitative data.

On the other hand, fieldwork in one province or county might suggest a
'common' underlying factor worth further investigation in other places. The
preceding chapters try to show that one such underlying factor is *social
capital*, i.e. the ability of economic actors to connect with each other, and
with those in control of scarce, non-tradable inputs, including political
power. If social capital is the driving force in the establishment of firms,
then the official data that pay no attention to such a resource must find it
hard to explain the direction and speed in the development of a private sector. Ultimately, if different formerly socialist economies started with different stocks in social capital, then to dismiss this as a crucial factor implies
forgoing the chance to explain the differences in socialist transformation.

Situational constraints

Unfortunately, the correlation between official guidelines and semi-official
communication such as interviews, remains high. For example, as long as
private entrepreneurs were not acknowledged by the official propaganda
(and policy) as crucial actors in the development of the Chinese economy,
their role, and even existence, was played down. The moment these actors
were proclaimed to be a part of the 'productive forces', they seem to be
mushrooming everywhere. This does not necessarily indicate a new wave
of entrepreneurship. It reflects rather the surfacing of existing entrepreneurship, where in the past entrepreneurs had found it safer to hide behind
other forms of firms, such as collective enterprises.

It is amongst other things for this reason that unofficial dinners with
colleagues and interviewees are such a valuable exercise. The informal
talks allow the interviewer to assess what is lip service, what is exaggerated
and what is indeed a 'fact'.

Chance dependency

Where to find personal accounts, or economic actors willing to be interviewed, is a major problem. Fieldwork would otherwise be confined to
the exchange of stories in hotel lounges and bars, conferences, or official

meetings. There is indeed a chance element in doing research in China. Once in a while one stumbles over some information that is intriguing enough to lead to further systematic inquiries. After all it was the enthusiastic description by one of the authors in this volume on entrepreneurship in Shanxi – and his generous willingness to part with his information – that stands at the beginning of the comparative analysis in entrepreneurship that forms the backbone of the book. More important than the chance element in finding a research topic is the importance of having access to colleagues within and outside China who can help to build up the necessary personal network infrastructure to sustain the fieldwork. Somebody who moves most of the time within the community of Western journalists in Beijing will for example be introduced to another group of economic actors willing to be interviewed: someone who knows managers of Western firms, or someone who has access to local universities. It is necessary to go for numerous and diverse groups of collaborators in order to build up a series of 'independent' sources. Though such a procedure might still not ensure representativeness, it is however superior to official data that are, after all, based on one source only.

Path-dependency

Two contradicting trends prevail in the 'Western' literature on China's economy. First, there are the quantitative studies that do not know a 'past' – or any institution for that matter. As is the case in the analysis of other countries, firms, or economies, they are all modelled as production functions. Institutional economics has argued long enough about the deficits of such approaches: they do not need to be repeated here. Second, there are the 'history matters' approaches. These can take the form of claiming that culture, mostly a Confucianist past, can explain the behaviour of individuals, politicians and firms, or, more recently, that the time and direction of the reform implementation in one place explains the further successive development. A lot was said about culture and path dependency in the preceding chapters. Here it will suffice to say that to claim only that the past or culture matters is not enough. The situations in which economic actors fall back on particular behavioural patterns and the extent to which those particular patterns reflect rational decision making or cultural roles also need to be analysed.

Experience with fieldwork in China therefore suggests three propositions.

Proposition 1
Close interaction amongst 'Western' academics representing competence in institutional knowledge of one or more regions in China and in different analytical concepts are a necessary requirement for fruitful research.

194

To give an example: three different kinds of economic interaction can be distinguished in the private business sector in China – control, competition, and co-operation. While economics offers the best analytical tools for analysing competition (and partly co-operation), political science and sociology understand better how to deal with control or political power. In a transitional period local political authorities and the bureaucratic machinery do not automatically lose the ability to coerce firms and individual actors into a certain kind of behaviour. Yet, as empirical research has shown, at one point, they need to search for a consensus or bargaining solution with firms – or to comply with the complete loss of control. This switch from one co-ordination mechanism (control) to another (co-operation) is crucial for the development of the private business sector, and needs to be systematically analysed. If empirical research should not get stuck in findings claiming that this switch occurred earlier in one province of China than another, then other systematic factors that explain the switch need to be considered. As this book demonstrates, such factors can be found in the interdependence of politics and the economic sector, or in the emergence of networks, business routines, or institutional identities which ask for different approaches.

Proposition 2
Close interaction between 'Western' and Chinese colleagues to discuss the suitability of selected models and to obtain access to interview partners are a necessary requirement for fruitful research.

To give an example: one of the strongest models in the 'Theory of the Modern Firm' is the 'Firm as a Nexus of Contracts' (Aoki *et al.* 1999). Taking this model to China will meet an immediate objection from Chinese colleagues who will point out that the ill-functioning legal system, and in particular non-contractual labour relations, does not promise fruitful results. The attempt to save the model by assuming that 'promises', i.e. non-written contracts, work as written contracts, is premature, to say the least, certainly so long as research has not yet established that this is the case. After all, the monitoring and sanctioning mechanisms are different. To claim that legal sanctioning in 'Western' economies corresponds to social sanctioning (by the family, village, or abstract norms) is correct but only at a too abstract level. At the operational level of the private business sector, the fact that long-term business relations cannot rely on state-provided law enforcement agencies, but need to be enforced by other means can be decisive. When such enforcement needs to be privately organized and privately financed then these costs can easily define a threshold so that entrepreneurship, or for that matter, foreign direct investment, will stay away. Chinese colleagues' insistence on searching for other, better-suited models ensures one does not fall into the availability trap of easy-at-hand models that have proved their usefulness only in an environment of integrated functioning markets, in the West.

Co-operation with Chinese colleagues is also a necessary requirement for overcoming asymmetric information. For example, in the case of research on private firms, access to managers or owners of such firms is crucial. As already indicated, the definition of a private firm is a question of registration rather than of ownership, risk-taking, or profit-maximization. Chinese colleagues and their networks of friends are needed to screen unofficially the pool of potential interview partners to make sure they manage firms which are independent enough to select suppliers or customers, transfer resources to other lines of production, conclude deals with business partners and the political authorities. In short:

Proposition 3
Fieldwork in China is a major exercise in cross-cultural, cross-disciplinary co-operation and the willingness to compromise on concepts, research design, and procedures.

Approaching Chinese economic reality II: being in the field

Fieldwork in China offers a plethora of delights that compensates for sometimes irritating situations. That there is no clear-cut strategy for fieldwork other than accepting that *nothing is as it seems* certainly adds to the impression that fieldwork in China is still an adventure. This is so because the outcome of empirical research depends not only on conceptual approaches, but also on co-operation with Chinese colleagues. Equally important, the outcome of fieldwork depends on connections, the acknowledgement of rules of courtesy while being in China, and a sensitivity that allows noticing and comprehending differences in behaviour. Some overview of a code of conduct for the experienced researcher might give an impression of the general problems involved.

How to establish personal competence

That China is the place where 'having face' (keeping face, gaining face) matters is almost a truism. How to get face, however, is often open to discussion. Two aspects seem to matter: familiarity with things Chinese, and status.

To marry a Chinese person is of course the obvious way to prove familiarity with China, yet a way not open to all non-Chinese academics. Language skill comes next and helps enormously, but in this case too the costs might be regarded too high for many. Thus, familiarity with other things Chinese need to be considered. A rough guide to the very important might include:

- food and its local variations
- local customs
- songs suitable for performances in karaoke-bars.

Knowledge about Chinese art, Chinese politics or Confucianism is less important.

While in the West status is linked to certain performance criteria such as income in the business world and authorship in academia, status in China is derived from the kind of people one knows. Certain exaggerations seem to be tolerable. Thus, it might come as a surprise to an academic who hears herself being introduced as a member of the Dutch Royal Household, a claim justified from the Chinese side because she was the recipient of a grant from the Royal Dutch Academy for Sciences. More surprising, however, would be to be introduced as a future Nobel Prize winner in Economics, based on having met several Nobel laureates. Equally, a claim that another academic who had met some of the top politicians personally in the past must also therefore have met Hu Yaobang, Mao Zedong, and any other eminent figure from Chinese history must be accepted with a straight face even though to do so defies the biological logic of the age of the person being introduced.

Whom are we talking to?

The approach that selecting respondents at random with the help of, for example, a telephone directory, in order to ensure high quality in data collection, becomes 'a Western belief' not generally shared by Chinese social scientists. They quite rightly point out that mailing questionnaires or phoning potential interview partners are exercises that test foremost the willingness of those contacted to answer. The willingness to answer, however, might differ between cultures and with specific circumstances. In this case, for example, it might seem that the active participation of local Party leaders creates an atmosphere of confidence so that the willingness of respondents to answer frankly increases. From their point of view the participation of the Party signals that nothing is wrong with answering questions about turnover, profit, and the firm's strategic behaviour to non-Chinese academics. The Party connection proved useful in a year in which some Chinese journalists had found an original idea to make some money on the side. After having visited the factory, and conducted some interviews, they had obviously threatened the management with publishing unfavourable photos and reports if appropriate payment was not made. This procedure was obviously so widespread that managers generally thought that anyone showing up for an interview expected gifts of money. In order to avoid getting flooded with bottles of Shanxi vinegar, leather purses, or other products of the local handicraft industry, one colleague had to visit the firms beforehand to make sure that the managers understood what a social science questionnaire is all about. Party connections are not always needed to ensure frank and competent answers; other networks will do.

To avoid a network-based bias a number of different networks must be employed. The Shanxi data set on which three articles in this book are based, for example, was collected with the help of local Party members, one state bank, and two universities. To guess which network was used for selecting respondents is an entertaining exercise for all fieldworkers, as the Chinese co-ordinator did not indicate the source of access, for various reasons. Thus, a common procedure during fieldwork is that the Western academics are picked up at their hotel and driven to one place where they find themselves introduced to somebody whom they might never meet again. That person in turn introduces them to a couple of others, one of which will accompany them further. Another half an hour will take them to another place where the procedure is repeated. Another person will join the entourage, who will take them to firms and respondents. These courtesy calls reveal the chain of personal connections. Business cards and the names at the office doors help the fieldworkers to guess the nature of the supporting network.

For example, the experience of having been shuffled around between several local tax offices found its explanation in the following story: one Chinese colleague knew a former PhD student who in the meantime had obtained a position at a university in another province. There he had helped to train local administrators, including some who worked for the local tax offices. Subsequently when approached to help to find respondents he turned to his new acquaintances. Taking into account that private entrepreneurs are probably the only economic agents who dutifully pay taxes, the tax registrar is certainly a good source for selecting interview partners, while the presence of a tax administrator made sure that the questions were answered frankly, with the understandable exception of 'real' profit. As a further incentive to spend time with the social scientists the respondents were also allowed to invite the research team and any other employee in the local tax administration for lunch.

To link job titles to a specific competence or status can be misleading. In China as elsewhere the owner of a company may not be the most qualified interview partner for example. Yet the owner is the major source for the life history of private firms. For this reason alone, the idea that a questionnaire should be filled in by just one person has to be abandoned, as must be the idea that answers should not be discussed by a number of respondents beforehand. In some cases it proved fruitful to wait until somebody better qualified was consulted. In other cases, one question, usually the one about ultimate ownership, was enough to cut the interview short, as either the company was not an independent firm or the respondent was not competent.

'Western' concepts of job titles are seldom more misleading than in the case of drivers. By chance, most drivers encountered and employed by the different universities or bigger firms had a military background. Their role is something in between that of the steward in a medieval court and the logistics manager of a modern company. They may

- select restaurants and food
- attend dinners, since they
- pay the bills
- control the mobile phone, i.e. place and answer phone calls on behalf of their employer
- organize sightseeing
- tell the research team when to get up and when to go to bed.

In other words, they need to be treated with respect as someone who amongst other things also knows how to drive a car. The description of the driver's job clarifies what modern Chinese managers would not do on the grounds that this would be incompatible with their status, namely ordering food, carrying cash for paying bills, placing phone calls, but also writing e-mails, cashing cheques in a bank or driving a car.

Why to amble aimlessly?

The quick answer is to avoid embarrassing situations. To signal to Chinese colleagues or interview partners that one waits for something to happen, or that one expects an explanation is bad manners. It creates stress for the Chinese who after all regard themselves as 'hosts' rather than colleagues so that any sign of impatience in their reading indicates that they have failed as hosts. Taking a sudden interest in the product of the company just visited is one way to spend the time until the driver reappears (from lunch, or a quick visit to a relative or his stockbroker). Such interest must, however, not be too enthusiastic if one does not want to get stuck in a quickly improvised tour around the factory site. Having a look at the plants and flowers that inevitably decorate the magnificent gates at the entrance, in the hallways and/or in the conference rooms offers a better background for ambling – in particular since one can rely on the fact that Chinese colleagues know no more about plants than (generally) visitors from abroad. To amble is a good strategy in situations in which:

- the man with the key is missing
- the address of the firm to be visited got lost
- the driver or car is missing
- the interview partner is still in another meeting, or sleeping or has changed his mind
- and in all other situations when something goes wrong.

Which question fits the answer?

The assumption that an answer should fit the question is based on the belief that the question is understood and regarded as relevant enough to deserve an answer. Yet, as fieldwork has clearly demonstrated, there are times when Chinese respondents would not answer a question, or fill in the questionnaire, if they regard the question as ridiculous, incomprehensible, too stupid or with a self-evident answer. Weird answers can further indicate that they have lost patience with the whole exercise or research team, that it is time for lunch, or that they regard the question as tactless. For example, when a question about a given respondent's number of children becomes a matter of major discussion for all present, then it is a sure sign that there is some problem best avoided, and the question rephrased, in this case to concentrate on the number of 'officially' sanctioned children with only one wife.

Similarly, the completion of questionnaires often needs to be monitored. No answer can indicate that a question was not understood, which the respondent does not want to admit. Offering an 'I do not know' option in the questionnaire is futile for the same reason. Other motives for not answering might be that the respondent finds the answers too obvious, or the whole exercise a waste of time. Subsequently, if not corrected on the spot, the distinction between 'I do not know' and a missing value in the database can become a nightmare once the data allow a quantitative analysis.

The anecdote as an argument

Politeness in China means foremost to be agreeable to somebody such as a foreign academic, with whom the Chinese colleagues expect to reciprocate. That can lead to confusion when Western academics who pride themselves on clearly distinguishing between social conversation and professional argument can no longer be sure whether they face polite talk or an academic exchange of thoughts. Chinese colleagues on the other hand judge the Anglo-Saxon competitive debating style aggressive. They wonder for example why two academics whom they have seen criticizing each other a couple of minutes earlier should be found sitting together at lunch exchanging pleasantries.

In turn, the compliments, which inevitably start any comment by Chinese colleagues, are seen by Westerners as flattering if not condescending, in any case inappropriate in an academic setting.

A rather common situation that illustrates the mutual misunderstanding are conferences in which a Westerner explains a special feature of Chinese business life, insinuating that his conclusions are of a general nature. Chinese colleagues who find it hard to see their reality reflected in this way will never straightforwardly say so. They will neither criticize the speaker nor his argument. Instead, they will try to illustrate the limitations of what had been said by offering an example that points to another line of reasoning. They leave it to the audience – and to the speaker – to decide whether the example given asks for a modification of what had been said or for another 'theory'. Often enough Westerners will react by dismissing the example as an 'anecdote', claiming that this is the exception that proves the rule, if not embarking on a lecture on methodology. What is not seen is that by giving an example the Chinese colleagues want – kindly and subtly – to tell the speaker that there are reasons to question his insights. Depending on the (lack of) sensitivity of the speaker this can lead to a situation in which the whole audience, knowing what is 'behind' the Chinese 'anecdote', looks embarrassed or pretends not to be in the same room (a version of the 'ambling aimlessly' tactic), while the speaker is still lecturing on how to treat examples and stories scientifically.

To confuse things further, an anecdote can be a way to express doubt and criticism of what has been said, it can be way of teasing the speaker, and sometimes an anecdote is, indeed, nothing but an anecdote. It matters to know what the intention in telling the anecdote is in order to respond appropriately. Yet this is something that cannot be learned either by reading books or by experience. Some people just 'don't get it'; they lack the ability to notice when something goes wrong, let alone to acknowledge the differences in style and content. In this sense, empirical research is, finally, also depending on a 'Fingerspitzengefuehl', i.e. the ability to notice, detect and comprehend differences in behaviour and communication styles.

Reference

Aoki, M. Gustafsson, B. and Williamson, O. (eds) (1999) *The Firm as a Nexus of Contracts*, Sage Publications.

APPENDIX

Background information on the interview
and questionnaire respondents

Table A1 Classification of respondents' firms by industry

Industry	Frequency	Percentage
Tourism	5	6.6
Retail and consumer service	5	6.6
Asset development and management	6	7.9
Construction	1	1.3
Primary products	4	5.3
Semi-manufactured goods	12	15.8
Car sales and components	6	7.9
Household apparel	9	11.8
Food processing	4	5.3
Fittings and bearings	2	2.6
Computer (hardware and software)	5	6.6
Pharmaceutical and chemical industry	4	5.3
Telecom and media	2	2.6
Textile	6	7.9
Other (education + missing)	5	6.6
Total	76	100.0

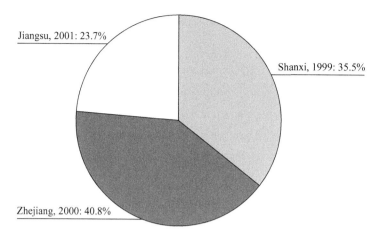

Figure A1 Year and location of interviews with managers/owners

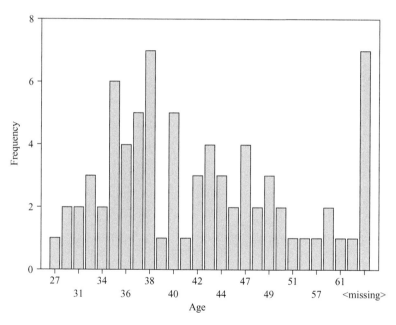

Figure A2 Age of interviewed managers/owners

203

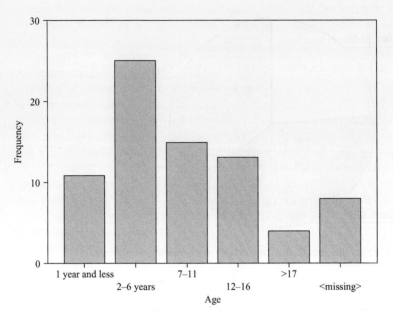

Figure A3 Age of firm at the time of the manager/owner's interview

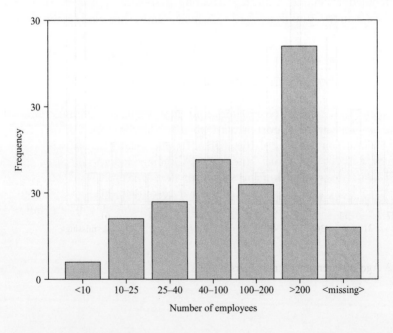

Figure A4 Size of the firm at the time of the manager/owner's interview by number of employees

204

INDEX

adaptation 39
agreements and disputes 13
alliances 51, 59–63, 83–4, 87, 119,
183, 124, 131, 173; multiplicity of
56, 63; with politicians 60, 119; as a
repository of knowledge 62
Asian financial crisis 23, 101, 125
assets: financial 1, 53, 54, 60, 86;
physical 1, 55, 60, 82, 86, 191;
transferable 59, 81, 88
authority 2, 5, 9, 25, 26, 31–3, 52, 78,
110, 114, 170, 183

banks 52, 53, 55, 59, 64, 102, 117,
179; Shanxi 179
Beijing 54, 64, 122, 141, 145, 194
bureaucracy 28, 40, 41, 81, 115, 119,
121
business relations 1, 3, 6, 9, 12, 52,
57, 73, 74, 78, 166, 172, 173, 176,
177, 179, 180–4, 195; entering 180;
success of 181–4
business system (comparative) 1–12,
16, 22, 24–8, 32, 33, 37, 45, 72

calculation 28–30, 33–6, 39, 43, 80,
180
capital: financial 60, 81, 106, 107,
191, 193; human 11, 32, 33, 37, 60,
83, 167, 168; political 61, 82, 83,
90, 91; social 1, 2, 11, 32, 33, 37,
59, 60, 62, 74, 78, 81–3, 86, 87,
97–113, 115, 124, 166–84, 193;
sourcing 1, 24, 53, 58, 123, 127,
129, 179; *see also* guanxi

chaebol 25
change: organizational 9, 86, 87
Chinese Communist Party (CCP) 3, 7,
21, 51, 52–5, 62–8, 73, 76, 105,
122, 123, 125, 139, 140, 144,
146–8, 151–60, 177, 179, 189, 197,
198
Chinese family business *see* family
codes: of behaviour 60, 170; family
106, 174; weakly enforced 75–6
collective memory 57, 77, 101
collectivism 4, 27, 169, 170, 173,
184
company law 87, 100–2, 108–11, 125,
128–31
comparative management 21, 22, 24,
44
competition 5–7, 12, 25, 35, 38, 40,
56, 63, 72–80, 84, 88, 90, 102, 106,
184, 195
concentration 58, 86
conceptual equivalence 10, 79
Confucianism 169–71, 183, 197
contracts 12–15, 40, 53, 54, 60, 66,
73–7, 81–3, 87–9, 100, 105,
107–10, 119, 122, 170, 182, 184,
191, 195
core competence 58–9, 192
corruption 30, 121, 191
cross-shareholding 12
culture (as an explanation for
entrepreneurship) 4–10, 14, 23,
26–8, 30–3, 36, 40–6, 84, 91, 140,
147–9, 171, 183, 194
cultural studies 1, 3–5, 7, 169–72

For Product Safety Concerns and Information please contact our EU
representative GPSR@taylorandfrancis.com Taylor & Francis Verlag GmbH,
Kaufingerstraße 24, 80331 München, Germany

Printed and bound by CPI Group (UK) Ltd, Croydon, CR0 4YY
08/05/2025
01864339-0001